The Green Movement in West Germany

Elim Papadakis

CROOM HELM
London & Canberra

ST. MARTIN'S PRESS
New York

© 1984 E. Papadakis
Croom Helm Ltd., Provident House, Burrell Row,
Beckenham, Kent BR3 1AT
Croom Helm Australia Pty Ltd, 28 Kembla St,
Fyshwick, ACT 2609, Australia

British Library Cataloguing in Publication Data

Papadakis, Elim
    The Green Movement in West Germany.
    1. Ecology – Germany (West) – Political aspects
    2. Environmental protection – Germany (West) – History
    – 20th century
    I. Title
    333. 7'0943   QH77.G/
    ISBN 0-7099-2071-7

St. Martin's Press, Inc., 175 Fifth Avenue, New York, NY 10010
Printed in Great Britain
First published in the United States of America in 1984

Library of Congress Cataloging in Publication Data

Papadakis, Elim.
    The Green Movement in West Germany.

    Bibliography: p.
    Includes index.
    1. Grünen (Political party) 2. Antinuclear movement –
Germany (West) 3. Pacifists – Germany (West) I. Title.
JN3971.A98G7236   1984   324.243'06   83-24728
ISBN 0-312-35009-0

Printed and bound in Great Britain

CONTENTS

TABLES

Tables

For Anya

PREFACE AND ACKNOWLEDGEMENTS

Between October 1976 and July 1977 I was able, as a visiting student at the University of Hamburg, to witness the genesis of a mass movement against nuclear energy and the division of the city between the supporters of nuclear energy and economic growth and protestors who issued dire warnings about the threat of technological developments to the lives and safety of the population.

These experiences prompted me to undertake, in autumn 1979, a research project on the Green Movement. I am grateful to Dr. Colin Crouch and Dr. Christopher Husbands at the London School of Economics and Political Science for their willingness to supervise the work even though there were only a few signs that the protest movement would exercise a powerful influence on contemporary West German politics. They both offered very useful advice on the original doctoral thesis and on the revised version which appears in this book. I should like to thank Dr. William Paterson and Professor Hugh Ridley for their helpful comments on various sections of the thesis. I am also indebted to many people in West Germany who were willing to be interviewed and to engage in discussions on the Green Movement. They include: Professor Peter Grottian and Professor Bernd Rabehl from the Free University of Berlin; Thomas Haertel in the Department of Health, Social and Family Welfare in Berlin; Klaus-Juergen Luther and Gisela Marsen-Storz in the Ministry of Education in Bonn; Anke Brunn, a member of the Berlin Senate who acted as an adviser to the government commission of inquiry on youth protest; several editors from the Tageszeitung alternative newspaper project; Corny Littmann, the leading candidate of the Green Party in Hamburg during the 1980 Federal Elections; and many other supporters and sympathisers of the Green Movement. In particular I should like to mention Elke Josties and Christiane Uschkereit both for their hospitality and for helping me to obtain information.

The Central Research Fund Committee of the University of London kindly agreed to provide me with a grant to carry out fieldwork in May 1982; other journeys, in September 1979, September 1980 and January 1982, were financed by myself and by my family.

Leytonstone, London

ABBREVIATIONS

AFAP	Arbeitskreis Finanzierung von Alternativ-projekten (Working Group for the Financing of Alternative Projects)
AFF	Anstiftung der Frauen zum Frieden (The Women's Initiative for Peace)
ASF	Aktion Suehnezeichen Friedensdienste (Action for reconciliation/services for peace)
BBU	Bundesverband Buergerinitiativen Umwelt-schutz (Federal Association of Environ-mentalist Citizens' Initiatives)
BDI	Bund der deutschen Industrie (Federation of German Industry)
Bunte Liste	Green or 'colourful' lists (parties)
CDU	Christlich-Demokratische-Union (Christian Democratic Party)
CSU	Christlich-Soziale-Union (Christian Social Union)
DFG-VK	Deutsche Friedensdienst/Vereinigte Kriegsdienstgegner (German Peace Society)
DGB	Deutscher Gewerkschaftsbund (German Trade Union Federation)
FDP	Freie Demokratische Partei (Free Demo-cratic Party)
GAL	Gruen-Alternative-Liste (Green Alterna-tive List)
GAZ	Gruene Aktion Zukunft (Green Action-for-the-future Party)
Jusos	Young Socialists (members of the SPD)
SPD	Sozialdemokratische Partei Deutschlands (Social Democratic Party of Germany)
Taz	Die Tageszeitung (a daily alternative newspaper)

INTRODUCTION

This book sets out to explain the evolution of the ecology, peace and alternative movements in West Germany and the emergence of a Green Party out of them. A large part of the work attempts to provide an original empirical contribution to a subject on which there currently exists no comprehensive work in English. Moreover, various themes are identified which are common to all the new movements and to the Green Party. Since the relationship between the various movements and the party-political organisation remains fluid, it is perhaps appropriate to refer to them all as the Green Movement.

The emergence of the Green Movement appears to confirm the thesis put forward by Ronald Inglehart in the early seventies that a 'silent revolution' was taking place in Western democracies and was founded on a 'change in values'. The new values related to matters of conscience, a desire for more participation in decision-making processes and an emphasis on creativity. These were contrasted to old materialistic values which stressed the need for economic security and for traditional attitudes to authority.

Hildebrandt and Dalton (1977) have shown that in West Germany around ten per cent of the population formed a reliable base of support for these new values. This was true, above all, of the young, well-educated middle classes who, in the early seventies, found an outlet for their aspirations in the Social Democratic and Free Democratic parties. However, over the past decade, the Social-Liberal Alliance lost the sympathy of many of these supporters because, in the wake of a worsening economic situation, particularly the oil crisis, it was unable to carry out its social policy and other reformist goals; towards the end of the decade its policy of intervention in the economy was less successful and there thus emerged an increasing dissatisfaction within the trade unions. These factors contributed to a general detachability of the Social Democratic vote and it is therefore of great interest to explore the relationship between the Green Movement and the SPD.

Equally important is the need to offer a framework for understanding why Green Politics have become so prominent in the Federal Republic and why the critique of Western democracy is combined with a stance against industrialisation which feeds both on Marxist utopian traditions and on Nietzschean antimodernist and romantic elements. Among the themes of Green Politics are ideas about how life could be fundamentally threatened by the deterioration of the environment, the destruction of community life and the continuous nuclear arms race. The fundamentalist and radical critique by the Green Movement of the prevailing economic and political conditions should not, however, obscure the fact that the movements may well serve an important function within the capitalist state. Therefore the simple distinction between new and old values, or between creativity and materialism, needs to be scrutinised more carefully by assessing the practice of the Green Movement in its attempt to fulfil its ideals and its efforts to organise the subjective elements of human experience. It is necessary to assess the extent and nature of the accommodation or co-optation of innovative ideas within the prevailing material and ideological framework of society.

Over the past few years there has occurred a broadening of the bases of support for the Green Movement. The most active support comes from young people, especially students, from towns and cities, who are dissatisfied with their position in society; and members of rural communities who have felt threatened by ambitious hypertechnological projects. The support of the so-called 'post-materialist' intelligentsia, who were increasingly disappointed at the lack of reforms which had originally been promised by the Social-Liberal Alliance in the early seventies, was also crucial to the successful evolution of the Green Movement. Hence radicalised students, farmers and traditional conservatives as well as the intellectual middle classes all took part in the early stages of the formulation of a Green Party Programme. The preoccupation with environmental issues arises firstly from a genuine concern about the direct physical threat posed to certain communities and secondly from a growing awareness conditioned by the publicity which emerged around studies on the 'limits of growth'. The theme of the limited resources available for the expansion of capitalism and of the self-destructive forces which had been unleashed by it played an important role in generating an 'environmentalist conscious-ness'. The material basis for questioning the motor of economic growth was of course the oil crisis in the early years of the previous decade.

The development of the Green Movement in West Germany has puzzled political scientists who have been impressed by the stability of the post-war party system in that country. Similar movements have arisen in other countries and have either faded away rapidly, or become co-opted by major political parties, or remained purely a mass movement without forming a party. The protest against nuclear energy in France in the mid-seventies only led to a short-lived success of ecological groups at local elect-ions. In West Germany the Green Movement has gradually gained in strength and attracted enough votes to upset the previous balance of power in several state, or regional, parliaments and to gain representation in the Federal Parliament.

It would be wrong to underestimate the strength of Green Politics in other Western democracies by making a straightforward comparison of the party-political strength of the Green Movement in the various countries. The scale and frequency of mass demonstrations against nuclear weapons in Britain, France, Italy, the Netherlands and West Germany shows that Green Politics motivate large groups of the population beyond the borders of the Federal Republic. The durability and level of organisation of the Green Movement has, none the less, been much more striking in that country. In order to explain this one needs to consider the vacuum that has existed on the left of the Social Democratic Party since the 1950s; the failure of this party to capture or to maintain the support both of middle-class radicals and of ordinary citizens who wished to take a more active part in politics as a result of the student protest movement in the late sixties; and the strength of an anti-modernist and romantic tradition in Germany.

The methods of inquiry and materials used to support the findings of this work include the following: interviews carried out by the author with government officials, politicians from various

parties and sympathisers of the Green Movement; an
analysis of primary and secondary literature including surveys on public attitudes both to the Green
Movement and to other related issues, as well as
policy statements, consultative documents and reports
by government Commissions of Inquiry and other
agencies; first-hand experience of the emergence of
the ecology movement between October 1976 and June
1977; an evaluation of around six hundred issues of
the daily newspaper _Tageszeitung_ (Taz) which forms
an integral part of the Green Movement; and an
assessment of relevant literature in the spheres of
sociology, politics, literature and philosophy.

Chapter One

ORIGINS OF THE GREEN MOVEMENT

The emergence of the Green Movement is, as I have emphasized, not based solely on features peculiar to the political climate in West Germany. Similar movements have risen and declined throughout the post-war period in different countries. However, the outstanding characteristic of the Green Movement has been its durability over a period of several years (ever since 1975) and its success in maintaining the support of those sections of the electorate that have become detached from the main political parties, particularly the Social Democrats. In this chapter I will only assess the relatively recent (post-war) origins of the Green Movement.

I   Post-war protest movements

In the post-war era the first generation of young people to protest against their society were the 'Beatniks' who, beaten by the system, sought 'beatitude' in another world.(1) Above all they were opposed to the threat of nuclear destruction and the corruption of society. Their alienation from the 'official' system was expressed by Jack Kerouac in his novel On the Road. In a famous passage, the narrator describes his feelings when he arrives back in his home town, having wandered as a hobo all over the United States:

> Suddenly I found myself on Times Square.
> I had travelled eight thousand miles
> around the American continent and I was
> back on Times Square; and right in the
> middle of a rush hour, too, seeing with
> my innocent road-eyes the absolute mad-
> ness and fantastic hoorair of New York

> with its millions and millions hustl-
> ing for ever for a buck among them-
> selves, the mad dream - grabbing,
> taking, giving, sighing, just so they
> could be buried in those awful cemetery
> cities beyond Long Island City. The
> high towers of the land - the other
> end of the land, the place where Paper
> America is born.(2)

This subjective analysis of the system tended to
overlook the social contradictions which existed in
the early 1950s. However, the Beatniks added an
'existential' dimension to political analysis.
Although they did not relate the emphasis on individual freedom to collective freedom, there was a link
between their beliefs and the way they lived their
lives in practice.(3) The 'beat' culture was later
to exercise a powerful influence on the American and
West European student movements.(4)
     In Western Europe the Beatniks formed groups in
which nationality was no barrier and they travelled
between all the major cities from North to South,
often depending on the season of the year. They
occasionally took part in demonstrations against
nuclear energy and militarism. Above all they provoked discussions over norms, values and ways of life
because of their rejection of the ethics of work,
achievement and consumption.
     Both in the United States and in the Netherlands
there emerged, in the early 1960s, groups which
sought to put these ideas into practice. The 'Provos'
in the Netherlands made demands similar to those of
the West German Green Movement in the 1980s. They
demanded free public transport, the disarmament of
the police, a ban on advertising for alcohol and
tobacco and the introduction of measures to curb
pollution of the atmosphere.(5) Hollstein notes a
similar attempt to offer constructive ideas by the
Hippies in the United States. He also stresses that
the idea that all those who joined the movement
simply wanted to 'drop out' is misleading since most
of them were not 'fleeing' from society but were
leaving it in order to build a new order of values.
In contrast to the earlier generation of Beatniks,
they tried to offer a positive counter-image to the
'negative' world. Whilst there were many different
types of Hippie - including those who were and
those who were not on drugs - they were all dissent-
ers.(6) Their missionary zeal and moral self-

righteousness meant that most of them did not have
material support from their parents, even though
they were mostly from a wealthy background. Thus
ten per cent were from upper class, fifty per cent
from middle class, twenty per cent from lower middle
class and five per cent from lower class families.
(7) Above all, they felt a general discomfort with
the American way of life. Most joined the movement
for emotional reasons such as a quarrel with their
parents, failure at school, the quest for adventure,
or because they had been influenced by the ideas of
writers like Ginsberg or Herman Hesse. Very few
joined as a result of a careful evaluation of
capitalist society. Their world-view was intuitive
and their search for truth was centred around themselves. The demonstrations against the Vietnam War
did, however, offer an important focus of unity for
this diverse protest.(8)

The Hippies' belief in the power of love and
understanding and other ideals was so powerful that
they seriously neglected building any infrastructure
and consequently the threat of hunger, sickness and
chaos in the Hippie communities became very real.
The idea of building shops, hospitals, restaurants
and clubs for the Hippie community came from the
so-called Diggers, who have been described as the
'politicised flower children'.(9) The Diggers established contact with existing land communes which led
to better organisation, the setting up of clinics
and self-help schemes as well as the opening of
'free shops' in various American cities and in Western Europe. The action by the Diggers was an important historical step in the formation of the
'counter-societal' or alternative movement.(10) The
solipsism of the Hippies gave way to a desire to
confront the political and economic power of the
'system'. Thus a Youth International Party (YIP/
Yippies) was formed and included people like Ginsberg, Hoffmann and Rubin. It was not a traditional
party; rather, it stood for action, street politics,
agitation and 'guerilla-theatre'.(11)

Whilst many Hippies had either taken to drugs
or gone home, many joined the YIP. In October 1967
the Hippie movement consciously buried itself because
of its own contradictions and the wave of commercial-
ism that had begun to make profits out of the Hippie
culture. Meanwhile the Yippies tried to carry the
values of this movement in to society. Politics was
understood existentially, growing out of the life of
the actors and indivisible from this life. There

Origins of the Green Movement

was however a tendency for political action to
assume the character of playfulness. Provocation
developed a dynamic of its own which hardly related
meaningfully to the reality of the United States.
As with the Hippies, the Yippies fell into the trap
of neglecting organisation and structures and rely-
ing too much on spontaneous and permanent revolution.

II Student movement

West European protest movements in the sixties were
strongly influenced by the Hippies and Yippies.
This reflected, moreover, the continuing influence
of the Beatniks. In the Federal Republic many young
people felt alienated from the political culture and
this was most clearly expressed by an introspective
movement, the Ohne-mich Bewegung, which turned its
back on a society which, only a few years after the
war, was discussing the issue of re-armament. Later
on, the anti-authoritarian movement of the 1960s was
influenced by the activities of intellectuals who
sought to link the disputes in Marxist theory with
the attempt to use psycho-analytic categories to help
with group-dynamic and individual problems. Communes
were seen as places in which an individual could
raise his or her 'consciousness' and also as a base
from which change could be carried in to society.
The practical experience of the well-known 'Kommune
1' and 'Kommune 2' showed how difficult it was to
achieve this. In the same manner as the Provos in
the Netherlands, and the Yippies in the United
States, the communards in West Germany relied on
their ability to 'ridicule authority'. When this
met with only limited success greater emphasis was
laid on the 'revolution of the self', and on
experiments in communal living. 'Kommune 2' was
actively involved in the opening of the first anti-
authoritarian 'kindergartens' in West Berlin.
Later communes, particularly feminist ones, were
mainly concerned with the creation of an alternative
to the nuclear family. Most communes sought to
change the 'consciousness' of the members. Thus the
'Linkeck' commune asked itself whether it was possible to develop and practice a form of life which
'can absorb if not totally abolish, the forces of
competition, fear of existence, pressure towards
achievement, and isolation, in a milder form of
living and working together'.(12)

8

The communal movement was absorbed into broader subcultural tendencies which were characterised by the separation of aims between those directed towards a change of the individual and his or her 'consciousness' and those directed towards social change. Thus the dialectical relationship between the two aims which the communes had encouraged was not realised. As with the Hippie movement in the United States many turned towards the use of drugs and psychedelic techniques and meditation as a means of self-liberation, and others, following the dissolution of the anti-authoritarian movement formed ad-hoc groups relating to factories and the process of production, internationalism, consumption, universities, environmental issues, schools, marginal groups, the media, art, the law and medicine. These groups tried to constitute, in their social practice, a counter-power to the one that prevailed in society. They then became the point of departure for efforts towards the formation of a variety of communist groups and parties. Peter Brueckner, an apologist for the original communal movement, described the process which occured from mid-1968 onwards as one of Entmischung (separation). Two intentions developed: on the one hand, to change 'consciousness' and the whole structure of inter-relationships and, on the other hand, to come to terms with relations in the sphere of production, political education and class analysis.(13)

III Citizens' Initiatives

Whilst the initiatives which were formed as a consequence of the disintegration of the anti-authoritarian movement attempted to come closer to social reality and 'proletarian consciousness', they only met with limited success. The gap between these groups and the rest of society was, to some extent, bridged by so-called Citizens' Initiatives (Buergerinitiativen) which had developed quite separately even though, as will soon become apparent, their emergence was facilitated by the actions of the protest movements in the late sixties. The origins of the Citizens' Initiatives can be traced back to the Citizens' Associations (Buergervereine) of the fifties and sixties. The Citizens' Associations were formed by well-educated, middle-class dignitaries in order to press for community or

special interests in a local situation which had
become 'de-politicised'. Through associations and
endowments, demands were made and projects set up to
deal with local needs. The claim of the major parties to represent people's interests was thus
modestly challenged and individuals showed that they
were not prepared to restrict their political activity to casting a vote periodically.(14) This challenge was broadened by the advent of the student
movement. As Roth has stated, the transition from
an initiative of dignitaries to a Citizens' Initiative 'would not have been conceivable without the
uncertainties caused by the extra-parliamentary
protest movements in the sixties and the defects in
the infrastructure which became apparent with the
recession of 1966-7'.(15) Liberal circles reacted
with the demand for greater democratic participation
and some of the pre-existing Citizens' Associations
became Citizens' Initiatives once the political and
social limits of the former had become apparent in
the new situation. This transition was marked by an
awareness of local conditions (such as the lack of
public services), a conscious widening of the social
base and a broadening of political fields of action.
There was much rational discussion, in contrast to
the subjective tactics of provocation employed by
the anti-authoritarian student movement.
        The transformation of the Liberal Free Demo-
crats (FDP) made them the party most open to the
citizens who wanted reforms through action by
Citizens' Initiatives. Reformers like Scheel, Flach
and Dahrendorf now replaced the national liberalism
of the earlier Liberals. The lack of a broad social
base and the lively youth organisation of the FDP
also made it easier for this party to attract the
support of the Citizens' Initiatives. Such was the
attraction of the FDP for these initiatives that
even in 1975 when the euphoria about reforms had
subsided, an FDP candidate was supported by them in
the communal elections in Kaiserstuhl, Baden-
Wuerttemberg, and gained seventy per cent of the
vote in a commune where there was strong opposition
to a planned nuclear power station.(16) Although
middle-class Citizens' Initiatives and other protest
groups were separate, the former were influenced by
the remains of the anti-authoritarian movement.
Thus an early publication on Citizens' Initiatives
referred to initiatives, on the one hand, by parents
who sought a more liberated educational system and
the creation of 'parent-child' groups and, on the
other hand, by groups which were concerned with

issues such as homelessness and squatting.(17)

The 'proletarian' orientation of many people within the New Left signalled a move away from what what were considered to be 'petty-bourgeois' and middle-class initiatives. The latter were only taken seriously when they were likely to involve 'mass actions': protests against price rises on public transport, battles with the authorities to prevent the eviction of squatters, or protest actions against the building of nuclear power stations. However, some left-wing groups were able to keep in contact with developments in the Citizens Initiatives. These were mainly groups which belonged to the 'undogmatic Left' whose motto was 'organisation according to interests'. Hence, anarchist and libertarian groups in Freiburg had co-operated with the villagers in Wyhl, Baden-Wuerttemberg, in opposing the plans of the Government and nuclear industry during the first major conflict between the ecology movement and the authorities.

As I have already suggested, the reason for the formation of Citizens' Initiatives generally arose from 'grievances and negative developments of a social and environmental kind'.(18) The initiatives were welcomed as a source of legitimation, providing a 'reformist mass base', especially for the FDP. In addition, the Citizens' Initiatives formed part of the 'dual strategy' for change by the youth wing of the SPD, the Jusos. Many initiatives, especially those concerned with education and social welfare, gained support from the government, but soon lost sight of their original aims. Other radical initiatives, for example the occupation of houses in Frankfurt, were quashed after being allowed to exist for a short period of time.

As Roth points out, many initiatives arose in marginalised social areas which had been excluded from participation in the political culture because of poor education and low social status.(19) Experimentation in these areas would not have been possible without professional help from social workers and groups like the Jusos. The sphere of politics was broadened as actions took place against high rents, lack of housing and other facilities, particularly in poorer areas where state institutions were not directly involved.

Most of the Citizens' Initiatives which arose at this time were organised and carried out their activities in accordance with the legal framework of the political system although, as P.C. Mayer-

Tasch has shown, they went beyond what the law had
foreseen: 'What had not been foreseen...was that
these legal possibilities would be used to the
extent that they have been used. Only this unexpect-
ed development led to the problem of legitimation'.
(20) Thus legitimated channels were used in innovative ways. In addition, officially sanctioned modes
of participation like citizens' forums (Buergerforen)
the amendment to the law to encourage urban constr-'
uction (Staedtebauforderungsgesetz), local advisory
bodies (Ortsbeiraete)and district representation
(Bezirksvertretung) in large cities all had an
ambivalent effect. The creation of these bodies at
a local level legitimated the activities of the
Citizens' Initiatives, and although they might have
led to an integration of the demands of the initiatives, during this period of conflict they did not
appear to have promoted the integration of the
opposition into the system.(21) Indeed the restrict-
ive character of the officially sanctioned forms of
participation and reforms led to the recognition of
the 'need' for less conventional forms of protest.
It was not long before the initiatives began to step
outside the legitimated channels, or to force the
state to restrict these channels, for example by
forbidding demonstrations around Brokdorf in 1977
and in 1981.

     As I have already suggested, the Social
Democratic-Liberal Alliance came into power in 1969
on the basis of a programme of reforms which meant
that for a certain period of time the Citizens'
Initiatives were welcomed. Moreover, their emergence was not only related to particular grievances
but to the different atmosphere at the time - one of
change and awakening political consciousness, partly
triggered off by the Grand Coalition and the anti-
authoritarian movement.

     The actions of the initiatives were directed
towards an improvement of disparate areas of need.
Claus Offe has described them as areas in which
labour-power and life are reproduced collectively
and not by individual acts of purchase. This occurs
in the spheres of housing, public transport, traffic,
education, health and leisure. The failure by the
state to deal with problems and changing needs in
these spheres ensured the survival of the initiatives.
The state had, according to Roth, re-directed funds
which were originally intended to help towards the
improvement of social services into economic programmes involving major investments:

A large portion of state funds went into
the building sector. The aim was to
create short-term employment and positive
growth and contradicted earlier aims for
reform. Projects for road-building with
an emphasis on (individual) private transport were carried out...the building of
private household dwellings was encouraged
whilst there was a fall in the rate of
building social accommodation; measures for
the protection of the environment were
made less rigid so as not to hinder
investment.(22)

The dissatisfaction at the lack of reforms, the
awareness - whether real or imagined - of the threat
posed by industrialisation to the environment, and
the pattern set by earlier by earlier protest movements and initiatives all led to the emergence of
a new extra-parliamentary mass protest movement in
the Federal Republic.

IV   Social Democratic and Free Democratic Parties

As extra-parliamentary movements, the groups which
applied pressure for changes in society did not pose
an immediate threat to the established 'people's'
or 'catch-all' parties. However, the formation of
the Green Party has meant that the Green Movement
threatens to attract the votes of the population at
elections and thereby undermine the basis for legitimation and power of the major parties. The
Social Democrats have suffered most from these
changes. Throughout the sixties the SPD, having
renounced its Marxist ideology, became a broadly-
based party of employees, rather than a narrow class
party. Yet, since then it has become vulnerable to
the loss of the group of people that helped into
power. For this reason, despite the loss of voters
both to the FDP and to the CDU at the 1982 Hessian
communal elections, the SPD stated clearly that it
perceived the Greens as the greatest threat.(23)
Large sections of the educated middle classes that
had joined the SPD in the fifties and sixties have
either taken up the issues raised by the Greens, or
gone over to join them. None the less the educated
middle classes form the elite group in the hierarchy
of the SPD. Those with a better formal education

and who work in the public service are over-
represented in the upper ranks of the party.

The SPD, as I shall illustrate, underwent a
crisis founded on the conflict between diverse
interests within the party and related to social
transformations outside the party. The question
then arises, whether the SPD, following its years of
success as a party capable of integrating various
groups with conflicting interests, can maintain this
success and reply to the challenge posed by the new
social movements and their organisations.

The changes undergone by the SPD in the 1950s
(and symbolised by the Godesberg Programme) and in
the 1960s (Grand Coalition with the Christian Democrats) set the stage for the SPD to form a government with the Free Democrats in 1969. A new party
elite had succeeded a traditional one which had
suffered a series of historical defeats - in the
1930s with the ascendancy of Hitler, at the end of
the war with the 'bourgeois restoration' and in the
1950s with the repeated success of the Christian
Democrats, based on a rapidly expanding economy
and on a powerful anti-communist ideology.(24) The
SPD reacted to these changes with conformity in the
sense that it saw an opportunity in the economic
boom to play a role in the distribution of the
recently accumulated wealth. By 1969 the SPD
appeared to many middle-class voters as the party
most capable of managing the economy, quite apart
from the attraction it held in promising reforms in
education and the 'quality of life'.

The dependence of people's parties on conflicting bases of support has been analysed by Joachim
Raschke, in a detailed empirical study of the Left
in the Berlin SPD, from which he concluded that the
people's parties:

> seek the broadest possible and most stable
> support (voters, pressure groups, also
> party members) which should provide the
> necessary legitimation in the system; the
> concrete content of their policies is, how-
> ever, primarily determined by the directing
> functions of the state apparatus in
> advanced capitalism.(25)

According to Raschke, the people's party becomes an
organisational carrier of the state apparatus which
extends the functions of the latter into society.
This contrasts with its earlier role, in the case of

the SPD, of wanting to overcome capitalism, and
hence, as an organisation which extended 'into' the
state. Thus the structure and inner-party conflicts
of the SPD are determined by the 'contradiction
between its social base and its directing functions
in the system'.(26) The people's party is thus
caught in a dilemma between its function of control
in the state apparatus and the imperative to gain
maximum votes at elections: on the one hand, it has
to reduce the claims which are made and, on the
other hand, it has to take up claims.(27) It should
not be overlooked that the study by Raschke was confined to the situation in West Berlin. However, the
conflict between Social Democratic government policy
and the aspirations of its bases of support were
brought into prominence by the demands of the Green
Movement, for instance during the controversy
surrounding the proposed extension of Frankfurt Airport. Thus in the 1981 communal elections in Hessen
the SPD lost votes both to the Left and to the Right.
According to Erhard Eppler:

> Some voters in Frankfurt did not vote for
> the SPD because the SPD in Frankfurt opp-
> osed the extension of the airport,
> although Holger Boerner [the Social Democrat
> leader in Hessen] supported the extension
> of the airport. They voted for the CDU.
> Other voters did not vote for the SPD
> because Holger Boerner was in favour of the
> extension of the airport, and they voted
> for the Greens.(28)

The division within the SPD over this issue
revealed that conflicts have emerged which have not
been easily subsumed into the people's party. It is
this that prompted Professor Richard Loewenthal, in
December 1981, to declare that the SPD must clearly
decide for 'industrial society with its division of
labour' and for the majority of working people
against marginal groups of dropouts. Loewenthal and
the right-wing of the party were increasingly
worried that the membership of the SPD was becoming
'infected' by the ideology of the Green Movement and
thus might attempt to offer simplistic answers to
problems that concerned no more than a few marginal
groups. In reality, more than half of the population was, in 1983, opposed to the construction of
further nuclear power stations and to the placement
of new missiles on West German soil.

The Left within the SPD was unable to attract the supporters of the Green Movement into its ranks. Moreover, throughout the seventies, the Left was unable to challenge the autonomy and strength of members who held important positions within the state apparatus, despite the fact that: 'Contrary to all... expectations, the period since 1969 has been one in which the role of the SPD has been subject to a constant and sweeping debate, of an intensity and scope not seen since 1914'.(29) William Paterson also points out that the SPD, in the early seventies, often 'seemed to dissolve into a governing party and a movement' because of the challenge posed by the Jusos and the educated, middle-class membership. The Left is thus composed mainly of the 'wage dependent middle class' which collides with the interests of the group whose its interests it claims to represent - the industrial working class.(30) Division and uncertainty within the Left culminated in defeats in the elections to the party executive committee in December 1979. The exclusion of the influx of left-wing members from the generation of the student movement from positions of power in the seventies is another reason for the weakness of the Left, although one has to consider the limited number of positions within any party that can be offered to a younger generation and thereby serve the purpose of integrating them.(31) This meant that at a time when the issue of ecology was capturing the imagination of increasing numbers of people, the SPD was lacking in people who were capable of carrying out a dialogue with the protestors. A central figure in the attempt by the SPD to communicate with the protest movements was Peter Glotz, who has become the General Secretary of the party.

Quite apart from these problems, to remain in power, the SPD had to make concessions to capitalist interests, to secure investment and the rates of profit. It also needed the support of the trade unions and to maintain their standard of living. It was obliged to consider the interests of the United States with regard to NATO and the role of the Federal Republic in the Common Market. This partly explains why the problems of youth and environmentalism as well as other related issues featured low in the list of priorities. Later I will indicate areas and initiatives which attempted to correct such an imbalance and how, by moving to the Left on these issues, it may have alienated voters on the Right, for example in the 1983 Federal Elections.

NOTES
1. W.Hollstein, Die Gegengesellschaft (Neue Gesellschaft, Bonn, 1980), p. 24.
2. J.Kerouac, On the Road (Penguin, 1972), p. 102.
3. Hollstein, Gegengesellschaft, p. 26.
4. G.Galli, 'The Student Movement in Italy', The Human Context, Vol. II, p. 494ff.
5. Hollstein, Gegengesellschaft, p. 37.
6. Ibid., pp. 43-4.
7. Ibid., p. 47.
8. Ibid., pp. 48-9.
9. Ibid., p. 51.
10. Ibid., p. 63.
11. Ibid., p. 56.
12. H.Bock, Geschichte des 'linken Radikalismus' in Deutschland, (Suhrkamp, Frankfurt, 1976), p. 262.
13. Ibid., p. 263.
14. R.Roth, 'Notizen zur politischen Geschichte der Buergerinitiativen in der Bundesrepublik', in R.Roth (ed.), Parlamentarisches Ritual und politische Alternativen (Campus, Frankfurt, 1980), p. 78.
15. Ibid.
16. BBU-aktuell Umweltmagazin, 3, 1978, p. 17.
17. Roth, 'Geschichte der Buergerinitiativen', p. 80.
18. P.C.Mayer-Tasch, Die Buergerinitiativbewegung (Reinbek, Hamburg, 1976), p. 12.
19. Roth, 'Geschichte der Buergerinitiativen', p. 85.
20. Mayer-Tasch, Buergerinitiativbewegung, p. 17.
21. Roth, 'Geschichte der Buergerinitiativen', p. 85.
22. Ibid., p. 87.
23. Guardian, 23 March 1982.
24. H.Kaste and J.Raschke, 'Zur Politik der Volkspartei', in W-D.Narr (ed.), Auf dem Weg zum Einparteienstaat (Westdeutscher Verlag, Opladen, 1977), p. 49f.
25. J.Raschke, Innerparteiliche Opposition. Die Linke in der Berliner SPD (Hoffmann und Campe, Hamburg, 1974), p. 13.
26. Ibid., p. 14. See also Kaste and Raschke, 'Zur Politik der Volkspartei', p. 50 who write that: 'State-theoretical and empirical analysis show a systematic privilege of capitalist interests - precisely where it is intended to limit them without affecting the basic principle of the profit-orientated realisation of capital: in social democratic activity in government'.
27. Kaste and Raschke, 'Zur Politik der Volkspartei',p.54.
28. Der Spiegel, Nr. 51, 1981, p. 29.
29. W.Paterson, 'Social Democracy - The West German Example' in M.Kolinsky and W.Paterson (eds.), Social and Political Movements in Western Europe (Croom Helm, London, 1976), p. 232.
30. Kaste and Raschke, 'Zur Politik der Volkspartei', p.69.
31. H.See, 'Strukturwandel und Ideologieprobleme der SPD'. in W-D.Narr(ed.),Auf dem Weg zum Einparteienstaat, p. 75ff.

Chapter Two

THEMES AND CONCEPTS (1)

The Green Movement comprises a wide range of groups which, although they seek to retain their autonomy, are united over certain themes and concepts. Table 2.1 attempts to provide the reader with a rough summary of the main trends that have either reflected or influenced the evolution of the diverse strands of the Green Movement. An assessment of the statements made by the intellectual inspirers of the movement does provide us with insights into the main themes and concepts which have influenced and arisen out of it. The intellectual inspirers exercise a decisive influence since they are often themselves activists and, if there is a lack of correspondence between their ideas and those of their supporters, they are subjected to heavy criticism.

In addition, it has been possible to monitor the themes and concepts which recur consistently because of the development of channels of communication within the movement itself, in particular the production of the daily newspaper _Tageszeitung_ (Taz) which enjoys a circulation of around 30,000 copies. Moreover, surveys carried out with representative samples of the population have measured both the level of support for some of the major themes and concepts and for particular groups. This chapter focuses on the contrast, evoked by the Green Movement, between 'technocracy' and 'community', and on the bases for the subjectivist critique of modernity.

I   Technocracy versus community?

Significant changes in the organisation of advanced capitalist societies have inspired theories about

18

the emergence of a 'post-industrial' society. The
theories were related to the adoption, in the late
sixties and early seventies, of programmes for long-
term planning. These appeared to reinforce the
power of executive decision-making bodies. It was
easy for many protestors against nuclear energy to
link these ideas to the concept of a 'nuclear state'
with its apparatus of supervision and control, which
could not be brought to account before the elected
representatives of the country.

One of the main proponents of a theory of
technocracy was Alain Touraine. He argued that the
conflict between those who rule and those who are
ruled, differs from the one which dominated 'industrial' society, namely between employers and workers,
since 'it is no longer situated inside an organisation at the place of work', but in the 'apparatus of
production' and the 'territory of consumption'.
Thus when

> investment is no longer limited to the
> distribution of products, as in the
> market economy, or to the organisation of
> labour, as in industrial society, but trans-
> forms production itself - thanks to scient-
> ific and technical progress, including the
> capacity to administer complex communication
> networks - it is then the organisations
> which become...the dominant actor. The
> main conflict takes place between these
> organisations and their social environment,
> between the apparatus of production and the
> territory of consumption.(1)

In West Germany the apparatus includes the state
administration and industrial interests; the territory is the 'community' which the Green Movement
seeks to defend against 'post-industrial' capitalist
investment.

The critique of 'technocracy' is based partly
on a rational assessment of the destructive effects
of the present organisation of industrial societies.
(It is also related to the disappointment of the
educated middle classes and the trade unions, as I
indicated earlier, with the role taken on by the
Social Democratic Party in regulating the economy.)
However, the contrast between apparatus and territory
or between technocracy and community overlooks the
conflicts that arise within the 'technocratic
apparatus.

Table 2.1 Summary of the main trends in the evolution

	Ecology Movement	Alternative Movement
1976	mass mobilisation against nuclear energy (Brokdorf, Wyhl)	emergence of Sponti student protest movement
1977	further mass demonstrations in Grohnde, Brokdorf and Kalkar	growing influence of Sponti ideas
1978	protests against nuclear reprocessing plant in Gorleben	peak of Sponti movement and attempts by Peter Glotz to hold a dialogue with it
1979	100,000 protest in Hannover and 150,000 in Bonn against government policies on nuclear energy	creation of hundreds of alternative projects, e.g. the Taz newspaper
1980	creation of alternative village in Gorleben; mass protest against extension of Frankfurt Airport	number of alternative projects estimated at 11,500; beginning of mass protest in support of squatters
1981	100,000 at Brokdorf and 100,000 at Wiesbaden; violence around Frankfurt Airport	squatters' protest and riots; squatters link up with alternative projects
1982	less prominent but continual protest activity at a local level	increasing debates over whether to accept funds from the state for projects
1983	main focus of attention is now on the peace movement, but environmental issues still important (e.g. debate over 'acid-rain' in Federal Elections	increasing pressure on projects both in terms of more members and less material resources

of the Green Movement   (1976-1983)

Green Party	Peace Movement	Established Groups
		no significant changes after Federal Elections: SPD-FDP Coalition continues
emergence of Green Lists at a local level		murder of Federal Attorney General Buback and of industrialist Schleyer by left-wing terrorists
Green Lists gain around 4% of vote in Hamburg and Lower Saxony state elections		Federal Parliament launches an inquiry into future energy policy
3.2% for a Green List in European Elections; another one enters Bremen Parliament with 5% of the vote	announcement of NATO dual-track decision signals start of the peace movement	SPD Congress: 40% of the delegates oppose party policy on nuclear energy
formation of Green Party; success in Baden-Wuerttemberg but not in the Federal Elections	emergence of decentralised protest, especially among church groups	success of SPD-FDP Coalition at Federal Elections; the state begins a dialogue with alternative projects
widespread support in Hessen and Lower Saxony local elections; 7.2% of vote in West Berlin	300,000 in Bonn rally; riots in Berlin against Alexander Haig	conflicts within SPD and trade unions over peace policy; government inquiry into youth protest
more than 5% of the vote in state elections; Greens hold balance of power in Hessen and Hamburg	mass protests in Bonn and Berlin; broad support from Social Democrats and trade unionists	Berlin CDU offers millions of marks to self-help projects; end of SPD-FDP Coalition
5.6% of the vote at Federal Elections and 27 seats in Federal Parliament	about half a million people take part in Easter protest activities	success of CDU/CSU-FDP Coalition and defeat for SPD under leadership of Vogel at Federal Elections

Giddens provides us with a more differentiated perspective, by referring to the growth of big corporations and the need for new policies by the state:

> ...the emergence of planning creates a whole series of potential new conflicts between state and industry on the one hand, and within the class structure more generally. There is a close link here with the role of social democracy. Social democratic parties have, at least in many countries, played an important part in initiating, furthering, or supporting planning - for obvious enough reasons. Not only do schemes of macroeconomic growth need the support of the trade unions in particular, and the acquiescence of the working class as a whole, but the ideology of social democracy is particularly conducive to the promotion of centralised economic regulation.(2)

For example, in West Germany there occurred throughout the seventies a series of 'modifications' to the administrative powers of the states, an increase in the provisions for 'joint tasks' and joint planning and financing which resulted in greater powers for the central government.(3) The interpretation of these changes divides those who are fearful of a technocratic post-industrial society and those who refer to differentiations within industrial capitalist society. The former interpret events in terms of alienation and human interests, whilst the latter emphasize the significance of exploitation.

In its attempt to move away from 'material values' the Green Movement has stressed the significance of general human interests as opposed to narrow class interests. There is also a tendency to adopt the standpoint of Touraine who maintains that if property was the criterion of membership in the former dominant classes, the new dominant class is defined by knowledge and a certain level of education.(4) In truth there is, as Giddens has pointed out, 'nothing new in the application of theoretical knowledge to productive technique'.(5) This emphasis on knowledge and education relates to the challenge to traditional elites by the Green Movement on the basis of these two factors. Giddens would argue that the ownership of wealth and property still play a fundamental role and that in capitalist

society 'the class system continues to constitute
the main channel of relationships of exploitative
domination'.(6) Although supporters of the Green
Movement are aware of the power of wealth and the
significance of the class system, they are particularly interested in the search for a new community
rather than the development of traditional trade
union struggles. Many would agree with Rudolf Bahro
that the struggle between employers' associations
and the trade unions 'shows all the signs of being a
stalemate'.(7) Bahro argues that the 'species
interest' should become the 'fundamental point of
reference' and that changes can only be achieved by
going 'beyond' Marx's own concept of class.(8)
He is therefore in favour of the creation of a class
of 'collective workers' which will encompass eighty
per cent of the population who belong to the 'wage-
earning class in the broadest sense'.

However, a precondition for the creation of
the 'collective worker' class is a shift from the
material to the creative values of 'self-affirmation
and self-realisation'. The observation by Inglehart
that a 'change in values' has been taking place in
Western democracies is transformed into a belief,
upheld by the supporters of the Green Movement, that
this new motivation is 'coming to the fore in _all_
strata of the collective worker'. This is often
further exaggerated into the assertion that 'the
most energetic people, and those strongest in their
mental demands, are at some point or other to begin
a creative life even if this means a reduction in
their living standards and external security'.(9)

The intellectual inspirers of the Green Movement are not so much concerned with the exploitative
but with the alienative effects of the capitalist
system:

> The psychological dimension of the problem
> of individuality in super-complex industrial
> society must be made completely clear. The
> different spheres of life - work, education,
> housing, recreation - are so separated from
> one another, almost all activities are so
> depersonalised and even private ties stripped
> of so many necessities, that the alienation
> of one person from another threatens to
> become the general fate...We find a loss of
> emotional connection even in the intimate
> contacts of the nuclear family, this last
> residue of the original community.(10)

This approach concurs with Touraine's view that new
conflicts have emerged between the structures of
economic and political decision-making and those who
are reduced to 'dependent participation'.(11) He
thus relates 'class struggles' to the 'alienative
effects of subordination to technocratic decisions'
rather than material exploitation.

These views are based on the assumption that
real exisitng trends within, for instance, the ecology
movement could be carried over to apply to the whole
of society. They tend to assume that because among
young people(Table 2.2) the Green Movement is supported by all classes, they can generalise this trend.

Table 2.2 Support among young people (16-24 age group) for
the ecology movement (compared to support for other groups)
related to class and education

| | Class | | (%) | Education | |
| | | Upper | Inter- | Modern | |
	Lower Middle	Middle	mediate	Secondary	Grammar
Committed protest groups					
environmenta-lists	38 31	31	37	32	31
opponents of nuclear energy	39 34	27	36	30	35
Non-committal groups					
football fans	58 28	15	60	25	17
disco fans	53 26	21	54	34	12
Youth culture groups					
music group fans	42 33	24	50	28	21
motorcycle fans	44 33	23	57	28	25
Total % of all young people	42 30	26	45	30	25

Source: Figures from Shell Studie, (1981), Jugend 1981,
Hamburg, Vol. 1, p. 494.

Joseph Huber has criticised this tendency to overlook the 'social question' since behind the issue of
'ecology' there lie the issues of economic disposal
and distribution.(12) As Giddens has pointed out in
his critique of theories on technocracy, it is still
useful to speak in terms of exploitation: that is
'any socially conditioned form of asymmetrical production of life-chances' or 'the chances an individual has of sharing in the socially created or

cultural 'goods' which typically exist in any given
society'. Thus, 'exploitation implies a separation
between the social creation of human faculties on
the one hand, and the denial of 'access' to those
faculties on the other'.(13)
Within a system structuredby class, 'the system
of exploitation operates through differentials in
market capacity'(14) which are related not simply to
economic modes but also access to education, the
type of work environment, as well as other benefits
and facilities which are potentially accessible.
According to Giddens these differentials do not
alter 'the central focus of class relationships as
founded in production'.(15) Differentiations within
the social structure, for example the different
situations, mobility chances, division of labour,
role in authority structures and patterns of consumption of white-collar and manual workers need to
be taken into consideration.(16) By placing the
question of 'survival' and the 'species interest' at
the centre of their arguments, supporters of the
ecology movement lose sight of these differentiations,
with the ensuing danger that instead of coming to
terms with the situation within the Federal Republic,
they identify with something distant as the extra-
parliamentary opposition in the sixties had done
with developments in the Third World.(17) For
workers it is not just a question of the interests
of humanity when their jobs are threatened; manual
workers are usually the first to be affected by unemployment. As Benson has pointed out, the threat
of unemployment is perhaps 'the greatest single
psychological burden of the worker'.(18)
Within the Green Movement the greatest psychological burden of its supporters is the fear of isolation and loss of personal and collective identity.
The creation of alternative communities forms part
of an effort to replace isolation with companionship,
fear with happiness and boredom with adventure. In a
letter to the Taz a reader offered his vision of the
future:

> We need love, peace and harmony in order
> to be able to live with and love each
> other. They go hand in hand. In a commun-
> ity, with which I am not yet familiar, love
> is possible, love is adoration, thanks and
> honour. There we love our bodies as we do
> our souls and as the cool mountain lake,
> the green forests with their birds with
> colourful feathers and the large sun which

grants us warmth and light. We no longer
experience ourselves as isolated individuals
in a community, but we are a living organism
...Let us become super-humans! Let us liberate ourselves and let us realise our dreams
and heroic and astonishing deeds.(19)

The term 'super-human' is the same as the one used
by Nietzsche in Unzeitgemaesse Betrachtungen
(Untimely Meditations). The relevance of the ideas
of Nietzsche will be explored more fully later in
this chapter.

For young people, the idea of 'experiencing
themselves as individuals' who are not isolated in
a community is of great importance. The slogans in
Table 2.3 express the desire among young people for
'life' and living together, and they enjoy widespread support. Even the last two slogans which
express a very negative view of the level of
isolation and alienation in society gain the
approval of about 45 per cent of all young people.

Table 2.3 Slogans from the youth culture which express
a desire for 'life' and living together (16-24 age group)

| Slogans | I consider the slogan... | | | |
	very good %	good %	less good %	not at all good %
to love, live, work together – without these walls everywhere – now!	38	46	13	3
to live – now!	34	39	14	3
why don't they simply let us be happy!	27	48	20	5
we won't let ourselves be done in, made small, equalized!	20	45	26	9
everybody here is shut in concrete!	13	35	37	15
everybody here isolates himself completely!	8	34	42	16

Source: Figures from Shell Studie, (1981), Jugend 1981,
Hamburg, Vol. 1, p. 465.

The search for meaningful and human relationships in a secularised and complex world has pre-
occupied people both within and outside the Green
Movement. This search has become increasingly
'politicised'. The interventions of the police and
legal apparatus, for example in the disputes about
squatting, are regarded as part of the continuous
intrusion of the system into further areas of 'life'.
Members of the Squatters' Council in Berlin Kreuzberg saw their activity as an attempt to win back
'time and spaces for living'. They wanted to have
more time for joking and chatting; for artistic and
creative work; for different relationships; and for
children and old people. They also wanted space
for working according to their principle of co-
operation rather than competition, and to achieve
self-determination in all spheres of life. Moreover,
this concept also favoured attempts to launch 'autonomous attacks from all sides against the state
system'.(20)
In contemporary society many groups, in their
search for collective identity, seek to create their
own community on the basis of ascriptive features
such as age group or sex or the occupation of empty
houses.(21) Women, for instance, are often encouraged to withdraw their support from men, to leave
them in the lurch so that they sort out their own
difficulties themselves.(22) Human fulfilment thus
becomes conditional upon 'finding oneself' after
withdrawing from conflicts which are conditioned by
sex.
Social and material problems are often seen as
an expression of alienation from oneself and from
the natural surroundings, and not in terms of social
structures and power relationships. Thus, in their
critique of modern housing, supporters of the alternative movement focus on the exclusion of nature and
of one's neighbours from modern houses rather than
on aspects of political economy.(23) This is
certainly a valid perspective, yet it is undermined
by a desire to interpret any problems as a sign of
the overall decay of the system. To overcome the
alienation of human beings from nature and from each
other it has been proposed that only when the archi-
tect, the builder and the occupant of a house are
'united', can one validly speak of 'architecture'.
(24) Since contemporary society does not meet these
standards, whether they are desirable and possible,
or not, the answer for many people is to withdraw

from it. This withdrawal is accompanied by a
rejection of the present in terms of a traditional
past and certain pre-industrial ideals. For
example, a far higher percentage of the young supporters of the Green Party than of any other party
would like to live in a solitary log hut in the
woods; or in a fishing village, living with
neighbours and without any industry at all; or on a
farm a hundred years ago. (Table 2.4)

Table 2.4 Favoured ideal places to live related to party-
political orientation (16-24 age group)

Ideal places (would like to live there much, or very much...)	CDU/CSU	SPD	GREENS
	%	%	%
Alternative idylls located in the past			
a solitary log hut in the woods	49	55	67
on a farm a hundred years ago	28	31	45
a fishing village, living with neighbours and no industry at all	54	61	83
Land of milk and honey			
a dream villa where every luxury exists	70	68	37
an island in the South Sea with palm trees and fruit	88	85	81
Narcisstic dream			
as a noble beast in the open wilds (e.g. a horse or panther)	20	21	30
on a sailing boat as king of the pirates	26	31	21
Civilised place of adventure			
at home in the night-life of a big city	33	40	25
Outer Space			
on a space craft or a planet in space	26	16	12

Source: Figures from Shell Studie, (1981), Jugend 1981,
Hamburg, Vol, 1, p. 684

Supporters of the Green Movement tend - more
than other groups of young people - to seek an ideal
located in nature which has not been affected by
industrial civilisation. To many people the triumph
of nature over destructive machinery and modern
civilisation becomes the general aim. A cartoon in
the Taz attempts to portray the campaign against
the West Runway near Frankfurt as the struggle
against the 'dictatorship' of the leader of the SPD
in Hessen, Holger Boerner, who was in favour of the

project. The cartoon shows a 'monument' of a tree
out of which there emerges a clenched fist within
which an aeroplane, a symbol of modern industrial
civilisation, has been crushed. The caption below
the drawing refers to the 'Monument in the Floers-
heim Forest, erected in the year...in honour of the
people who fought the Boerner dictatorship'.(25)
    The Green Movement has contributed to an inc-
rease in awareness of certain problems. However,
the contrast between technocratic society and alternative communities serves as a model for its supporters to justify their efforts to bring about an
alternative civilisation based on new values. This
contrast is founded on the questionable assumption
that technocracy is alien to the creation of a fruitful community life. In reality anti-technocratic
ideas like the critique of consumerism are easily
integrated into existing society. Anti-materialist
ideas or values may in effect only symbolise a
change in consumer habits. Huber has commented
that the critics of consumerism do not consume less
than anyone else, only differently.(26) On the
basis of 'utopian' ideas about communal living,
participation and creativity, new businesses
'colonise the informal sector' of the economy.(27)
Furthermore, the prophets of doom may serve an
important function in warding off the occurrence of
catastrophes by alerting an allegedly technocratic
society to the dangers which threaten the environment and community life.(28)

II Bases for the subjectivist critique of modernity

Recently, sociologists have become increasingly
concerned about the effects of modernisation on the
identity of the individual. Peter Berger has drawn
our attention to the fact that modernisation has
led to a 'progressive separation of the individual
from collective entities' and that:

> at the same time as these concrete communi-
> ties have been replaced by the abstract
> megastructures of modern society, the
> individual self has come to be experienced
> as both distinct and greatly complicated -
> and, by that very fact, in greater need of
> personal belonging which is difficult in
> abstract institutions.(29)

According to Dreitzel, people experience a gap
between, on the one hand, 'economic and scientific-
technological activity', and on the other hand,
'personal life and interaction'.(30) The concern
which is expressed by these authors about the evolution of industrial society and its effects on the
individual is echoed by the Green Movement in West
Germany. However, neither the sociologists nor
supporters of the protest movements give us any
clear indication of when these changes date from.

In Germany they can be traced back to the
response by the German middle classes to the arrival
of industrialisation in the late nineteenth century.
Hugh Ridley and Keith Bullivant, in their assessment
of how the middle classes viewed industrial expansion between the middle and late nineteenth century,
have noted that:

> the national ideology emerging in Germany
> in the late nineteenth century was not, as
> one might have assumed, a direct reflection
> of the nation's increasing military and
> industrial strength, but took on the form
> of Kulturpessimismus [cultural pessimism]:
> a rejection of the present in terms of a
> traditional past.(31)

They also point out that the people who rejected the
conditions of Germany's industrial expansion were in
no hurry to renounce the results of it, namely an
increase in the international prestige of their
country. Hence, because 'their hands were tied in
this way, their social protest never became fruitful
social criticism'.

The Green Movement has shown similar signs of
rejecting the present in terms of a traditional
past. In contrast to the middle classes in the late
nineteenth century, it is not tied down to a natio-
nalist ideology. However, most of its supporters
appear to enjoy the material benefits of industrial
civilisation whilst rejecting it as such. For
example, the Taz uses micro-computers to ensure the
successful operation and distribution of the newspaper. As one editor explained, no significant
sections of the ecology and alternative movements
want to give up technology which would save work.
He admitted, however, that it was 'not at all clear'
how certain heavy industrial processes which are
absolutely necessary, for example to manufacture
ploughing equipment for fields, could fit into a

concept which favoured exclusively small, graspable,
decentralised units.(32) The lack of clarity over
the consequences and implications of the critique
of modern civilisation poses serious problems for
the Green Movement, as I shall illustrate by compar-
ing it to other expressions of disquiet at the path
of industrialisation.

In the late nineteenth century Nietzsche had
expressed the view that science and excessive historical knowledge had destroyed life-giving mythical
forces, that the accumulation of knowledge had no
relation to fruitful life.(33) Nietzsche felt that
the moral and logical problems posed by the rationalist outlook on life (that is, that God no longer
existed) had not been confronted, and that the in-
compatibility of Christian love with the Darwinist
struggle had left a 'nihilist gap'. In his view,
life could only be guaranteed in the future if it
was dominated by human instinct and powerful myths.
He nurtured the idea of the 'superman'(or, 'supra-
historical man') who could experience the fulness of
life and who belonged to the German tradition of
assent to the world as it is, the world of the flesh
and physical realities. Such a notion can be traced
back to the Promethean myth of the eternal warmth of
man who has great power. This was contrasted to the
Judaeo-Christian tradition of Adam and Eve, who were
banished from paradise and condemned to eternal toil
and miséry because they had not been able to resist
the temptation of physical and earthly goods.

Nietzsche himself was not an anti-Semite and he
loathed anti-Semitism. However, his ideas about the
importance of a life dominated by human instinct and
powerful myths were taken up and politicised in an
uncritical manner by writers of that period. His
cult of the 'superman', his emphasis on the fulness
of human life and on the fact that life alone, not
justice, truth or objectivity, was the true judge
of the past(34), were transferred by others into the
economic sphere. Nietzschean imagery was used to
depict the successes of the 'captains of industry'
and self-made men of that era.(35) It was also
used by writers like Julius Langbehn to provide fac-
ile answers to the social problems of the time.
Langbehn and other 'cultural pessimist' writers
offered to the middle classes an escape from their
feeling that they were outcasts and uprooted individuals in the emergent industrial nation by idealis-
ing nature and reviving a spurious German tradition
of community and racial purity. The racialist

solution to social conflicts was later taken up by
the National Socialists who encouraged the idea that
authenticity could only be found in the 'natural
racial being' rather than in the 'social self'. (In
Britain, at the turn of the century, social tensions
at home coincided with jingoism, extreme nationalism
and the idea that the Empire belonged to everyone.)
Although Nietzsche did not support the 'literary
racists', they felt, as Fritz Stern has shown, a
particular affinity for the 'lonely prophet'. In his
best-selling work, Rembrandt als Erzieher (1890),
Langbehn attacked intellectualism, science and
modern culture. He sought to revive a 'true Germanic past', and in the words of Stern, to restore old
German virtues which had been lost: 'childlike
simplicity, subjectivity and individuality'.(36)

The work of Langbehn reflected widespread feelings of pessimism among the middle classes at the
time. The themes which he raises, the search for
simplicity, subjectivity and individuality were of
great importance to the German Youth Movement
(Wandervoegel) at the turn of the century. When the
movement was formed in 1896 the youth of suburban
Berlin took off into the countryside, whilst decry-
ing a 'souless materialism'. After World War One
many young people, mainly from middle-class, professional families from the cities, and who found no
attraction in the politics of Social Democracy,
continued the movement. The critique by the movement and its ideologists was aimed, not at the
'remote' world of the factory, but at the urban
environment, the modern city, with its concrete and
traffic and corrupting effects, and the adult world,
which lacked understanding and respect.(37) In
contemporary society, the protest by young people is
similarly directed against the urban environment,
the adult world and the loss of communal bonds.
In addition, the protest is mainly supported by a
similar group of people, namely the young middle
classes. Does all this make it particularly
susceptible to a right-wing ideology based on a critique of modernity, or to a utopian left-wing
ideology?

In a recent publication on right-wing tendencies within the ecology movement, Jan Peters tried
to illustrate the intellectual continuity of ideas
between movements in the 1920s and contemporary
movements by showing how the flight from the city,
the critique of technology, cultural criticism and
the yearning for nature can be found within the

Green Movement and are traditional elements of
German Romanticism and pre-nationalist ways of
thinking.(38) This approach is rejected out of hand
by the producers of alternative ideology in the Taz.
(39) Yet, despite their firm repudiation of any
connections with fascism, they do not hesitate to
assert that mythology, an essential element of
German Romanticism, will play a vital role in bringing about the transformation of society:

> The myth of fascism is not of any danger
> to us. What is dangerous is if the Left
> does not take up mythology and thereby throws
> out emotionality. Fascism was a combination
> of myth and technocracy, centralisation and
> military apparatus, which did not contain
> individuality and the destruction of centr-
> alised structures. We refer to folk myth-
> ology in the sense that within a region,
> mythological ways of thinking are conveyed
> in the relationship to the countryside, in
> the relationships which I have with others,
> and that is so far removed from fascism as
> anything else.(40)

Few people will deny that mythology is an essential
ingredient of community life. Yet the same author
goes on to praise the older generation, which is
usually criticised by the Left for its involvement
with Fascism, for being much more aware of certain
aspects of mythology because 'in those days they had
not been so undermined by television and technocracy'.
    Blinded by its vision of a 'technocratic'
society, the Green Movement proclaims the revolt of
life and individuality. In some instances it veers
towards dangerous ground in its efforts to combine
subjectivity, the liberation of instincts and social
criticism. An intellectual sympathiser of the Green
Movement declared:

> The youth protests have rediscovered the
> body. They feel that it is not there for
> indolent self-reflection or for self-
> destruction but for expressive public display,
> for fighting, for trying out one's powers in
> order to experience things. This discovery
> is one of the main reasons for the use and
> support of violence...A young demonstrator
> says: 'You don't know this liberating feel-

ing when the windows of a boutique selling
furs or of a bank shatter'. This is no
senseless brawl, but rather the effort to
change the room for manouevre in a world
that is bureaucratically covered in glass
and concrete...In a house occupied by
squatters in Berlin one can read the slogan:
'In dubio pro libido'. That is why it makes
sense when young people demonstrate in the
nude. They are placing their naked bodies
against the concrete, against the law and
against self-destruction.(41)

The search for a better, future society in which
human needs are fulfilled, is partly based on a
tradition which has been inherited from Nietzsche.
The latter shares with the utopian socialists and
Marxists the view that all of history so far is
only one stage in the process leading to the emergence of the true man; whilst he had faith in the
emergence of a 'superman', the Marxists believe that
the 'new man' will emerge in a classless society.
(42)
      Of course it is important to distinguish bet-
ween the attempt by the National Socialists to combine technocracy and certain myths and supporters
of the contemporary movements who are tempted into
transforming popular feeling into mythology and
subjectivity. The mythology that exists in the
Green Movement retreats into the irrational and
subjective past whilst looking forward to the future,
towards a utopian society. The radicalism of the
supporters of the Green Movement often resembles
that of the movement of Expressionist writers and
poets in the 1920s who, having been born into the
industrial world, had to come to terms with it but,
in their search for meaningful relationships and
'humanity', were inclined to make absolute judgements
about the social world in an emotive, theological
manner and style of language.
      The effort to combine the 'authentically human'
with a transformation of industrial society is
shared by the Expressionists and large sections of
the new movements. Expressionist poets and dramat-
ists like Ernst Toller and Georg Kaiser devoted much
of their work to the theme of industrial society.
In the play Maschinenstuermer (1922), which is
about the Luddite Movement in Nottingham, Toller
concentrates on the objective political problems,
for instance on how machinery should not be

destroyed but used to serve human purposes. However
the message of the play is often undermined by un-
differentiated subjectivity in the dialogue. In
another play, Masse Mensch (1920) which, according
to the author, is about the 'social revolution of
the twentieth century', Toller never gives a clear
indication as to who the 'masses' actually are,
since the perspective of 'humanity' predominates and
overrides any social divisions; the search for a
community in relationships is, moreover, combined
with a tendency towards social regression, towards
a subjective idyllic view of the world. The plays
of Georg Kaiser, like Gas I (1918), a synonym for
the cruelty of industrial society, and of Ernst
Toller, were concerned with the visionary transformation of the world and not based on sociological
or analytical arguments. Later on, the disappointment that the transformation of society had not
occurred, resulted in pure nihilism, for example
in Kaiser's Gas II (1920).

The link between the German Youth Movement, the
Expressionists and contemporary movements is even
acknowledged in a publication of a key alternative
project, the Netzwerk self-help initiative, in
which Hans Koch, born in 1897, gives an account of
how the present alternative movement 'stepped into
its children's shoes'. Koch describes how he, the
son of a high-ranking civil servant in Berlin,
experienced the First World War and later contacted
members of the German Youth Movement. He took part
in various communal projects and even persuaded the
dramatist Georg Kaiser to finance him and his
comrades to set up a commune in the countryside.
Later he took part in the events surrounding the
short-lived Socialist Republic in Munich and came
into contact with the Expressionist dramatist Ernst
Toller, and with Erich Muehsam, a well-known
anarchist. Hans Koch felt that he had more in
common with young people in a variety of alternative
projects today than with people of the older
generation.

The article by Hans Koch is accompanied by two
cartoons by Fuchsi, a well-known cartoonist in the
contemporary alternative movement, which link up in
an unmistakeable manner the existing movement with
the Nietzschean critique of Christian morality,
which had been contrasted to the Germanic notion of
assent to the physical world. The first cartoon
shows naked characters from the alternative movement
enjoying a feast in the garden of Eden. Adam has
baked an apple pie for the other members of the

community; Eve is not clearly identifiable, but
could be the woman who is doing exercises to try and
lose weight after having eaten too many apples. Even
the serpents of paradise have joined in the feast.
The second cartoon shows God with his sword drawn
at the gates of paradise and the group from the alternative movement (including Adam and Eve as well as
the jaded snakes) who have all just been expelled
for their misdeeds. They do not appear to have any
remorse for their sins since one of them is shown
making a rude gesture at God, whilst the others have
set off in search of another paradisical orchard.
The cartoons bear the title, 'The alternative people
have more tradition than they imagine', and allude
to the links with the German Youth Movement, as
embodied by Hans Koch. Yet they are also either a
conscious or subconscious reference to the traditional beliefs which are taken up by, and inherited
from Nietzsche.(43)
    A more direct source of inspiration for the
alternative movement in Germany was the so-called
Sponti movement which emerged at the same time as
the ecology movement in the mid-seventies. The
Spontis made a major contribution to the creation of
the Taz newspaper project. Whilst their ideas
exercise a powerful influence on the Green Movement,
they were aware of their debt to the Nietzschean
critique of the rationalist outlook on life. The
Spontis also shared with the Expressionists of the
1920s the idea and experience that the direct
expression of subjective feelings is more important
than 'abstract theorising'. They regarded the
student movement of the sixties as 'too theoretical'
in its preoccupation with the revolutionary ideas of
Marx and Marcuse. They reflected the disappointment
of the student population with dogmatic communist
splinter groups, traditional politics, and large
organisations. The Spontis posed a number of
problems for the Left. One of their popular slogans
declared that 'Marx is dead, Lenin is dead, and I'm
not feeling too well either'.(44) In Vulkantaenze
- linke und alternative Ausgaenge two of the Sponti
theoreticians criticised Marxism because it 'repressed the instincts' and failed to take up the
subconscious elements of human experience.(45)
    The Left, argue the Spontis, has failed to take
part in the 'revolt of life' against the 'world of
death', which they describe as prison, lunatic
asylums, family structures, schools and war. This
failure is caused by its over-estimation of
'analysis and knowledge'.(46) 'Dogmatic' politics

is far too engrossed in the state. To the Spontis
the 'best state, is no state' since it is the
manager of death' which destroys everything and
maintains repressive structures.(47) 'Dogmatic'
politics, in its preoccupation with theory, the
state and analysis fails to perceive that 'instinct
produces a social sphere, that society presents a
network of a countless number of desires which are
mixed together'.(48) The Spontis conveyed this
perspective with their own very personal and
anarchic brand of humour and satire which often
puzzled people who sought to identify its serious
political meaning: 'Germans leave Germany and then
there will be peace', 'God knows everything but says
nothing, I know nothing but say everything', 'We
have nothing to lose apart from our fear' and 'The
Communist Party is the foreskin of the working
class, when things get serious it draws back'.(49)
The Spontis were also influenced by the 'Autonomist'
movement in Italy; their emergence formed part of an
effort to revive some of the cultural revolutionary
practices of the sixties as well as to combine
religious, mystical and idealist elements with
radical social practice. They reflect the writings
of Ernst Bloch who, in <u>Principle of Hope</u>, had
called for an alternative relationship to nature
and to technology, and also of Nietzsche in his
critique of knowledge and rationality.
    In <u>Vulkantaenze</u> the authors stress the decisive
nature of mythology in politics. Mythology, they
state, foresees the dominance of the will over
reason. They refer to the saying by Nietzsche that
the theorist understands as much about mythology as
a deaf person does about music.(50) The authors
feel that mythology needs to be embraced by progressive political forces, that neither 'bourgeois
rationality' nor Athenian dialectics nor Christian
laws 'could extinguish the irrational, the intuitive
and the imaginary world that people create'.(51)
We are told that the 'volcanic violence' generated
by the power of mythology in this century has filled
people with 'perplexity and fear' because Fascism was
able to use the power of mythology. The Spontis now
want to re-direct this power because, in their
opinion, it is the only force which can 'move things'
precisely because it is irrational and 'because it
does not allow itself to be criticised, because it
cannot be defined'.(52) And in a phrase borrowed
from Nietzsche, they describe their myths as
'beyond good and evil'.(53)

Mythology is contrasted to rationality. The latter is seen as a destroyer of life-affirming forces:

> There are experiences, ecstasies, powerful feelings, sweet wicked desires, which are better kept to oneself. If they are put into words, if one begins to discuss them the power of their intensity is destroyed; they are transplanted into the sphere of reason. Isn't that one of the tragedies of the discussion on sexual liberation?(54)

This critique of rationality echoes the writings of Nietzsche, particularly in Unzeitgemaesse Betrachtungen in which he is critical of the way modern man is burdened with undigested knowledge and resembles a walking encyclopaedia.(55) Nietzsche feared that too much knowledge would distort human emotions. In a sentence that sums up the situation of many people within the Green Movement, he complains that the 'young person has become so homeless, and calls into question all customs and meanings', because of the excess of knowledge which he or she is expected to absorb.(56) Nietzsche's critique was aimed at the German education system and its 'scientific factories'.(57)

His message is politicised by the Spontis who wish to bring about social change by awakening human desires. Purely political groups are criticised for their 'paranoia of reason'.(58) In contrast, 'anti-authoritarian collectives' will make people aware of the 'irrational vibrations' which travel through a community. The ideal society will thus, according to the Spontis, consist of collectives in which people will recognise the 'differences of others'. (59) The inevitable breakdown of collectives, as contradictory desires lead to the dissolution of groups, will not however lead to individual isolation and loneliness: 'Rather new collectives will be formed with other contents and other people'.(60) We are not told how these collectives will be organised, how they will co-operate with other collectives. The superiority of mythology as a determinant of life is simply affirmed:

> All large uprisings had much less to do with strategy, tactics, agitation, organisation - they were above all a feast of the masses, a devil's ball which upset all normalities and a cornucopia of feelings. Even the French

> Revolution could not escape from the
> mystery of the feast.(61)

These ideas were highly popular among the Sponti and
alternative subcultures in the late seventies, and
they continued to influence the subjectivist elements
in the Green Movement.(62)
      The subjectivist critique of modernity has also
been based on certain images of the state and large
organisations. They derive not so much from any
analysis of the Constitutional State of the Federal
Republic, parliamentarism, wage and social policies,
but from direct experiences with the bureaucracy,
judiciary and the police. This subjective approach
has led some protestors to describe the police as
'fascist'. A journalist from the <u>Taz</u> has described
the attitude of many protestors towards the state:

> the state first of all, comprises the pigs.
> More broadly it involves all those who don't
> leave you in peace...The state is everywhere
> ...The state is nuclear power stations,
> Schmidt's mug, rockets and war, the empty
> chatter of politicians...The state is Germany:
> narrow, annoyed, philistine, mad about work
> and everything always in order. Their Order.
> The order in which you never have a say, the
> street traffic order, the Free Democratic
> Basic Order...The state is practically
> always stronger. They plan and do things
> obdurately. What they want is unclear,
> distant, alien...The state functions. Like
> a machine, an apparatus, a computer...The
> state is omnipresent and superior. But one
> can annoy it: just like a teacher. It has
> power, but for that reason it is vulnerable
> to attack. We can play a trick on it, tease
> it, make it look ridiculous, resist it.(63)

The state is presented in terms of a monolithic
power which functions in a completely different way
to the loosely structured forms of organisation
within the Green Movement. The contrast between the
casual life-style, for instance, of young squatters
and the discipline of the police apparatus is under-
standable since the police is in fact 'a fairly
monolithic, centralised bureaucracy with a strict
allocation of roles, duties and obligations'.(64)
None the less the fear of an 'omnipresent and
superior' state is based less on an analytical
assessment of the functions and powers of the state

and more on an instinctual and purely psychological
response. Hence we are told by the protestors that
the state can be annoyed 'just like a teacher'.
    These images of the 'police state' are reinforced
by the experiences of protestors with the judiciary.
The first two people to be sentenced after riots by
squatters in December 1980 in Berlin were given un-
usually severe prison sentences even though it was
only their first conviction. Professor Wesel has
shown how the judiciary, with the severity of its
sentences, continually poured oil on to the fire of
the squatters' protest and undermined the moderate,
reconciliatory approach of the Social-Liberal Coalition in trying to negotiate with the squatters.(65)
It is widely acknowledged that, of all the German
elites to survive the changes from a dictatorial to
a democratic state, the judiciary and the Church
have remained the most unbroken. According to
Anke Brunn, a Social Democrat member of the Berlin
Senate, the courts issued less severe sentences
once the Christian Democrats were elected into power
in West Berlin.(66)
    The state and large organisations are criticised
because of their 'double standards' and their
excessive reliance on rules and regulations. In
August 1980 the Taz announced that it had been
'excommunicated' from the press conferences of the
metalworkers' union, IG Metall. The executive
committee of this trade union felt that it did not
have any chance of being treated fairly by the Taz.
The newspaper was reproached because it repeatedly
accused all trade union leaders of being traitors to
the workforce. In reply, journalists from the Taz
claimed that they were neither dogmatically nor
fundamentally opposed to the trade union apparatus,
although they were increasingly sceptical about it.
Discussions between the two sides failed to bridge
the gap between the different interpretations of the
'democratic rules of the game'. The newspaper
accused IG Metall of practising 'democratic centralism'; being far too defensive, especially towards
people like Strauss, the leader of the CSU; and
not looking beyond the next round of pay negotiations, towards the problems of women, foreigners and
young people, and to the possibility of more meaningful forms of production. It felt that co-
operation could not be achieved by administrative
measures, and that the union had to recognise that
it needed to become more democratic and accountable
to its members' wishes.(67)
    Yet the Green Movement is not itself immune from

such problems. For instance when the Netzwerk
project which helps to raise money for other projects
refused to set aside a large proportion of its funds
exclusively for women's projects it was criticised
for being bureaucratic and partiarchal.(68) Laws,
formal rules and bureaucratic structures are all
regarded as barriers to commitment for a cause.
Netzwerk, a project who main aim is to finance other
projects, is criticised because it sometimes functions like a large organisation which stifles spontaneity and personal needs. This form of criticism
is an important element in the sceptical attitude
among members of alternative groups towards the
concept of 'rationality'. Within the alternative
movement, as in the ecology movement, there exists
an ambivalent attitude to science and technical
progress. Many of its supporters fear that industrial civilisation causes alienation and the destruction of community life; yet there is an appreciation
of the possibilities of using science to 'liberate'
people, for instance from repetitive work on a production line, by the use of new technology. There
is also a strong awareness that a vacuum exists
between, on the one hand, economic and social life
under the belief of technical progress and, on the
other hand, the personal and moral aspects of human
activity. The critique of the modern state and
large organisations has led many people to question
the idea of industrial progress. The ecology movement rejected aspects of industrial progress on the
assumption that the earth could not survive the
level of exploitation of raw materials; supporters
of the alternative movement believe that industrial
progress and alienation are closely linked.

In his recent work Juergen Habermas has been
concerned with new conflicts which have arisen in
the spheres of cultural reproduction, social integration and socialisation, on the borders between the
'system' and the 'world of life' or, in the terms
used earlier in this chapter, between the technocratic apparatus and the community:

> Hitherto the processes of destruction which
> have delayed the path of capitalist modernisa-
> tion, have proceeded in such a way that new
> institutions arose which transferred social
> matter from the sovereign territory of the
> world of life into areas of action which are
> steered by the media and organised in a formal
> legal manner. That was a success as long
> as it was concerned with functions of material

reproduction which do not absolutely need
to be communicatively organised.
In the meantime it does however appear that
the systemic imperatives intervene in spheres
of action, of which it can be shown that in
relation to the structure of their tasks,
they cannot be solved, if they are withdrawn
from communicatively structured areas of
action. This concerns the task of cultural
reproduction, social integration and socialisation. The borders between the world of
life and the system then gain a new relevance.
Today the imperatives of economy and administration which are communicated by means of
money and power are forcing themselves into
spheres which somehow come to pieces if one
cuts them off from action orientated towards
understanding and switches them to such
interactions guided by the media.(69)

None the less the rejection, even if only in ideological terms, of capitalist modernisation by
supporters of the Green Movement leads them to
identify 'rationality' with manipulative and dominant action by the system on the human and natural
environment, or world of life. Reason itself is
often rejected because, as Habermas points out,
rationality is 'equated with the preservation of
economic and administrative systems of action'.(70)
This failure to make a distinction between different
levels of rationality has been a major obstacle to
the formulation of coherent alternative concepts by
the new social movements.
    In the prologue to a book which offers advice
on 'every-day' ecology, the author explains how she
originally intended to write a completely 'unscient-
ific' book without figures and statistical tables
since she had no need for 'academic (alibi-)research'
to identify problems. The use of statistics was
chosen 'deliberately to strengthen and support the
impression which can be observed every day, of the
'emancipation of human beings from nature' with the
result that the bases of life are destroyed'.(71)
This approach to scientific data results from a one-
sided critique of the rationality of industrial
civilisation and a desire to reaffirm the importance
of subjectivity. The same author stresses that
although she is not an expert on traffic, food or
physics, she is an expert on her own 'subjective
feelings', which bring about the 'transposition of
knowledge' in these disciplines into technology and

social structures. In her opinion, the 'large-scale technological developments increasingly present a problem and a threat'. The protest by the Hippies against the 'computerisation' of post-war American society has re-emerged in a powerful form in the Federal Republic. In response to the threat posed by some technological developments to the world of life, alternative groups have attempted to construct and defend their own particular communities. Any threat to these is regarded as part of a technocratic misuse of power by outside forces.

NOTES

1. A.Touraine, 'Crisis or Transformation?', in N.Birnbaum et al., Beyond the Crisis (Oxford University Press, 1977), pp. 35-6.
2. A.Giddens, The Class Structure of the Advanced Societies (Hutchinson, London, 1973), pp. 163-4.
3. N. Johnson, Government in the Federal Republic of Germany (Oxford, 1973), p. 102.
4. A.Touraine, The Post-Industrial Society (Butler and Tanner, London, 1971), p. 51.
5. Giddens, Class Structure, p. 262.
6. Ibid., p. 294.
7. R.Bahro, Socialism and Survival (Heretic, London), p.57.
8. Ibid., p. 65.
9. Ibid., p. 119.
10. Ibid., p. 33.
11. Touraine, Post-Industrial Society, p. 9.
12. J.Huber, Die verlorene Unschuld der Oekologie (Fischer, Frankfurt, 1982), p. 61.
13. Giddens, Class Structure, pp. 130-1.
14. Ibid., p. 131.
15. Ibid., p. 221.
16. Ibid., p. 108.
17. O.Negt, 'Alternative Politikformen als politische Alternative' in R.Roth (ed.), Parlamentarisches Ritual und politische Alternativen (Campus, Frankfurt, 1980), p. 165.
18. L.Benson, Proletarians and Parties (London, 1978), p. 124.
19. Taz, 8 Oct. 1981, p. 4.
20. Taz-Journal Nr.3, p. 196f.
21. Taz, 23 April 1982, p. 8.
22. See reader's letter in Taz, 23 March 1982, p. 12.
23. Taz, 20 Nov. 1981, p. 14.
24. Taz, 29 April 1981, p. 11.
25. Taz, 20 Nov. 1981, p. 14; see also Taz, 22 Oct. 1981, p. 12.
26. Huber, Verlorene Unschuld, pp. 156-7.
27. Ibid., p. 156.

28. H.Jonas, Das Prinzip Verantwortung (Insel, Frankfurt, 1979), p. 218, makes a similar point.

29. P.Berger, Facing up to modernity (Penguin, 1977), p. 106.

30. H.Dreitzel, 'On the Political Meaning of Culture' in N.Birnbaum et al., Beyond the Crisis, p. 116.

31. H.Ridley and K. Bullivant, 'A Middle-Class View of German Industrial Expansion, 1853-1900', Oxford German Studies, 7, 1973, p. 107.

32. Interview carried out by the author with editors of the Taz newspaper in January 1982.

33. F.Nietzsche, Unzeitgmaesse Betrachtungen (Goldmann, Munich, 1964).

34. Ibid., pp. 91-2.

35. For example in F.Spielhagen, Hammer und Amboss (1869), and in W.Sombart, Haendler und Helden (1915).

36. F.Stern, The Politics of Cultural Despair, (Berkeley, California Library, 1961, reprinted 1974), p. 98.

37. P.Gay, Weimar Culture (Penguin, 1974), pp. 80-1.

38. J.Peters, Nationaler 'Sozialismus' von Rechts (Klaus Gruhl Verlag, Berlin, 1980).

39. W.Dombrowsky in Taz, 10 March 1981, p. 8.

40. H.Roettgen in an interview in Taz, 19 March 1981, p.9.

41. J.Bopp, 'Trauer-Power. Zur Jugendrevolte 1981' in Kursbuch 65, (Berlin, 1981), pp. 157-8.

42. Jonas, Prinzip Verantwortung, p. 280ff.

43. Netzwerk Rundbrief Nr.15, (Dec. 1981) p. 11ff.

44. W.Hau, Sponti-Sprueche, (Eichborn, Frankfurt, 1982). This fifth edition of the book led to the publication of 56,000 copies overall.

45. H.Roettgen and F. Rabe, Vulkantaenze - linke und alternative Ausgaenge, (Trikont, Munich, 1978), p. 84.

46. Ibid., p. 95.

47. Ibid.

48. Ibid., pp. 84-5.

49. Hau, Sponti-Sprueche.

50. Roettgen and Rabe, Vulkantaenze, p. 10.

51. Ibid., p. 11.

52. Ibid., p. 15.

53. Ibid., p. 18.

54. Ibid., p. 34.

55. Nietzsche, Betrachtungen, pp. 7-216.

56. Ibid., p. 115.

57. Ibid., p. 116.

58. Roettgen and Rabe, Vulkantaenze, p. 59.

59. Ibid., p. 63.

60. Ibid., p. 64.

61. Ibid., p. 114.

62. For example, this is reflected in the long interview with Roettgen in Taz, 19 March 1981, p. 9.

63. B. Haerlin, 'Von Haus zu Haus - Berliner Bewegungs-studien' in Kursbuch 65, (Berlin, 1981), p. 10f.

64. P. Rock, <u>Deviant Behaviour</u> (Hutchinson, London, 1973), p. 186.

65. U. Wesel, 'Der friedliche und der unfriedliche Bruch des Friedens' in <u>Kursbuch</u> <u>65</u>, (Berlin, 1981), p. 29ff.

66. Interview by the author with Anke Brunn in May 1982.

67. <u>Taz</u>, 8 Oct. 1980, and 28 Aug. 1981, p. 8.

68. <u>Taz</u>, 29 Sept. 1981, p. 6.

69. J.Habermas, 'Dialektik der Rationalisierung' in <u>Aesthetik und Kommunikation</u>, <u>45/46</u>, (Oct. 1981), p. 140.

70. Ibid., p. 161.

71. S.Bahnemann, <u>Ein Tropfen auf den heissen Stein</u> (Freunde der Erde, Berlin, 1981), pp.8-10.

Chapter Three

THEMES AND CONCEPTS (2)

The critique of technocracy on the basis of ideas
about the reaffirmation of subjectivity and community has given rise to concepts which seek to transc-
end and, at times, to transgress, the prevailing
order. In its more optimistic moods the Green Movement has attempted to combine its utopian demands
with specific proposals for alternatives in economic
and social policies, whilst in its more despondent
moods it has encouraged an atmosphere in which
people resort to violence in their efforts to
achieve 'liberation'.

I Hope, pessimism and violence

Throughout the 1970s the disillusionment of the Left
was most acutely expressed by the activities of left-
wing terrorist groups. Violence, fruitless theoretical discussions and conflicts with their immediate
surroundings led many students to search for a new
context in which to overcome their own isolation.
The ecology movement provided an important outlet
for them to express their dissatisfaction. The
issue of violence, however, still remained high on
the agenda of discussions because of confrontations
between the police and groups within the ecology
movement as well as the attacks by the extremist Red
Army Faction on prominent people like the chairman
of the BDI, Hans-Martin Schleyer. Many young people,
particularly those influenced by the ideas of the
Spontis, became torn between their realisation of
the futility and counter-productivity of the murder
of Schleyer and their belief in the 'inhumanity of
the system'. The Spontis claimed that, on the one
hand, the terrorists had robbed them of their future

46

hopes for socialism because they had used violence and, on the other hand, the older generation had betrayed them about their past because they had not opposed or had actually supported Fascism. In an appeal to one of their congresses they declared that in the future people might divide the history of the Federal Republic into the period before and after the death of Schleyer and that 'socialism will not be able to prosper here until the year 2000'.(1) The attempt by the Spontis to renounce violence did signal, according to Peter Glotz when he was Senator for Education in West Berlin, a change in attitudes among large sections of the student population.(2)

None the less the subjectivist critique of technocratic society and the adoption of mystical traditions has allowed violent tendencies to rise to the surface of the Green Movement. According to Bahro, 'clear-headed mysticism' leads to a 'profound mobilisation of emancipatory forces in the human psyche' and is a 'phenomenon that has nothing other-worldly about it, and should be made accessible to everyone, for example in the practice of meditation'. (3) Yet the unleashing of such forces does not of necessity produce 'clear-headed' perspectives, even among groups that have claimed they are practising the clear-headed version in the interests of human emancipation.

In November 1980 the Taz launched an appeal for 'Weapons in El Salvador' to further the 'struggle for self-determination' by church, christian demo-cratic, social democratic and revolutionary groups in that country, against the intervention by the United States in support of the military dictator-ship.(4) Within less than a month 207,239 marks had been raised; by the end of March 1981 the sum had risen to one and a half million; and by June 1982 the total was three million. Throughout this period the newspaper had severe financial difficulties of its own and it barely survived after constant appeals for donations and subscribers; yet its appeal for funds in support of a violent response to the un-doubted brutality of the El Salvadorean regime met with a stupendous response. What needs to be high-lighted is that the defence of the environment, the protest against the oppression of life in the city, the fear of a nuclear holocaust and the politicisa-tion of subjectivity provoke feelings which are channelled into ideologies that are sometimes nourished on the use of violence and simplistic ideas about social conditions, thereby widening the gap between alternative groups and large sections of society.

Experience of the anti-authoritarian student movement has shown how a large number of groups that emerged from it espoused a new form of authoritarianism. According to a former leading figure in the student movement, Bernd Rabehl, the inclination towards violence by some groups within the new movements has led to the danger of a 'new Right' which does not emerge from old conservative circles but from the non-proletarians, the uprooted intelligentsia and the uprooted unemployed,

> who actually don't know where they want to go to, who are proletarianised, thus expropriated, poor, but are full of ideas, and who morally and ideologically overcome their decline in an atmosphere of fundamental change.(5)

This statement is directed mainly at those who seek to oppose the monopoly of violence by the state with their own counter-violence; it is not intended as a general condemnation of the efforts and ideas of everyone who is involved in the Green Movement. It does, however, illuminate tendencies within it which create an atmosphere whereby people are inclined to opt for a strategy of counter-violence, or simply react violently because of the deep sense of moral outrage which they experience at events around them.

Table 3.1 Slogans which express the will to resist (16-24 age group)

Slogans	I consider the slogan... very good/ good %	I consider the slogan... less good/ not at all good %
those who don't defend themselves are living the wrong way!	72	29
we are we - and we'll do what we feel like doing!	40	61
it's cheaper to travel without paying your fares!	34	66
ruin whatever is ruining you!	34	67
they have ordered us about, watched over our houses, punched us in the face enough!	28	72

Source: Figures from Shell Studie, (1981), Jugend 1981, Hamburg, Vol. 1, p. 465.

The Shell survey established the popularity of certain slogans used by young people which proclaimed the will to resist the system. This is illustrated in Table 3.1. The aim of individual and collective liberation and the attempt to construct an alternative reality becomes entangled with apocalyptic ideas about the collapse of the system and the need to speed up this process by the use of force, or at least to resist the 'violence of the system': 'Those who do not defend themselves are living the wrong way'. These ideas are clearly illustrated in the following extract from an open letter from the Schoeneberg Squatters' Council to the 'citizens of Berlin' following riots in the city:

> You say that we are violent. But where does the violence come from? Did we destroy the city uninterruptedly in the process of modernisation? Do we build motorways through residential areas? Did we build the 'silos' for accommodation which destroy people?...It was not us but the other side which refused to engage in a dialogue for decades. Until we began to speak their language, that of violence. You say that policemen are also people. Of course, when they are not on duty. But is it human to allow oneself to be shoved into a uniform like a puppet, and when given orders, to hit people with a truncheon and to fire tear-gas at them, irrespective of who they are?...It is a question of the future of everyone. Without policemen, no riots!!! You must understand that we must defend ourselves, if we don't want to perish.(6)

Within the Green Movement there is a continual debate over these issues. Moreover, opposition to industrial society in its present form and the search for a new community and style of living do not inevitably produce a new authoritarianism. None the less, the search for a simpler way of life, for a community in which meaningful social relationships can develop, needs to have certain criteria if it is to assume a form to which most groups within the population can also relate; it is unlikely that most people would even understand some of the contrasts which were evoked in the letter from the squatters in Schoeneberg between the 'violence of the system' and the need to resist it. There is a

lack of consideration of existing social contradictions and only a tentative development of the links
between individual and collective freedom. The lack
of commonly accepted criteria for social behaviour
and organisation has made the Movement susceptible to
certain forms of regression for which there are pre-
cedents in German social and cultural history. I am
referring not only to the mythology of violence, but
also to the widespread feelings of pessimism.

In the Shell survey 42 per cent of the respon-
ents held an optimistic view of the future, 58 per
cent, a pessimistic view. There was a striking
difference in attitudes between supporters of the
Green Party and those of the main political parties.
The pessimists outnumbered the optimists by more than
3:1 among supporters of the Greens.(7) Statements
about the possibility of a nuclear war, the threat
posed by technology and the isolation of individuals
provoked the greatest number of pessimistic replies
from supporters of the Green Party. (Table 3.2)

Table 3.2 Pessimistic statements related to party-political
orientation (16-24 age group)(%)

Statements	CDU/CSU	SPD	GREENS	NO PARTY
the world will come to an end in a nuclear war (definitely/probably)	32	44	76	49
people will become more sociable (definitely/probably)	44	36	18	40
technology and chemicals will destroy the environment (definitely)	19	24	52	28
there will be more equality among people (probably/definitely)	33	26	10	21
people will be totally controlled by computers (definitely/probably)	47	56	70	53
wars will cease (definitely not)	60	68	79	63
people will again adapt to a life related to nature (probably/definitely)	46	37	32	39
people will increasingly isolate themselves and only think of themselves (definitely/probably)	53	54	76	62
raw materials will become increasingly scarce, economic crises and famines will break out (definitely)	28	33	52	38
there will come into existence a society with no worries, in which everything one needs is available (definitely not)	60	62	84	63

Source: Figures from Shell Studie, (1981), <u>Jugend 1981</u>,
Hamburg, Vol. 1, p. 678.

Table 3.3 Attitudes to the possibility of a third World War,
future prospects of children, economic situation and ability
of parties and politicians to solve problems (%)

A third World War is...	1979	1981
unlikely	80	47
possible	17	46
likely	2	6
Children will be...	1980	1981
better off	22	14
able to live like adults do today	43	44
worse off	33	41
The economic situation is...		
good, or very good	48	15
partly good, partly not so good	43	51
bad, or very bad	9	33
The large parties...		
are no longer in a position to solve the countless problems in our society		59
Most politicians...		
don't know any more what ordinary people are thinking		78

Source: Figures from Der Spiegel, Nr. 50, (1981), p. 87 and 97.

According to a survey in Der Spiegel, pessimism
and fear has increased among the population as a
whole.(Table 3.3) More and more people believed
that a third World War was possible and increasing
numbers felt that their children would become worse
off in the future. This increase in fear and pessimism about the future occurs against the background
of a decrease in confidence with regard to the
economic situation. Between April 1980 and October
1981 the proportion of people who regarded the
economic situation as bad or very bad rose from nine
per cent to 33 per cent. Most people, 59 per cent,
felt that the large parties were no longer in a
position to solve the countless problems in society,
and even more of them, 78 per cent, felt that most
politicians did not know what ordinary people were
thinking.

All these factors contribute to a bleak vision
of the future among significant layers of the
population. Yet fear alone is not enough to motivate people; it can often paralyse effective action.
Those who actively oppose the placement of nuclear
weapons in their country must have some hope that
their action will have some effect. The following
extract, written by an activist in the peace move-

ment, conveys the mixture of pessimism and hope
which typifies the 'apocalyptic' attitude of many
people. However, only a committed activist could
have expressed it in this manner:

> The period before 12 December 1979 has been
> called the period after the Second World
> War. The period after the NATO decision to
> place nuclear medium-range rockets in
> Central Europe can no longer be called the
> post-war period; rather we are living in
> the period before the Third World War...
> Many people are already talking about the
> war we are conducting against nature, of
> the Third World War which year after year
> costs the lives of millions of people in
> the Southern Hemisphere. And they look on
> with horror at the way in which we rob our-
> selves of our own basis for existence. How
> much more unimaginable would the global
> suicide be, introduced and prepared by the
> nuclear Super-powers, supported and encour-
> aged by all those people who have fallen
> for the ideology of 'disarmament by further
> armament', 'the balance of terror'...
> Whilst in this scenario there creeps in a
> growing lack of perspectives and resignation,
> even among circles of left-wing established
> academics, there emerges out of the various
> initiatives a many-sided movement for peace.
> This grass-roots movement which gives hope,
> votes - as the smallest common denominator
> of an ideologically broad spectrum - for
> unilateral steps towards disarmament.(8)

The widespread fear and pessimism among supporters of the Green Movement contradicts the quest for
happiness, for a more creative and convivial society.
Those who are constantly fearful of and angry with
the evolution of society may in turn cause themselves as much hurt and sorrow as the society with
which they are at odds. The only way out of this
contradiction is to invent forms of protest which
chase away sorrow and involve other people; to
enable individuals with the help of a group to understand better the world that surrounds them; and to
act as mediators in a world that is divided in many
ways. The consequent transcendence of helplessness,
despair, negative attitudes, and the feeling of
strength which often results from participation in
groups and in imaginative and cheerful activity is

one of the most powerful forces which carries the
Green Movement forward. The prospect of overcoming
fear is offered by participation in group activities.
Various issues, for instance the opposition to
nuclear weapons, often provide a new channel into
which anxieties can be diverted. The danger of such
a path is that the level of protest is often determined by the fears and uncertainties of individuals
in their immediate situation, and this may clash
with any rational assessment of an appropriate long-
term plan of action. This does not imply that
committed individuals, driven on by their fears and
hopes, weaken the aims of the peace movement; often
they are the motor of such movements, although at a
later stage there is very likely to occur a clash
between some people who perceive the need for careful consideration of future forms of activity and
specific 'utopian' proposals and others who thrive
on the immediacy of more spontaneous activity which
offers possibilities for the 'liberation of the
Self'.

II Utopian ideas

One of the underlying assumptions of the Green Movement is that in a different civilisation the problem
of alienation will cease to exist because of a radical change in values from materialism to creativity.
There is a widely-held belief that an 'accumulation
of material values' runs contrary to individual
development. This approach fails to consider that
people who work are not necessarily only concerned
with earning money to keep alive, but may do so for
the sake of leisure as well as family and social
life. The idea of the 'quality of work' exercises
a powerful influence on supporters of the Green
Movement; yet the 'quality of work' does not exclude
material values, and despite hopes that there
should no longer exist a division between work and
leisure most people are well aware of the gap between the two spheres, even in an alternative community. There is always an element of necessity in
work even in the most unalienated conditions. Hans
Jonas, in a critique of the utopian Marxist, Ernst
Bloch, has argued that there is no realm of freedom
outside the realm of necessity, and that Marx and
Bloch make the basic error of assuming that freedom
begins where necessity ends.(9)
     The basis for the belief in the fulfilment of

human needs in the realm of freedom is as follows:
in a model ecological society fundamental needs will
no longer be perverted by consumer society and thus
it will be possible for them to form the basis for
human activity. These needs, however, are only
defined in the most general terms. Bahro simply
refers to 'the basic needs of the human species as
quite reliably ascertained by anthropology'.(10)
This reveals one of the main weaknesses of the ecology movement: its critique of the existing structures, especially with regard to the loss of communication between people and the deterioration of the
environment, won over many citizens to its ranks;
there remained, however, a lack of clarity over the
creation of practical alternatives which can serve
more than a limited number of social groups. At
this comparatively early stage in the development of
a mass social movement it was perhaps too much to
demand of it a blue-print for an alternative society.
None the less, one is struck by the manner in which
similar assumptions about the world of work re-
emerge, at a later stage, in the programme of the
Green Party, when sections of the movement had
established more clearly defined organisational
structures.

In November 1981 Manfred Coppick, a left-wing
member of the SPD who had a seat in the Federal
Parliament, wrote a letter to a 'thousand friends'
in which he asked them to call into question the
existing organisational structures of the party.
The letter was published in the Taz and invoked the
fury of a reader who was 'fed up to the teeth' with
the 'question of organisations'. The reader asked
Coppick finally to understand that the 'movement'
did not want to organise itself and appoint treasur-
ers and chairpersons but sought to bring about peace,
justice and humane living conditions in the manner
described by Ernst Bloch. We are assured by the
same person that the alternative movement has all
the answers, but only lacks the willpower to carry
out its plans; and that Andre Gorz and many other
people have described the possibilities of a post-
industrial society.(11)

Whilst the works of Bloch and Gorz are read by
some activists who wish to put forward plans for a
rational utopia, most supporters of the Green Movement gain inspiration from writers and visionaries
like William Morris. News from Nowhere, which
conveys Morris' vision of a utopian society, has
been read widely because, according to a review in
the Taz, 'this novel, which is nearly a century old,

touches on highly topical developments and discussions, precisely in the ecology movement'. In his
review of the book, Wolfgang Haug writes that Morris'
portrayal of a future state describes how the freedom of an individual can be fulfilled in an anarchist-
communist community. Money, the state, parliaments,
laws and pollution are all things of the past.
People live in harmony with nature. Decision-making
processes have been simplified and decentralised,
and people are provided with goods on the basis of
their needs. However, the greatest changes are in
the sphere of human relations; marriages have been
replaced by partnerships which can be dissolved
without disadvantages for the woman, and the'future of
all children is safeguarded by the community'. Haug
concludes that Morris' utopia is not a 'utopia of
the state' because he is not only concerned with
changing power relations but with the 'true liberation of people in all spheres'.(12) It is no coin-
cidence that the book by Morris is as popular as
other novels which set out to portray utopian forms
of social relations and conditions. Within a short
space of time the 'Black Roots' publishing house in
Reutlingen had to produce a second edition of the
book.
    The social idealism of Morris, the efforts by
Bloch to combine mystical and idealist elements with
dialectical Marxism (with the introduction of concepts like 'concrete utopia' and the 'principle of
hope') and the works of authors like Bahro, Gorz
and Touraine are all based on a considerable capacity to perceive certain changes and propose new
models for sociological analysis. When their ideas
are taken up by groups within the Green Movement,
who feel that time is running out in the race to
save humanity from a final disaster, there is often
a lack of understanding of the complexities of
social reality.
    For instance the Taz has experienced many
difficulties in its efforts to analyse and interpret
events. Despite the conflicts among various tendencies within the project, and the continual flow of
readers' letters which are critical of the editors,
the paper has become financially viable and gained
the support of more and more readers. It has managed to do this because individual editors tend to
act as spokespersons for various tendencies within
the Green Movement and because of the 'monopoly'
which the paper enjoys; there is no other equivalent
daily newspaper for people who are highly dissatisfied with all the established parties and institut-

ions and who wish to be informed about particular
subcultures.(13) However, even if one bears in mind
that the press is traditionally partisan, the Taz
is a long way from fulfilling its own aims to provide
the public with information and not just propaganda.
Some editors left the project because of the manner
in which it constantly sought to 'serve the movement!
(14) Movement 'lobbies' reach into the newspaper
because many editors form their own identity as
journalists on the basis of this idea.

Editors who seek to attain higher standards in
reporting political events often come under attack
from readers who feel that the Taz is far too pre-
occupied with conventional political dialogue. One
reader criticised the reports on the SPD Congress as
the reproduction of 'bourgeois press reports from an
opposite direction'.(15) This critique is based on
the assumption that any initiatives within the SPD
which opposed nuclear energy and nuclear weapons
were 'insignificant'. This gives rise to ideas
which constantly evoke the failure of the dominant
parties and institutions to solve problems. Readers
are reminded that government commissions of inquiry
and parliaments cannot take free decisions since big
business has already decided on investments in various
spheres. A government commission of inquiry on
future energy needs was thus described as a farce, a
'useful alibi for a reckless policy in favour of
nuclear power', and an attempt to throw sand into
people's eyes in order to blind them from seeing the
real power relationships.(16)

The rational basis for the critique of industrial society, namely the defence of the world of life
or of communities against the real endangerment of
the environment, psychological isolation and the
threat of nuclear weapons is thus often undermined
by certain misconceptions and mythological interpretations of the social and political system. Many
people beyond the Green Movement agree with some of
their criticisms of the existing culture and society.
However, they are not convinced that this movement
can offer a coherent alternative. Many other people
- and they form the majority of the population -
reject most of its ideas because they focus their
attention on its mythological rather than its
rational characteristics. This section of the population experiences the life-style of the movement
as a great challenge to the moral and material
foundations of the prevailing order. The extreme
attitudes of many protestors tends to reinforce
this feeling rather than to create an atmosphere

in which new and alternative concepts can form the basis for discussions.

The Green Party, in its efforts to capture the popular vote, has stressed the need for specific alternative policies. However, there exists within it an uneasy relationship between pragmatic and utopian tendencies. In their 1983 electoral programme the Greens wished to abolish the 'basic conditions of capitalist production', to 'totally restructure' the social system by changing property relations in the sphere of production and to step out of the 'automobile society'. Decisions on how and when things are produced would be determined by those who are 'directly affected' and not by the laws of profit. Voters were assured that the creation of 'ecologically and socially meaningful alternatives to the production of damaging products does not pose a serious problem'.(17) One of their long-term aims is to increase 'self-reliance' and reduce the level of international trade. Not surprisingly, it was only over short-term aims that there were strong parallels between the programmes of the Greens and the SPD: for instance over the introduction of a shorter working week and the creation of 'ecologically sensible' employment in the spheres of public transport and the conservation of energy.

Differences of opinion about the value of work in parliaments still prevail among the Greens despite their relative success in the 1983 Federal Elections. Attempts to bridge the gap between these differences, between uncompromising utopian demands and pragmatic radical reforms are a distinctive feature of debates within the party and the Green Movement. One of the intellectual inspirers of those who seek to reconcile pragmatic alternatives and utopian demands is Ernst Bloch, the author of <u>Principle of Hope</u>. The critique by Hans Jonas of Bloch's utopian ideas helps to explain why there is an uneasy rapport within the Green Party between fundamentalist and utopian tendencies and pragmatic radical reformism. In <u>Das Prinzip Verantwortung</u> (The Principle of Responsibility) Jonas takes up some of the themes which preoccupy the Greens, although he rejects the utopian Marxist attempt, for instance by Bloch, to 'solve' these problems with the help of technology.

Jonas points to the 'critical <u>vulnerability</u>' of nature firstly because of the intervention of technology and secondly because, hitherto, ethics never had to take into consideration the conditions of human life and the future existence of the human

species.(18) He shows how man has become the 'object
of technology', and how new developments in cell
biology, behaviour control and manipulation of genes
have raised new moral problems which require a new
ethics to cope with their implications.(19) He
appears also to share the basic concern of the Green
Movement that the 'future' has not been represented
in any lobby or representative institution, even
though technological changes have far-reaching
implications.(20) The limits to the exploitation of
nature, the potential shortage of food, raw materials
and energy, and the dangers which face the entire
biological sphere because of excessive heat energy
which is produced by human beings and machinery, are
all themes which prompt Jonas to call for a new
ethics of responsibility.(21). He stresses that the
future of mankind is the first duty of collective
behaviour in an age when the negative mode of technical civilisation has become 'all-powerful' over the
biological sphere and over the future.(22) The
'ethics of responsibility' does not, however,
involve a utopian attempt to use progress and perfec-
tion to overcome problems but sets itself the more
modest task of preserving and protecting what
already exists.(23) Whilst utopian Marxism does
take up responsibility for the future, it wishes to
do this with the aid of technology.(24)

The Marxist alternative is based on progress
and an increase in accumulation.(25) Jonas, however,
argues in favour of a politics of 'constructive
prevention' and of the need for caution.(26) He
identifies the utopian Marxist ideas of Bloch with
a very incautious approach to the solution of problems, since the first requirement of utopianism is
material plenitude to satisfy the needs of the population and its second requirement, the ease with
which this plenitude will be acquired.(27) In the
Principle of Hope Bloch has great faith in the ability of human beings to use technology to arrive at
this state of plenitude.(28)

Later, I will illustrate how, despite their
critique of the existing system, sections of the
Green Party still have faith in technology to solve
problems, although many of them adopt a slightly
more cautious approach than Bloch. However, they do
imply that we have arrived at the conditions which
are necessary for the creation of a utopian society
when they state that:

> Our starting point is that the existing
> productive force of the economy can guarantee

an adequate material existence for all
members of society. This, however, requires
a radical change both in the direction of
production and the distribution of the products. In particular, the existing level
of production allows for a reduction in
working hours without a reduction in wages,
as well as an expansion of social services.(29)

One of the weaknesses of the utopian perspective which is often adopted by the Greens is that it
does not consider enough that even in a utopian or
alternative society there will be dissatisfaction,
greed, unrest and temptation.(30) The 'inhumanity'
of the present system is repeatedly evoked in cut
and dry terms: 'The existing social conditions shape
the relationships between people: the search for
power, violence and repression are not the exception
but the rule'.(31) As Jonas points out, the utopian
trust in the human being of the future is coupled
with mistrust of people in the present society.(32)
Above all, people who repeatedly evoke the importance of ideal conditions are likely to regard anything that falls short of this ideal as 'inhuman'
or 'undignified'.(33) The programme of the Green
Alternative List (GAL) in Hamburg reflects this
attitude. In the section on social policy, we are
told that:

> The dominant parties are tightening our
> belts so much that large sections of the
> population already hardly get enough air to
> be able to live in a humanly dignified manner.
> But the party bosses and bureaucrats shove
> millions into their own pockets, allowing
> themselves to be bribed.(34)

Investment policies are similarly divided into
'human' and 'inhuman' categories. Hence there are:

> more important spheres for investment than
> increasing the space for business conventions
> and building harbours and airports, and
> parking places for visitors to the opera.
> There are also investments which help people
> to live and learn in a humanly dignified
> manner.(35)

The existence of the homeless, the victims of the
system of production, the handicapped, and the
elderly is repeatedly described as 'inhuman'.(36)

The implication is that in a new society goodwill shall prevail. There will be no need for prisons, and competition, which destroys imagination and creativeity, will also cease to exist.(37)

As I have attempted to show, the Greens believe to some extent that the conditions of production already make it possible to satisfy all material demands. This allows the belief to emerge that once material goods are more justly distributed, the realm of freedom can develop without any hindrances. Aware of the powerful utopian impulse among activists, some members of the Greens have attempted to develop concepts which might reconcile 'irresponsible' demands with 'responsible' actions. There emerged a trend among Green and Alternative Lists to try and draw up 'progressive, practical alternatives to financial and budget plans'.(38) In its alternative approach to parliamentarism the Bunte Liste in Hamburg wished to set out positive goals and 'formulate a social utopia which becomes more and more concrete'. (39) In Baden-Wuerttemberg the Greens admitted that their alternative dream of trusting everyone fell on its face when the harsh realities of politics had to be confronted.(40) They criticised the lack of clarity in their original programme, which did not explain how tangible policies would be carriedout and resolved to 'develop the art of working out programmatic demands which create bridges between the bad reality and the good utopia'.(41) In Bielefeld the Bunte Liste felt that it was no use developing an 'abstract analysis' of society without linking this to tangible alternatives, 'transitional demands' and 'concrete utopias'.(42)

It is not entirely clear whether the Greens often play down their utopian demands for purely tactical reasons or because they sense that their demands may contradict some of their original aims. The theorists and activists within the party often appear to embrace the attitude of Bloch, whilst at the same time there is a greater amount of scepticism about the possibilities offered by technology to fulfil the utopian dream. Many clearly reject the idea of a 'super-industrial' breakthrough to solve existing problems.(43) Some place much emphasis on uncomprising, fundamental demands which imply a rejection of a more cautious path towards change, whilst others are gradually modifying their demands in the face of the realities of the strength of the system. Their sense of responsibility for the future of mankind is often undermined by their lack of consistency in taking up responsibilities in the existing situation because of their fear of compromising their fundamental demands. To some extent, they are trapped by an excessive emphasis on a utopian view of how to solve social and environmental problems. They believe in the goodwill of human beings, yet regard with suspicion and distrust the 'greedy' and 'repressed' citizens of the Federal Republic. They believe in the power of individuals to change their situation, yet they are afraid of the power of individuality and of charismatic individuals. As I will illustrate in the following chapters, they many well be striving for irreconciliable aims: to introduce grass-roots democracy into a parliamentary system; to combat certain aspects of economic growth whilst seeking to satisfy most material and social needs; to uphold the idea of the charisma of the group and the community, whilst still being influenced by and individualist culture and forms of protest and action.

NOTES

1. P.Glotz, Die Innenausstattung der Macht (Fischer, Frankfurt, 1981), p. 210.

2. Ibid., p. 216.

3. Bahro, Socialism and Survival, p. 70.

4. Taz, 3 Nov. 1980, p. 1.

5. B.Rabehl, 'Im Kampf gegen die Polizei werden sie die Gestalt der Polizei annehmen' in J.Bacia et al. Passt bloss auf! Was will die neue Jugendbewegung? (Olle und Wolter, Berlin, 1981), p. 81.

6. Taz, 12 Oct. 1981, p. 6.

7. Shell Studie, Jugend 1981 (Shell, Hamburg, 1981), Vol. 1, p. 386.

8. C.Bartolf, Etwas fuer den Frieden tun (unpublished discussion paper, Berlin, Jan. 1982), p. 7.

9. Jonas, Prinzip Verantwortung, p. 364.

10. Bahro, Socialism and Survival, p. 104.

11. Taz, 13 Nov. 1981, p. 16.

12. Taz, 28 July 1981, p. 10.

13. See Taz, 23 April 1982, p. 16 for a letter from a reader who is critical of the 'monopoly' position of the paper; and Taz, 24 March 1982, p. 7 where an editor, Max-Thomas Mehr, criticises the different factions in the paper for their bias.

14. Interview carried out by the author with 'Sabine' from the Netzwerk self-help project.

15. Taz, 23 April 1982, p. 16.

16. Taz, 23 March 1982, p. 10.

17. Der Spiegel, Nr. 2, 1983, p. 34ff.

18. Jonas, Prinzip Verantwortung, p. 26ff.

19. Ibid., p. 47ff.
20. Ibid., p. 55.
21. Ibid., p. 329ff.
22. Ibid., p. 245.
23. Ibid., p. 249.
24. Ibid., p. 229.
25. Ibid., p. 258.
26. Ibid., p. 321.
27. Ibid., p. 327.
28. E.Bloch, Das Prinzip Hoffnung (Suhrkamp, Frankfurt, 1959), p. 1055, cited by Jonas, Prinzip Verantwortung, p. 407.
29. GAL Hamburg, Programm fuer Hamburg, (Hamburg, 1982), p. 9.
30. Jonas, Prinzip Verantwortung, p. 383.
31. GAL Hamburg, Programm, p. 50.
32. Jonas, Prinzip Verantwortung, p. 411.
33. Ibid., p. 341.
34. GAL Hamburg, Programm, p. 4.
35. Ibid., p. 10.
36. Ibid., p. 31, p. 34, p. 41 and p. 43.
37. Ibid., p. 25 and p. 38.
38. T.Langer and R.Link, 'Ueber den Umgang mit Defiziten linker Politik in Hamburg' in R.Schiller-Dickhut et al., Alternative Stadtpolitik (VSA, Hamburg, 1981), p. 141.
39. Ibid., p. 143.
40. Taz, 10 Nov. 1980, p. 12.
41. W.Kretschmann, 'Die Gruenen im Landtag von Baden-Wuerttemberg' in R.Schiller-Dickhut et al., Alternative Stadtpolitik, p. 106.
42. R.Boch et al., 'Die alternative Wahlbewegung und die Kommunalpolitik' in R.Schiller-Dickhut et al., Alternative Stadtpolitik, p. 22.
43. Taz, 13 April 1982, p. 11.

Chapter Four

ECOLOGY MOVEMENT

Public awareness of environmental problems grew
throughout the 1970s, and it focused not only on the
potential destructive effects of nuclear power
stations and chemical factories but also on the gradual increase in the pollution of air, water and
land. These and other themes formed the basis for
the critique by the ecology movement of industrial
society. Fears about the deterioration of the
environment were shared by the population at large.
Mayer-Tasch has pointed out that in surveys carried
out in 1972 and 1973 around fifty per cent of the
population felt that more effective measures should
be introduced to protect the environment even if
this endangered their own job. In the latter survey
eighty per cent felt that effective measures should
be introduced even if this had an adverse effect on
the rate of economic growth.(1) This appears to reflect the discovery by Inglehart of a 'change in
values' in the early seventies among the populations
of Western democracies. In West Germany many people
also expected the SPD-FDP Alliance to carry out
reformist environmental and social policies. Moreover, as I have argued in previous chapters, the
idea of defending nature against the excesses of
modernity has held a great appeal both for post-war
protest movements and for the inhabitants of Germany.
The work of Dennis Meadows and many other authors on
the 'limits of growth' provided 'scientific' proof
that the natural environment was under great threat.
    Sociologists in the Federal Republic decided
that 'nature' had become a significant variable in
any paradigm which sought to explain social development. Volker Ronge, in Die Gesellschaft an den
Grenzen der Natur, found that it was difficult for
people to agree on what scientifically constitutes
an environmental crisis. He argued that the

'objective social, environmental problem' had to be
seen in connection with public consciousness and
public activity 'without the objective extent of the
problem having to correspond exactly to the level of
awareness'.(2) None the less, the extent to which
people are in fact prepared to risk their security
of employment or to renounce economic growth in order
to save the environment remains open to question,
and will be assessed in this chapter in relation to
the ecology movement.

The main forces within the ecology movement -
the first major piece in the Green Movement jigsaw -
comprised: firstly, opposition by various communities
to specific projects which were likely to lead to a
deterioration of the quality of life in their neighbourhood; secondly, a rejection - especially by
young well-educated people - of the 'evils' of
economic growth and consumerism; and thirdly, a
questioning of the prevailing parliamentary democratic order because of its failure to consult people
on issues which related to the worsening condition
of the human and natural environment. The first
clear expression of these forces was the mass mobilisation of the population in various regions. This
was followed by attempts to organise the heterogeneous protest initiatives by creating conventional
political groups and less conventional alternative
communities and subcultures. Thus I will examine
the background to the emergence of the Green Party
by referring specifically to events in locations
where the ecology movement was at its most powerful:
Wyhl in South-West Germany, Brokdorf in the North,
Frankfurt in the Centre and Gorleben in the North-
East. The geographical spread of these locations
has not been chosen deliberately; it merely reflects
the breadth of the activities by Citizens' Initiatives across the country.

I Mass mobilisation against nuclear energy

The general politicisation which occurred in the
late sixties in the Federal Republic contributed to
the emergence of the SPD-FDP Alliance which encouraged social experimentation and the arrival of
Citizens' Initiatives whose actions were directed
towards disparate areas of need. As I explained
earlier on the initiatives did not disappear from
the political stage because of the critical increase

in the significance of the sphere of reproduction
and the disappointment at the failure of the SPD-FDP
Alliance either to carry out or to further a variety
of reforms.

Throughout the Federal Republic it was not un-
ususal to hear of popular opposition in small towns
and villages to the aims of planners and politicians
to set up large-scale projects. The latter argued
that they intended to serve the needs of entire
regions for the benefit of the population as a whole,
not only for the benefit of specific communities.
However, when the planners and politicians in the
state of Baden-Wuerttemberg in South Germany chose
a site for a nuclear power station near the village
of Wyhl, they confronted a rural population with
hyper-technology which was perceived as an immense
threat to their social and physical existence.(3)
The wine-growers in the area were concerned that the
quality of their wine would be impaired by radiation
from the planned nuclear power station. The initial
impulse to resist came from a conservative rural
population which sought to preserve its way of life.
Moreover, the original intention of the local people
was to seek a reversal of the plans for the project
through the legitimate adminstrative and legal
channels. They did this, but to no avail.

Instead, they discovered that the Minister
President of Baden-Wuerttemberg, Hans Filbinger, had
a special interest in carrying out this project
since he was the chairman of the supervisory board
of the Badenwerk company. One of the subsidiaries
of this company, Kernkraftwerk Sued (KWS), was
awarded the contract to build the project. Seventy
five per cent of Badenwerk was owned by the state of
Baden-Wuerttemberg, and the KWS was subsidiary of
both Badenwerk and Energieversorgung Schwaben. The
Minister of Economics in Baden-Wuerttemberg, Rudolf
Eberle, was Filbinger's representative on the supervisory board of the construction company Hochtief
which had been commissioned to carry out a large
proportion of the construction work on the planned
project. Thus the persons applying for permission
to build the nuclear power station and the authority
responsible for granting permission for work to go
ahead were almost identical insofar as Filbinger and
Eberle were involved in the manner which has just
been described.(4)

Thus the fear of the local farmers and wine-
growers about the threat of radiation to their products, the anger at the manner in which the state
government tried to introduce the project without

proper consultation of the local community and the
subsequent loss of faith in legal channels as a
means of reversing the planning decision explains
why a peaceful demonstration by about 150 people
took place in February 1975, when they occupied the
site of the planned project. The demonstrators
made a strong impression on the police since they
sought to discuss the issues with them rather than
to hurl abuse. They were not social revolutionaries
but ordinary people who were shocked that the state
should use the police to 'solve' what they saw as a
political problem. The eviction of this small group
of people only gave further publicity to their cause.
    Two new factors emerged out of this: firstly, a
rediscovered awareness of the traditions of the
Baden region and secondly, support for the opponents
of the project from students and other young people
in Freiburg, who were involved in non-violent, grass-
roots and socialist or anarchist initiatives.(5)
The region of Baden had a common language, history
and culture. In the past its population tended to
view the inhabitants of Wuerttemberg with great suspicion. The capital of Baden-Wuerttemberg, Stuttgart, is situated in what used to be Wuerttemberg.
It was only after the last war that the two states
were merged into one.(6) A tradition of resistance
by the population of Baden to the dominance of the
Swabians in Wuerttemberg was thus revived in a more
modern context. In addition, the rural quality of
the area around Wyhl was more pronounced than in
most other regions. Thus the population identified
closely with the countryside and nature as well as
their own history and culture. All groups, including the social revolutionaries from Freiburg, were
united in the desire to maintain the principle of
non-violent resistance in the campaign. This
intention was strengthened by the participation of
Evangelical priests and by the experiences in neigh-
bouring communities in the Alsace where non-violent
resistance to industrial projects had been very
successful.(7) People from Alsace also took part in
this campaign.(8) The use of force by the police in
evicting the demonstrators only ensured that tens of
thousands became involved in a campaign which encompassed an entire region. Moreover, a fine
balance was maintained between locals and outsiders,
old and young, conservatives and left-wingers.(9)
    The authorities in Baden-Wuerttemberg had
seriously misjudged the situation in Wyhl and various historical factors appeared to coincide, so that
although people all over Germany were informed about

what was happening in Wyhl, no one imagined that
these events were the stirrings of a far-reaching
campaign against similar projects. Yet it is highly
significant that one of the main catalysts of the
Green Movement was the revolt by a traditional conservative and rural community against the 'technocrats'. Hence the issue of opposition to alien,
technocratic forms of rule was a common denominator
of the subjectivist protest by both the young well-
educated middle classes and conservative elements.
At that point in time the ruling 'technocrats' were
the Social Democrats and the Free Democrats.

In 1976, the year following the events at Wyhl,
the Social-Liberal Alliance was re-elected into
power, and as Peter Glotz pointed out in an election
speech, instead of being concerned about the problems
of the 1980s, with the build-up of nuclear weapons or
the deterioration of the environment, the major
parties fought over the 'fears of the 1950s', over
the election slogan 'freedom or socialism', namely
over whether or not the Social-Liberal Alliance was
destroying freedom.(10) Even though the major parties did not campaign on these issues - the statement
by Glotz being the exception that confirmed the rule
- there was a growing sentiment among Citizens'
Initiatives all over the country of the need to
oppose planning measures which threatened particular
communities.

The announcement, in November 1973, by the
Nordwestdeutsche Kraftwerke AG (NWK) of its intention to build a nuclear power station near Brokdorf
in Schleswig-Holstein, led to the formation of a
Citizens' Initiative for the Protection of the Lower
Elbe (Buergerinitiative Umweltschutz Unterelbe -BUU).
In August 1974, over a period of four weeks, the BUU
collected over 30,000 signatures for a petition
which opposed the project. However, the BUU only
had 160 members in April 1975 and there appeared
to be little prospect of preventing the construction
of the project by legal means. In October 1976, the
NWK, shielded by the police, and in the middle of
the night, surrounded the site at Brokdorf with
barbed wire. To the Citizens' Initiatives this
indicated the start of construction work on the project, and on the following Saturday, on 30 October,
about eight thousand people attended a demonstration
in Brokdorf that had been organised by the BUU.
Around two thousand people then clambered over the
barbed wire and on to the site, and were then
evicted by the police on horseback. Tents and
building materials which had been brought on to the

site were burnt and destroyed and many people were
apparently treated with brutality by the police.

These events signalled the beginning of a
campaign that attracted people from all over the
Federal Republic. Whilst in Wyhl an entire region
had stood behind the campaign, in Brokdorf the regional aspect of the protest was overshadowed by the
interest shown by people in the city states of Bremen and Hamburg, and in the capital of Schleswig-
Holstein, Kiel, as well as Citizens' Initiatives and
opponents of the 'system' all over the country. In
addition, the principle of non-violence on the part
of the demonstrators, which had hitherto been upheld both in Wyhl and in Brokdorf, was ignored as
the reality and the myths surrounding the 'battle of
Brokdorf' mobilised more and more people. The mass
movement found it difficult to conceive any method
by which agreement could be reached among thousands
of people on how to remain entirely non-violent.
Following the events on 30 October 1976 the authorities erected more barbed-wire fences and even dug a
moat around the site of the planned project. Individual communist groups in university towns like
Hamburg sensed a great opportunity to lead the masses against the authorities, and anticipated a violent confrontation at the next demonstration.

Their opportunity arrived two weeks later when
around 40,000 people, many of whom had travelled
tens and hundreds of miles, approached the site which
to many people resembled a modern version of a medi-
eval fortress. Some isolated and well-organised
groups proceeded to provide a spectacle for the
other demonstrators by crossing the moat and trying
to cut their way through the barbed-wire fence.
This prompted the police to fire water-cannons and
tear-gas grenades at these groups and into the crowd
of people who were not actually trying to get on to
the site. All this incensed the crowd and many who
had come to stage a protest without wanting to become involved in any violence simply joined in a
collective effort to pull down fences and protest
angrily against the use of force by the police.
Thus many became involved in what had begun as a violent confrontation between a small minority of the
demonstrators and the police. Hundreds of people
ended up in need of medical treatment and others
ended up in court.

Apart from passing sentences on some of the
demonstrators, the courts were kept busy by environmentalists who questioned the legality of the plans
by the electricity supply industry to provide energy

from nuclear power. The decision by the administrative court in Schleswig-Holstein to call a halt provisionally to any further work on the site in Brokdorf came too late (17 December 1976). Huge demonstrations had already been planned and most people were convinced that the authorities simply intended to use police force in order to carry out the nuclear energy programme. An immense campaign in self-education in the dangers of nuclear power occurred in thousands of neighbourhoods, and although the authorities presented coherent arguments about the need for nuclear power stations to ensure prosperity and the growth of the economy, many people were won over by the sound arguments of the protestors about the potential dangers of such projects to the health and safety of the population.

Opinion polls between September 1976 and December 1976 showed how the publicity surrounding the massive campaign against the project in Brokdorf had swayed people towards a different opinion. Between these dates the number of people who were opposed to the construction of a nuclear power station in their neighbourhood rose from 36 per cent to 47 per cent, and more people felt that these projects posed a risk to the health and safety of the population. (Table 4.1)

Table 4.1   Attitudes to nuclear power (1973-1976)(%)

Question: If electricity was produced by nuclear power, do you think this could be done in a way that did not endanger human health or do you fear that it does entail certain risks?

	June 1973	September 1976	December 1976
a risk	48	65	70
no danger	40	24	19
undecided	12	11	11

Question: If there were plans to build a nuclear power station in your neighbourhood and the population took a vote on the issue, how would you vote personally - for or against?

	May 1975	September 1976	December 1976
for	40	35	35
against	28	36	47
undecided	32	29	18

Source: E.Nolle-Naumann (ed.), Allensbacher Jahrbuch der Demoskopie, (Allensbach, Institut fuer Demoskopie, 1977), Vol. VII, p. 186.

In 1977 there took place a series of demonstrations, some of which ended in violent confrontations (for instance in Grohnde, Lower Saxony) and this ensured the maximum publicity for the new movement and a polarisation of views among the population. Most of the protestors were opposed to the violence, but they rejected appeals by the authorities for them not to take part in any further demonstrations. One demonstration near Brokdorf was banned by the state government; none the less, well over 20,000 people took part in it. By mid-1977, when 40,000 people demonstrated against the planned nuclear reactor in Kalkar, North Rhine Westphalia, where they were supervised by tens of thousands of police from all over the country, many people seriously believed that they were witnessing the advent of a new form of totalitarianism as described by Robert Jungk in his best-selling book, The Nuclear State. In the 'nuclear state', the supervision of highly sophisticated, technological projects can only take place under a huge security apparatus and security industry. The idea of opposition to the 'nuclear state' played a significant part in the protests in Gorleben (the planned site for a nuclear fuel reprocessing plant) which led to a demonstration in Hannover (March 1979) attended by 100,000 people; and in Bonn (October 1979), when 150,000 people took part in the largest protest rally in the history of the Federal Republic up to that date.

This level of support reflected the popularity of Citizens' Initiatives. In January 1980 it was estimated that around five million people were loosely organised in 1,138 regional and 130 supra-regional environmentalist groups.(11) Surveys had shown that Citizens' Initiatives enjoyed, within the population, a much higher level of credibility than commercial and political interest groups relative to environmental issues. In a survey carried out in Berlin, most people (48 per cent) expected these initiatives to make an effective contribution to the protection of the environment, rather than industry (38 per cent), the Federal Government (31 per cent), the main political parties (8 per cent) and the trade unions (2 per cent).(12)

II Attempts to organise the protest movement

The activities of the Citizens' Initiatives and the mass mobilisation against nuclear power stations increased people's awareness that certain interests

Table 4.2 Popular awareness of lack of representation
of interests (%)

	February 1976	June 1978
despite numerous interest groups in the Federal Republic, there are many people whose interests are not really represented by anyone	40	62
I would count myself among those people whose interests are not really represented by anyone	16	31

Source: Figures from Der Spiegel, Nr. 24, 1978, p. 31, and
cited in D.Murphy et al. Protest. Gruene, Bunte und Steur-
rebellen (Reinbek, Hamburg, 1979), p. 141.

were not adequately represented by the main political parties. Between February 1976, before the mass
mobilisation against nuclear power stations had
taken place, and June 1978, the percentage of people
who felt that their interests were not represented
by any interest group rose from 16 per cent to 31
per cent. (Table 4.2) A survey carried out in 1978
showed that if Citizens' Initiatives and other
environmentalists were to found an environmentalist
party for the whole of the Federal Republic, 47 per
cent of the population would welcome it, and 32 per
cent would not. When asked if they might vote for
this party at a state election, 33 per cent said
they would and 51 per cent said they would not.(13)
Another survey showed that 6.6 per cent of the population belonged to a narrow circle of sympathisers
who were most likely to vote for an environmentalist
party both at state and National (Federal) Elections.
This group considered environmental protection to be
the most important political problem; it had enough
trust in capable politicians to solve it; and it
could not perceive any potentially successful initiatives on this issue within the established parties.
(14) Early survey results suggested that the bulk
of support for an environmentalist party would come
from young people; 67 per cent of the 18-23 age
group said that they would welcome this kind of
party and 44 per cent that they would vote for it.
(Table 4.3) In the 1978 state elections 66 per cent
of the vote for environmentalist groups in Hamburg
came from young people; in Lower Saxony it was 22
per cent; in Hessen; 79 per cent; and in Bavaria,
20 per cent. In all these states none of the major

parties gained more than 13 per cent of the vote
from the 18-25 age group.(15) The Green Party, once
it had been formed, enjoyed the support, above all,
of young people with a higher level of education.
(Table 4.4)

Table 4.3 Potential support for an environmentalist party
related to age groups (1978) (%)

	18-23	24-29	30-49	50-64	65+
would welcome it	67	63	54	47	28
would vote for it	44	51	39	32	19
would not welcome it	13	24	27	35	37

Source: Figures from R.Wildemann, 'Protestpotential'
in Capital, (Aug. 1978), p. 125, and cited in D.Murphy et al.
Protest, p. 147.

Table 4.4 Level of support for political parties related to
level of education (16-24 age group) (%)

	Intermediate (n=482)	Modern Secondary (n=317)	Grammar (n=338)
CDU/CSU	19	16	18
SPD	27	25	17
GREENS	15	22	29
NO PARTY	35	29	28

(Level of education relates either to actual level attained, or
level likely to be attained in the future)

Source: Figures from Shell Studie, (1981), Jugend 1981,
Hamburg, Vol. 1, p. 675.

The environmentalist groups that competed in
the 1978 state elections in Hamburg and Lower Saxony
gained votes from all the major parties. This confirmed the trend which had been shown in a survey in
Hessen where 18 to 25 per cent of the voters from
the established parties said they might vote for
a Green Party, and 3 per cent, definitely vote for
it.(16)In the Hamburg state elections environmentalist
groups made the greatest net gains from the SPD,
although they also won over many voters from the
other two established parties. A similar pattern
occurred in Lower Saxony.(Table 4.5)

Table 4.5   Votes from established to minor parties (Hamburg and Lower Saxony state elections, 1978)

Hamburg

Main parties	No. of votes to minor parties	Minor parties	Total no. of votes	% of vote	1974 vote
SPD	9,000	environment-alist groups	43,253	4.5	(-)
CDU	3,900	Communist Party	9,378	1.0	(2)
FDP	2,900	National Democrats	3,230	0.3	(1)

Lower Saxony

Main parties	No. of votes to minor parties	Minor parties	Total no. of votes	% of vote	1974 vote
SPD	66,400	environment-alist groups	157,666	3.9	(-)
CDU	27,500	Communist Party	12,708	0.3	(-)
FDP	19,800	National Democrats	17,593	0.4	(1)

Source: Figures from Der Spiegel, Nr. 24, 1978, p. 33.

Table 4.6 Gains by environmentalist groups at the expense of the established parties (1978 state elections)

	% of total vote for environmentalists
Hamburg electoral districts	
—with relatively small SPD gains	3.9
—with the greatest CDU losses	4.0
—with the greatest FDP losses	3.3
Lower Saxony electoral districts	
—with the greatest CDU losses	4.3
—with the greatest SPD losses	4.3
—with the greatest FDP losses	4.8

Source: Figures from INFAS 'Report fuer die Presse vom 5.6.1978' (Bonn, 1978), p. 3, and cited in D.Murphy et al. Protest, p. 145.

The outlook for an environmentalist party which might be formed at a national level appeared favourable in the light of the relative success of environmentalist groups at a communal and state level, and the results of the nationwide elections to the European Parliament. In June 1978 a Green List secured 3.9 per cent of the votes in the Lower Saxony state elections and contributed to the exclusion of the

Table 4.7 Local opposition to projects and environmentalist vote (European Elections, 1979)

Location	Project opposed by local population	% of vote
Gorleben	Nuclear fuel reprocessing plant	27.8
Luechow-Dannenberg	Nuclear fuel reprocessing plant	14.4
Tuebingen	Nuclear power station (Wyhl)	12.0
Freiburg	Nuclear power station (Wyhl)	10.0
Ahaus	Nuclear power project	44.1

(The Greens also gained about 4% of the vote in the following towns and cities where there were many groups that opposed nuclear power: Bremen, Bonn, Cologne, Frankfurt, Hamburg, Hannover, Munich.)

Source: Figures from BBU—aktuell Umweltmagazin, 10, 1979, p.10.

FDP from the state parliament. In Hamburg two Green Lists competed in the state elections and secured 4.5 per cent of the vote; once again, this ensured that the FDP lost its seats in the state parliament. Whilst the results in Hessen and Bavaria - less than 2 per cent of the vote - were less encouraging for the environmentalists, in March 1979 the Alternative List in Berlin received 3.7 per cent of the vote and gained ten seats in four (out of twelve) district councils. In June 1979 an alliance of various environmentalist groups, under the leadership of the former Christian Democrat Member of Parliament, Herbert Gruhl, attracted 893,510 voters, 3.2 per cent, in the elections to the European Parliament. The best results were achieved in areas where strong local opposition - often by a conservative, rural population - to specific projects was combined with the support of young, well-educated protestors from nearby university towns and cities. An analysis of aggregate data on the social and economic characteristics of all the different areas might have helped to explain the variation in the strength of the environmentalist vote. It should be borne in mind, however, that the higher percentages relate to small rural districts. In large towns and cities the vote averaged around 4 per cent. (Table 4.7) The federal structure of West Germany and the proximity of rural enclaves to urban centres meant that the protest was likely to erupt in several areas. On the whole, whenever this combination of factors did not exist, there was little or no durable protest activity against hyper-technological projects.

The combination of a strong anti-modernist
urban protest movement in Bremen and local opposition
to the nuclear power project in Brokdorf led, in
October 1979, to the success of a Green List in
Bremen when it secured just over 5 per cent of the
vote and four seats in the state parliament. (An
Alternative List, which had campaigned on similar
issues, secured a further 1.5 per cent of the vote.)
The Greens were only short of a few votes which would
have denied the SPD a majority in the parliament, in
a state where the Social Democrats are traditionally
very powerful. This was the first occasion on which
a Green List had gained representation in a state
parliament since the electoral system allows parties
to send representatives into a parliament if they
obtain more than 5 per cent of the vote. The federal
structure of parliamentary democracy in West Germany
had therefore enabled the voice of significant
regional opposition groups to be heard at an influential - even if far from decisive - level of state
power. The supporters of Green Lists now had to
consider the possibilities of uniting the various
initiatives at a national level.
The conditions for uniting everyone who was involved in Citizens' Initiatives and in communal and
state elections under one political and organisational umbrella were not entirely favourable. In Hamburg, Hessen, Bremen and in many other locations,
Green Lists had often competed against each other.
In addition, many left-wing supporters of the initiatives were reluctant to 'play the parliamentary
game'. There was a widespread fear that any effort
in this direction would drain the resources and
energy which were needed for extra-parliamentary
campaigns and direct action, especially since the
Greens were likely to exercise only a limited influence on the formulation of policies in parliament.
At any rate many people were suspicious of 'representative' as opposed to grass-roots politics. Others,
however, argued that the population would only take
the ecology movement seriously once it had formed a
party with a recognisable rationale and mode of
behaviour, especially because politicians had not
taken up the issues raised by the environmentalists.
As Claus Offe pointed out:

> the political public of a parliamentary
> democracy is primarily determined by the
> disputes of parties in parliaments, in the
> media and in elections. These institutions
> are the 'tribunes' on which themes and

> conflicts appear as 'political'...the
> political form of a party could, under the
> conditions of local structures of conflict,
> serve the purpose of bringing into relation
> with each other the thematically, regionally
> and socially isolated fields of conflict,
> and bring out and make people aware of the
> rationality common to them. (17)

Offe describes this rationality as the 'struggle
against the social consequences of capitalist modernisation, against the social dictatorship of those
with power to invest'. He stresses that, hitherto,
there had only been attempts to generalise a single
theme, for example the dangers of nuclear energy, or
social categories like the student movement. In his
opinion, only the structure of a party allows the
support of citizens to be expressed in conflicts
in which they are not directly affected, but whose
rationality and significance they recognise.(18)

Two further factors influenced the decision by
many supporters of the ecology movement to try and
form a party. Firstly, despite the heterogeneous
origins of the supporters of the Citizens' Initiatives and Green Lists many people were aware of a
process whereby various standpoints were becoming
integrated; for example, Wolfgang Sternstein described how this had come about during the campaign in
Wyhl:

> Today there are many wine-growers and
> farmers who have at heart the issues of
> environmental protection and democratisa-
> tion of our society as much as their wine
> and their tobacco. There are environment-
> alists who have at heart the preservation
> of the basis for existence of the Kaiserstuhl
> [Wyhl] wine-growers and the democratisation
> of our political system as much as the
> preservation of the natural bases for life
> of human beings. And there are socialists
> and communists who today campaign as
> passionately for the protection
> of the environment and the interests of the
> population of Kaiserstuhl as for the change
> of society. This process of integration of
> various standpoints and attitudes is one of
> the most remarkable results of the common
> struggle against the nuclear power station
> and the ensuing industry on the Upper Rhine.(19)

Secondly, people with different political backgrounds were able to look forward to the formation
of a Green Party in the hope that they could
influence, or even lead it, since there did not yet
exist any Green Programme. No single group had been
powerful enough to overcome the 5 per cent electoral
hurdle consistently and in different regions. Whilst
the events in Brokdorf had offered to some 'professional revolutionaries' the opportunity to lead the
'masses' against the state and the police, the
prospect of the formation of a Green Party attracted
people with varying degrees of political experience
(including many former Social Democrats) who wished
to organise the same 'masses' into a political party.
When people like Herbert Gruhl did not get their way
they eventually left the party; this feature will be
explained more fully later on. Those who strove to
form a party imagined that it would be able to
represent the variety of Citizens' Initiatives. It
has been pointed out that in the Hamburg state
elections (1978) more than 150 Citizens' Initiatives
took part in the formulation of an electoral programme.(20) Yet the parties were not whole-heartedly
accepted as representatives of the interests of
these initiatives because many people were in favour
of less conventional forms of organisation. This
became apparent in the environmentalist protests
in Gorleben and around Frankfurt Airport and the
creation of loosely-organised alternative communities which went further than Citizens' Initiatives
in their opposition to 'technocracy'.
    Citizens' Initiatives were usually formed at a
local level in order to oppose particular projects
which might directly affect the quality of life.
The emergence of a mass movement in the campaign
against nuclear energy meant that new forces were
at work which transcended particularist interests.
New groups emerged to sustain the wave of protest,
and they were not only interested in giving up a
little of their spare time to oppose a particular
project but rather in living an alternative way of
life and in fundamentally opposing the evolution of
industrial society. These groups did not constitute
the majority within the Green Movement, yet they
gained the support and sympathy of most people
within it. The movement could not have grown at
such speed without this committed activity which
strove to unify the spheres of personal existence
and objective social reality. These groups, which
were supported mainly by young, well-educated people,
made one of their most dramatic appearances in the

protest in Gorleben. In contrast to Citizens'
Initiatives, they heralded the arrival of groups of
people who were held together not only by their
opposition to a particular project, but by the
search for personal and collective identity in a
community.

When the Federal Government decided to build a
reprocessing plant for nuclear waste in Gorleben,
which was partly a nature reserve, members of the
local community - particularly farmers - were supported in their opposition to these plans by protestors
from large cities (West Berlin, Hannover, Hamburg).
These protests culminated in a mass demonstration by
100,000 people in Hannover, the centre of the
regional government in Lower Saxony, in March 1979.
In Gorleben itself repeated efforts were made to
prevent the destruction of the forest. When trees
were felled on the planned site of the project, the
protestors planted thousands of saplings to make up
for the loss. In another initiative one million
marks were raised to help prevent the purchase of
land by the nuclear energy industry.

The strength of the protest forced the Christian
Democrat Minister President of Lower Saxony to
announce that, for political reasons, the area around
Gorleben would not be used as a site for a nuclear
waste reprocessing plant. Nevertheless, the authorities did not give up plans to store radioactive waste
in the underground salt deposits in the area. This
led to plans by the protestors to occupy a drilling
site which was being used by the nuclear energy
industry to investigate the salt deposits. The
occupation was organised by groups outside the region
although activists in Gorleben were also involved in
the preparations. The activists wished to carry out
a non-violent protest and to create loose structures
- for instance 'reference groups' which would be
represented in a 'Speakers' Council' - in order to
reduce the isolation and fear of individuals and to
encourage dialogue and participation.

When 5,000 people arrived on the site on 4 May
1980 they were supported by local farmers and, above
all, by women of all age groups from the local community. Their arrival had, to a large extent, been
made easier by publicity in the Taz which provided
contact addresses and practical suggestions in
support of the non-violent occupation.

The efforts to practice grass-roots democracy
and non-violence were inspired by the belief that,
on the one hand, the machinery of consultation and
structures of parliamentary democracy did not

facilitate the participation of ordinary people in decision-making and, on the other hand, certain groups in the movement against nuclear energy had tried to instrumentalise this protest to further their own political aims and thus made it difficult for unity to emerge over the principle of non-violence. The essence of this form of grass-roots democracy lies in the belief that trust and solidarity can only emerge when individuals form groups in which majority decisions are not allowed to over-ride individual opinions. The weakness of this concept is that decisions can often only be reached after an arduous process and that it may only be possible to fulfil on a small scale.

Around four hundred people remained on the site in Gorleben for an entire month. They had organised themselves into reference groups of up to fifteen people. Each group sent a representative to the Speakers' Council where, once unanimity had been achieved, decisions were made on matters which affected the entire site. All groups were free to initiate their own activity, although they were requested to consult the Speakers' Council. Some groups had decided 'autonomously' to build barricades and dig trenches, whilst the majority were in favour of passive, non-violent resistance. Some militant groups adhered to a non-violent form of protest since they did not wish to cause divisions among the occupants. (21)   Others, who were disillusioned by the ideas of passive resistance, simply left the site.(22)

The Speakers' Council helped to coordinate activities. Whenever a particular task had to be undertaken, for instance the clearing of rubbish, a loudspeaker would ask for volunteers to do it. The constant availability of volunteers meant that it was easier to avoid the emergence of leading figures and that individual and group responsibility played an important part. Volunteers were constantly needed for fire-watching duties, for parking duties (to cope with all the visitors), and for providing information to new arrivals on the site. The latter received leaflets on the dangers of lighting fires near the forest, the times for clearing rubbish and the latest paper of consensus from the Speakers' Council. Yet it was not easy to arrive at a consensus and to implement decisions. For example, the Speakers' Council was unable to agree on how to deal with autonomous initiatives that led to the construction of a tower on the site and the erection of barricades in the surrounding woods. Agreement had been reached on a concept of passive resistance.

Yet some activists - it is not known whether they were from the occupied site - damaged fencing around another drilling site and lit a small fire.

Most occupants worked hard to maintain good relationships with the local community in Gorleben. The main topic of discussion at various meetings was how to practise non-violent resistance when the police arrived, since most people had little or no experience in this. This led to the introduction of 'training in non-violence'. Occupants divided themselves into groups of 'occupants' and 'policemen'. The latter then proceeded either to drag or to carry off the former in a mock eviction of the site. This training, as well as the solidarity and trust that had been created in the reference groups, ensured that when the police did actually arrive there was 'no violence at all from the demonstrators'.(23) The eviction took place with the arrival of six thousand police and border patrol troops in a convoy of trucks, army vehicles, horses, helicopters and bulldozers. The reporter from Die Zeit commented that the occupants 'disarmed the irritated police and their huge potential of violence almost imperceptibly so that it did not explode. Everything could have exploded at one command: tear-gas, water-cannons and guns'.(24) The demonstrators showed immense self-discipline as they were removed from the site, occasionally urged away by a police truncheon.

The non-violent form of protest won great sympathy for the occupants of the site from a local population that had been highly sceptical about the illegal nature of their action. Many farmers began to consider the police and the drilling teams from the nuclear energy industry to be a far greater intrusion in the area that the presence of the occupants.(25) The farmers made very generous contributions of food to the occupants and some even had to be returned to them.

The occupation of the site in Gorleben brought into the public eye the attempts of certain groups within society to create an alternative context for the realisation of personal and collective identity. The campaign to protect the environment grew into one which sought to create a meaningful context for human relationships. A large placard in the village warned the authorities that they could 'destroy the tower and the village, but not the strength that had created them'.

The site was visited by thousands of people on every weekend throughout May 1980. There were

at least two kinds of visitors: those who wished to
support in an active manner the occupants and those
who were either curious about or generally sympathetic to their cause. The latter group included families, school classes, old people's clubs and even new
recruits from the West German border police. It was
thus possible for the villagers to engage the visitors in discussions which usually centred more around
the life in the village than the initial aim of the
villagers, namely to oppose the plans of the nuclear
energy industry.(26) In fact the village appears to
have had the effect of publicising and generating
interest in the aims and life-style of the alternative (counter-cultural) movement rather than the
particular issues raised by the ecology movement.
This is hardly surprising since the occupants themselves declared the site to be the 'Free Republic
of Wendland' which was neither 'a government, nor a
state, but a model of grass-roots decision-making'.
The occupants had called the village 'Wendland'
after a traditional name of the region. Everyone,
including the visitors, was issued with a passport
which bore a close resemblance to the one carried by
the citizens of the Federal Republic. The alternative passport, however, contained the following
lines: 'attitude to life: positive; capacity for
thought: good; this passport may be presented when
one is arrested and is valid as long as the bearer
can still laugh'.
    Visitors were struck by the immense amount of
work and creativity involved in the construction of
an entire village and the introduction of 'alternative technology', for instance a windmill powered by
a car battery and a unit for the transmission of
solar energy. Whilst most of the visitors were
impressed by the material results of the occupation,
people on the site emphasized the strength of their
ideals, their desire and ability to live happily
away from a consumerist culture. Even though they
shared a middle-class background and were thus able
to afford the materials needed to construct the
village, they stressed the cultural aspects of their
life-style. Work on the site was often accompanied
by music. Theatrical displays, the composition and
singing of songs as well as sport and other creative
activities all stressed the importance of 'life'.
In one of their songs, the protestors proclaimed:
'We wish to live, and in the face of death,life
means resistance; we wish to live, yet they beat the
flowers out of our hands'.(27) The occupants also
wished to convey the image that they were the 'happy'

ones and the police the 'unhappy' ones.(28) When
special units of the police climbed the towers on
the site which, according to some newspapers,
harboured militants armed with molotov cocktails,
they were greeted with chocolates and wine. The
clearing of the site was punctuated by moral appeals
to the police to ask themselves if they could feel
responsible for their action.(29)

The eviction of the occupants prompted acts of
solidarity all over the country. In Berlin and
Hamburg around 20,000 people took part in protest
marches. In sixty other locations there were small-
scale protests;around 35 churches were occupied.
The events in Gorleben showed the close links between
the ecology and alternative movements. Many young
people who observed these events found here a model
for an alternative life-style. The emergence of
youth protest, especially the squatters' movement,
in the months to follow, was influenced by events at
Gorleben. On the one hand, romantic ideas about a
simple way of life were adopted in an uncritical
manner, on the other hand, passive non-violent
resistance was regarded as a feeble and naive strategy relative to the use of force by the authorities. Whilst in Gorleben the supporters of a non-
violent strategy had succeeded in carrying out a
peaceful protest, the events around Frankfurt Airport showed how easy it is for militant groups to
undermine a loosely-organised social movement.

Following the events in Gorleben many protestors noticed that despite their efforts towards
peaceful protest and passive resistance, neither
the authorities nor the population at large
suddenly became happy and peaceful. Since the gap
between their ideals and social reality remained a
large one, many of them, in their search for personal and collective identity, constructed their own
sheltered communities which often reinforced the
distance to society at large. There thus developed,
within the Green Movement, an increasing tension
between some people who wished to plan ahead ration-
ally for a utopian transformation of society and
others who sought meaningful contexts in the
immediate situation. This became apparent in the
conflict around Frankfurt Airport and contributed to
the tensions between pragmatic, radical reformists
and utopian and fundamentalist tendencies within
the Green Party.

In the area around Frankfurt Airport the
authorities had, for several years, aroused scattered
opposition from nearby communities to their plans to

construct a new runway and thus to destroy a large
section of woodland area. The advent of the ecology
movement and the tradition of violent urban protest
in the nearby city of Frankfurt (for instance the
squatters' protests in the early seventies) provided
the added ingredients for another prolonged confrontation between protestors and the authorities. Another
factor was the strength, among certain groups, of
anti-American sentiment. They were convinced that
the new West Runway was not only part of national
infrastructural plans, but would also serve American
long-range military aircraft which can reach the
Middle East. These urban protest groups regarded
West German politicians as puppets in the hands of
a power that was planning for war at the expense of
the opponents of a technocratic 'colour television'
culture.(30) The opposition to the runway was
regarded as an uprising of marginalised groups
against the centres of power, as an attempt to resist
the 'South Americanisation of entire regions through
the creation of antiquated mono-maniacal large-scale
projects'.(31)

The conflict around Frankfurt Airport also
reflected a growing disappointment by broad layers
of the population with the policies of the Social
Democratic-Liberal Alliance. Efforts by Social
Democrat politicians to postpone the construction of
the runway did not placate the opposition because,
even whilst a formal inquiry was being held in the
state parliament on the effects of air traffic on
the surrounding area, the Free Democrat Minister of
Economics in Hessen continued to insist that this
would not affect the decision in favour of going
ahead with the construction of the runway.(32) The
opponents of the project felt that the inquiry
failed to deal with the 'fundamental question as to
what people need and the questions of living and
quality of life'.(33) The language and level of dis-
course conducted by experts frustrated many of them.
Although they were granted the opportunity to express
their views, they felt that they had been given much
less time to argue their case than those who were in
favour of the project.(34)

By 3 November 1980 the protest against the West
Runway had gained the support of local DGB trade
union groups, the _Jusos_, the _Judos_ and groups within
the church. About 15,000 people took part in a protest which, according to the _Taz_, was the scene of
discussions between squatters from the city and
ordinary citizens; workers and owner-occupiers; and
the grandmother who pleaded with a policeman that,

for the sake of her children, the woodland area should be retained.(35) A year later, on 14 November 1981, more than 100,000 people took part in a rally in Wiesbaden against the extension of the airport and in autumn 1982 the Green Party gained enough votes in Hessen to enter the state parliament in Frankfurt and hold the balance of power between the SPD and the CDU. In 1981 the environmentalists had gained an impressive proportion of the vote in communes around Frankfurt Airport: 25 per cent in Moerfelden-Walldorf, and in Buettelborn, 17 per cent in Ruesselheim, 15 per cent in Kelsterbach and 13 per cent in Gross-Gernau. In all these communes the main political parties were often opposed to the West Runway; if they had been in favour of it, they might have been faced with a local government run by an environmentalist group.

The protest encompassed all layers of the population. At the Opel car factory around one third of the workforce, out of a total of 30,000, took part in some form of protest activity.(36) The works council sent a letter to Holger Boerner about the excessive use of force by the police against the demonstrators.(37) Many Social Democrats and trade unionists were also highly dissatisfied with the Social Democrat Administration in Hessen. According to a survey carried out by Frankfurt University, 86 per cent of the population in Moerfelden-Walldorf was opposed to the project; 50 per cent took part in demonstrations; 80 per cent took part in general campaign activities; 94 per cent were in favour of non-violent opposition; and 70 per cent were in favour of a spontaneous occupation of the site to prevent the felling of trees.(38) The growing strength of local and regional opposition to the project was one of the main reasons why many many protestors called for a plebiscite over this issue.

Mass demonstrations and impressive gains at local elections were not sufficient to provide a legal basis for the opponents of the project to reverse planning decisions. The Citizens' Initiatives in the vicinity of the airport decided to try and collect 800,000 signatures to bring about a plebiscite which might result in a defeat for the planning authorities. The Hessian State Constitution allowed for this measure to be introduced over certain issues. By September 1981 the protestors had collected 120,000 signatures which were required for the first stage of an appeal for a plebiscite. The efforts to bring about a plebiscite were not regarded as an alternative to direct action to prevent the

project. The protestors did, however, repeatedly
point out that the Hessian state authorities were
constantly breaking the law, for instance over the
infringement of 'Water Rights'.(39) The authorities
argued the question of the legality of the West Runway could only be dealt with by Federal Law and was
therefore beyond the competence of the Hessian State
Constitution.   In January the Supreme Court of
Jurisdiction in Hessen decided that the state
government of Hessen was not acting illegally by
refusing to carry out a plebiscite since Federal Law
precedes State Law and the controversy over the the
project could only be dealt with by Federal Aviation
Law. At a Federal level, however, there are no
provisions for a plebiscite.
     The efforts to bring about a plebiscite form
part of a populist critique of parliamentary democracy, because it did not take into account the
wishes of broad layers of the population in the
region around Frankfurt Airport. Initially the
protestors whole-heartedly took up the form of popular protest which had been adopted in Gorleben. The
police who were sent in to carry away the demonstrators from the site were totally disarmed by their
attitude, and by their gifts of chocolates and cigarettes. A publication of the alternative scene in
Frankfurt, Pflasterstrand, noted the difference in
attitudes between young protestors from the city
like themselves and local people: 'We propagate the
idea of seeing the human side of every cop. However,
the people of Walldorf speak to them and in such a
manner that they can hardly bear to carry out their
duty.'(40) This prompted the authorities to send in
what some protestors described as 'battle-hardened
troops from the big cities' who would not allow
themselves to be influenced by offers of chocolates
and the good humour of the demonstrators. Many
citizens thus felt that their peaceful intentions
had not been acknowledged by the other side. From
then onwards there was a marked increase in verbal
radicalism within the local population and greater
scope for the militants from large cities who wished
deliberately to provoke the 'violence of the state'.
     Whilst the demonstrators often exaggerate the
level of police brutality, there is much evidence
to support the assertion that the escalation of the
conflict was often caused by the use of force rather
than sound arguments by the authorities. (This was
partially acknowledged by the Government Commission
of Inquiry on Youth Protest which I refer to later.)
The Citizens' Initiatives, although they were pre-

pared to 'break the law collectively', remained
committed to the principles of non-violence. They
stated that any attacks with explosives or fires
were acts of provocation which played into the hands
of those who sought to build the West Runway.(41)
However, the resort to direct action, the lack of
consensus over a long-term strategy and the loose
structural forms that held the movement together,
led to a growing belief among many protestors in the
need for violent resistance and expressionistic
spontaneous protest. There appeared to be little
control by the Citizens' Initiatives over the pace
and dynamic of the social movement.(42)

There was an increasing conflict between those
who sought to coordinate and control the activities
of the movement and those who felt that constant
expressive protest and action would somehow make the
authorities shift their position. The regualr demonstrations were seen as part of a gratifying effort
to 'loosen up the asphalt jungle'. (43) However,
the desire to resist the consequences of modernisation 'here and now' came into conflict with longer-
term strategies: for instance, the efforts to bring
about a plebiscite, participation in elections and
the attempt to replace the exisiting government.(44)
The overwhelming majority of Citizens' Initiatives
supported non-violent direct action, and they stressed that their aims were political and not military.
(45) Yet among activists and militants who held an
apocalyptic view of the future there developed a
feeling that only violence could counter the 'brutal
terror of the state'. This feeling is linked to the
idea that the survival of the human race is at stake
and is most clearly expressed by the statements by
young people involved in the conflict. A sixteen
year-old schoolboy explained that his future prospects were bleak and that he could not commit himself to his work at school; his only source of hope
and commitment lay in opposing the extension of
Frankfurt Airport.(46) Another protestor believed
that the conflict over the runway gave people 'a
feeling for the woods' which was in sharp contrast
to the pollution in the city, the power of the police
and the machinery of war' that was going to unfurl
itself on the runway.(47) The contrast between a
dead city and a living forest which has to be defend-
ed in order to preserve life and civilisation is a
compelling one and reflects the earlier expressions
of disquiet at the path of modernisation.

This feeling of unease and the desire to defend
nature and 'humanity' against the 'violence of the

state' prompted a group of students from Marburg to
try and justify the need for counter-violence.(48)
The potential for counter-violence against the monopoly of violence by the state has so far not been
instrumentalised by any organisations. The violence
has been sporadic and based on loose structures, for
instance a network of informal contacts, and on a
philosophy which has only been politicised in a
general manner. Despite the mutual support which
exists between the protest movements there are
significant differences of opinion over how the
unifying themes and concepts can be converted into
a specific political strategy. One of the most
poignant themes is the desire to defend the world of
life and communities; in this sphere the protest
movement has devised its own structures which do not
rely on the organisational framework provided by the
Green Party.

The Citizens' Initiatives and organisations like
the Green Party provided an organisational point of
reference for the protest movement against the West
Runway. However, as I have already stated, the
conflict around Frankfurt Airport was not simply
related to a rational calculation of the actual level
of environmental destruction but to a deep yearning
for a change in life-style. The search for meaningful relationships in a communal context, for the
warmth and friendship of a group of similarly-minded
people was a common feature of the campaign against
nuclear power in Brokdorf, the ecological village in
Gorleben and the squatting and alternative movements
in Berlin. Around Frankfurt this desire to recreate
a lost community was expressed in the construction
of a 'village of resistance' in the woods near the
planned West Runway. The village was supported and
visited not only by members of the alternative
'scene' in Frankfurt but by housewives and other
people from the surrounding communities. Ute Scheub,
a correspondent for the Taz, felt that the warm
atmosphere which held together 'the extended family'
in the 'village of resistance' was largely attribut-
able to the presence of the women on the site.(49)
One housewife drew parallels between the atmosphere
in the alternative village and the solidarity which
held people together during and after the last war.
She felt that this feeling of unity had been lost
'as a result of the affluent society'.(50) The
villagers experienced similar problems to those that
occur in other arrangements for communal living.
The correspondent for the Taz did, however, assure
the readers of the newspaper that the problems were

exactly the same as those which are 'produced by the plastic and concrete society, problems like alcoholism, lack of awareness of responsibilities and so on'.(51)   The importance of the village as a unifying force is beyond question: when the authorities destroyed it, a new one, comprising ten huts was erected within twenty-four hours.(52)

The dispute around the West Runway was part of a general conflict between dissident groups and what they regarded as 'established society'. It took on a particular form in different regions: in North Germany the opposition was directed against the plan to build a nuclear power station at Brokdorf; in West Berlin it focused on the rights and life-style of squatters; and in Frankfurt the attention of the protestors was directed towards the West Runway. The links between the various movements were maintained through an informal network of contacts, through organisations like the BBU and the Green Party, that coordinate rather than direct the actions, and through the publicity in the alternative and the 'established' media. The main centres of activity were large cities where the Green Movement brought to the surface the tensions between the participatory and the governmental elements in the Social Democratic Party. I will now go on to assess the response of this and other established groups to the challenge posed by the Green Movement on environmental issues.

NOTES

1. Mayer-Tasch, Buergerinitiativbewegung, p. 26.

2. V.Ronge, Die Gesellschaft an den Grenzen der Natur (AJZ, Bielefeld, 1978), p. 22.

3. W.Sternstein, Ueberall ist Wyhl (Haag und Herchen, Frnakfurt, 1978), p. 206.

4. Ibïd., p. 27.

5. Ibid., p. 33.

6. Ibid., pp. 194-5.

7. Ibid., p. 32.

8. Ibid., p. 50.

9. Ibid., p. 19.

10. Glotz, Innenausstattung der Macht, p. 10.

11. Taz, 30 Jan. 1980, p. 1. The groups formed part of four umbrella organisations:'Deutscher Naturschutzring', 'Bundesverband Buergerinitiativen Umweltschutz', 'Bund Umwelt- und Naturschutz' and 'Deutschbund fuer Lebensschutz'.

12. B.Guggenberger, Buergerinitiativen in der Bundes- republik (Kohlhammer, 1980), p. 28.

13. F.Mueller, 'Das Waehlerpotential' in D.Murphy et al., Protest. Gruene, Bunte und Steuerrebellen (Reinbek, Hamburg,

1979), p. 143.

14. Ibid.

15. Ibid., p. 148.

16. Der Spiegel, Nr. 25, 1978, p. 90.

17. C.Offe, 'Konkurrenzpartei und kollektive politische Identitaet' in R.Roth (ed.), Parlamentarisches Ritual und politische Alternativen (Campus, Frankfurt, 1980), p. 41.

18. Ibid.

19. Sternstein, Wyhl, p. 2.

20. Meuller,'Das Waehlerpotential', p. 143.

21. G.Zint, Republik Freies Wendland – Ein Dokumentation (Zweitausendeins, Frankfurt, 1980), pp. 62-3.

22. Ibid., pp. 54-5.

23. Frankfurter Rundschau, 6 June 1980.

24. Die Zeit, 13 June 1980.

25. Frankfurter Rundschau, 9 May 1980.

26. Zint, Freies Wendland, p. 90.

27. Ibid., p. 83.

28. Taz, Gorleben-Dokumentation, 21 June 1980.

29. Zint, Freies Wendland, p. 208.

30. Taz, 15 Oct. 1981, p. 3.

31. Taz, 31 March 1982, p. 9.

32. Taz, 3 Feb. 1981, p. 4.

33. Taz, 4 Feb. 1981, p. 3.

34. Taz, 6 Feb. 1981, p. 10.

35. Taz, 4 Nov. 1980, p. 12.

36. Taz, 13 Nov. 1981, p. 4, in an interview with the deputy chairman of the works council (IG Metall) at the factory.

37. Taz, 5 Nov. 1981, p. 11.

38. Taz, 21 Oct. 1981, p. 6.

39. Taz, 13 April 1982, p. 10.

40. Taz, 28 Oct. 1981, p. 11.

41. Taz, 27 Oct. 1981, p. 10.

42. Taz, 6 Nov. 1981, p. 3.

43. Taz, 6 Nov. 1981, p. 3.

44. Taz, 13 Nov. 1981, p. 3.

45. Taz, 8 Dec. 1980, p. 3 and 16 Dec. 1981, p. 9.

46. Taz, 13 Nov. 1981, p. 4.

47. Taz, 13 Nov. 1981, p. 4.

48. Taz, 13 Nov. 1981, p. 5.

49. Taz, 21 Oct. 1981, p. 9.

50. Taz, 14 Oct. 1981, p. 11.

51. Taz, 14 Oct. 1981, p. 9.

52. Taz, 5 Nov. 1981, p. 4.

Chapter Five

THE RESPONSE OF ESTABLISHED GROUPS

I The Social-Liberal Alliance

In 1970 the Federal Social-Liberal Government introduced a broad catalogue of aims in their 'Programme
for the immediate protection of the environment'.
Yet, as Ronge has shown, this was narrowed down
considerably when it came to the implementation of
specific policies.(1) Ronge shows how, in the Federal Republic, the law on the amount of lead in petrol
was passed without great resistance from economic
interests; however, the law on the emission of waste
water met with strong opposition from the chemical
industry. He suggests that this was due to the dominance of economic imperatives over political considerations.(2)
     This partly explains why the protest against
the deterioration of the environment found much
sympathy among supporters of the SPD. In Schleswig-
Holstein the SPD came out in support of the protest
around Brokdorf; in Lower Saxony it called for a
'moratorium' on the further construction of all
nuclear power stations(3); similarly, in Hamburg the
party revised its original opinion that a nuclear
power station at Brokdorf was essential for the
supply of electricity.(4). The ecology movement had
brought to the surface the tension between the SPD
in government and the party at a local level where
members sought to achieve greater levels of participation. The latter were anxious to take up some of
the issues raised by the Green Movement.
     This led to tensions with trade union elements
within the SPD since they had given their full
support to Chancellor Schmidt. In some instances,
the trade unions actively opposed the ecology movement since the opposition by the latter to economic
growth and to the development of nuclear energy was
seen as a serious threat to the employment prospects
of the workforce. In 1977 the union which represents

90

workers in the public service, transport and traffic
sectors, supported a demonstration by a thousand
workers who were given the day off from work in
order to take part in a rally in support of the plan-
ed nuclear power station at Brokdorf. These tensions
between participatory and governmental elements within the SPD were overcome, to some extent, several
years later with the emergence of the peace movement
and the withdrawal of Helmut Schmidt as leader of the
party.

During the early stages of the ecology movement
any efforts by the Federal Government to hold a dialogue over the issue of nuclear energy were regarded
as insincere because it continued to stress that
this form of energy would still be required in the
future (Government Speech by Chancellor Schmidt,
December 1976). In March 1977 a leading newspaper
quoted an internal report from the Ministry of Economics which reaffirmed that nothing would change in
the basic direction of the government policy on
nuclear energy.(5) The contrast and conflict between
the movement outside parliament and the government
and other institutions was intensified by the confrontation between demonstrators and the police.
The latter were identified with the state apparatus
and hence any credibility of the strategy of dialogue was undermined. The adoption of direct action
had intensified the level of mistrust between both
sides. The protest movement only lost some of its
momentum when conflicts emerged within it over the
use of violence, and when the courts repeatedly took
decisions out of the hands of the politicians by,
at least provisionally, calling to a halt the proposed construction of various nuclear power stations.
In this instance, the courts certainly reduced the
potential conflict even though they were only
passing judgement on technical matters relating to
the levels of safety of nuclear power stations.

The formation of Green and Alternative parties
represents the failure of the Left within the SPD
to attract the protestors into their party. In
addition, the issue of nuclear energy did not easily
fit into classical modes of interpretation; the
traditional Left in the party was divided over the
issue. Yet, despite the defeats that it suffered
at the 1979 party congress, 40 per cent of the
delegates voted against the government policy on
nuclear energy. Nevertheless, the general scepticism by young people was hardly articulated at this
congress. Helmut Schmidt described their lack of
interest in established forms of political dis-

course as 'pure escapism' and Holger Boerner felt
that they simply did not pose the right questions.
(6) As I have shown, there are escapist tendencies
within the Green Movement; however, these and other
politicians failed to recognise the political relevance of the questions raised by them. Three years
later, during the campaign leading up to the 1983
Federal Elections, Hans-Jochen Vogel admitted that
the Greens did pose the right questions, although
he added that his party had the right answers.(7)
One of the few politicians to recognise the need to
develop a new strategy in the face of the Green
Movement was Peter Glotz. He identified as one of
the major tasks of the SPD the need to bridge the
gap between the trade unions and the Green Movement
- a gap which had arisen as a result of a 'profound
dispute over the ethics of progress and accumulation
which has prevailed since Descartes'.(8)

Later, I will show how Glotz sought to re-
establish the role of the SPD as a mediator between
the established institutions and the Green Movement.
In the meantime the government was forced to respond
to the challenge posed by the ecology movement which
was proving to be more than just a passing trend.
The pressure from the ecology movement led to the
introduction of a major inquiry into future energy
needs. On 14 December 1978 the Federal Parliament
voted in favour of setting up a commission of inquiry
which would investigate the nuclear technologies as
well as different concepts for the supply of energy.
Further acts of parliament went on to determine how
the commission would be composed of members of the
three established parties and a number of scientific
advisers appointed by each party group.

Considerable work went into the inquiry with
twenty-two meetings of the commission (including two
'hearings' and ten meetigs which lasted two days
each) as well as twenty-four meetings of working
parties. Delegates from the commission went on
journeys to France, Austria and the United States to
gain further advice and information. Experts on
alternative technology, for instance Amory Lovins,
were asked to talk about 'soft energy and decentral
supply as alternative solutions for energy policy'.
(9) The commission appears to have been sensitive
to the fact that political decisions on energy
supply determine, to some extent, how people do or
do not want to live. They developed four criteria
for assessing energy needs: economic requirements,
international suitability, effects on the environment
and social aspects.

The commission tried to assess in great detail what resources will be available to the world and to the Federal Republic in the future, and remarked that although there was no certain knowledge on the possibility of using renewable resources of energy, the potential was great and had not been used sufficiently.(10) Many of the recommendations could easily be mistaken for parts of the programme of an environmentalist pressure group. In fact in their detailed summary of the results of their research, the members of the commission traced four possible paths for the energy policy of the future, two of which actually excluded the use of nuclear power. (Table 5.1) The commission also referred indirectly to the criticism by many environmentalists of two government agencies, the Commission for Reactor Safety and the Commission for Protection from Radiation. It recommended that these two agencies - which play a crucial role in offering advice to the Minister of the Interior - should in future include qualified experts with different standpoints on nuclear energy issues, so that they too would offer advice to the government.(11)

Unanimity could not be achieved among members of the commission over all the issues under discussion. The Social Democrat members took a much more cautious view than the Christian Democrats about the safety of nuclear reactors, and the accident at the Harrisburg nuclear power station in the United States.(12) The commission did not take up a definite position on the safety of nuclear reactors. It felt that a clearer standpoint could be worked out around 1990 and that, in the meantime, existing nuclear power stations should be allowed to continue to operate. The commission spoke out in favour of a 'moderate' expansion of the number of 'light-water' nuclear reactors; further work on the fast breeder nuclear reactor at Kalkar; a depot for the final storage of nuclear waste in Gorleben; the construction of a reprocessing plant for nuclear waste; and a series of depots for the 'intermediate' storage of waste.(13) To many people it appeared that the commission was recognising the various fait accomplis of the nuclear energy programme, and was even encouraging the development of some projects which had been opposed by the ecology movement. However, it had been cautious not to reccomend wholeheartedly the development of nuclear energy and to encourage the promotion of alternative strategies.

In a separate initiative, leading Social Democrats in North Rhine Westphalia discussed plans

Table 5.1 Calculations by a Government Commission of Inquiry of four possible paths for the supply of energy (in millions of tons of bituminous coal)

		'Hard' paths		'Soft' paths	
		Path 1	Path 2	Path 3	Path 4
Economic growth before 2000 A.D.		3.3%	2.0%	2.0%	2.0%
Economic growth after 2000 A.D.		1.4%	1.1%	1.1%	1.1%
Structural changes in the economy		average	average	strong	strong
Growth of manufacturing industry		as GNP/2	as GNP/2	zero	zero
Saving on energy		trend	strong	very strong	extreme

Year	1978	2000	2030	2000	2030	2000	2030	2000	2030
Demand									
primary energy	390	600	800	445	550	375	360	345	310
energy	260	364	446	298	317	265	250	245	210
elecricity*	36	92	124	47	57	39	42	36	37
non-energy usage	32	50	67	43	52	34	34	34	34
Supply									
bituminous and brown coal	105	175	210	145	160	145	160	130	145
oil and gas	265	250	250	190	130	190	130	165	65
nuclear power in GWe	10	77	165	40	120	0	0	0	0
renewable sources	8	40	50	40	50	40	70	50	100
Other									
electricity from coal	65	80	80	29	22	76	77	52	33
synthetic gas from coal	–	18	50	18	56	–	–	–	–
% of electricity									
for heating houses	3	14	17	5	7	3	2	2	0
for industrial use	7	19	17	8	8	8	8	7	6

* The need for electricity refers to the final energy requirement and not to the gross total for electricity production. Here it is given in millions of tons of bituminous coal.

Source: Figures from Deutscher Bundestag (1980) Bericht der Enquete-Kommission: Zukuenftige Kernenergiepolitik, Bonn, Drucksache 8/4341, p. 38.

for the conservation of energy and for alternative
methods of supplying it. Dieter Haak, a Minister in
the Federal Council, presented to the state cabinet
in North Rhine Westphalia a programme for saving oil
by an extension of the network which uses waste heat,
for example from industry, and the construction of
small coal power stations adapted to the structure
of housing estates.(14) His proposals did not include the use of nuclear power. They emphasized that
within a few years every second household in West
Germany could benefit from 'district heating' by
using waste heat (Fernwaerme), and that this could
lead to the creation of many new jobs. Both the
Minister of Labour, Farthmann, and the Minister of
Economics, Jochimsen, presented energy concepts which
foresaw an extensive development of a network for
'district heating'. While Farthmann thought that
nuclear energy still had an important role to play,
Jochimsen wanted to move away from the use of oil
but not towards nuclear power. The delay in the
development of nuclear power because of the activities of the protest movement, and the rising cost of
oil partly explain this interest shown by leading
Social Democrats in alternative methods for the
supply of energy. Farthmann had calculated that
eighty billion marks would be required for the network of 'district heating'. Since Haak wanted to
avoid the use of large-scale power stations, his
proposals would only have cost fifty billion if they
had been implemented. Moreover, more than 200,000
jobs might have been created in the coal, steel pro-
cessing and building construction industries. The
increase in tax revenue and saving in the payment of
unemployment benefit would finance part of the project. The remainder would come from money which was
going to be spent on new roads, from an increased
tax on mineral oil or through public borrowing.(15)
    Plans for the use of 'district heating' were
drawn up throughout the Federal Republic. In the
Ruhr area there were plans to provide 800,000 households with energy from 'distirict heating' during
the 1980s; this would be in addition to the 400,000
households that were already benefitting from it.
Whilst Minister Haak proposed that a decentral system
of supplying energy in this way would be most effective, the electricity supply industry put forward
proposals for large-scale centralised projects in
its attempts to maintain control of the energy
market. The chief of 'STEAG' (a subsidiary of
Ruhrkohle AG) wanted to build several huge coal power
stations, so that each one could produce 750 MW of

electricity in North Rhine Westphalia and be linked
up to a common network which distributed 'district
heat'. In Bonn, the Minister of Economics, Graf
Lambsdorff, and the Minister of Reasearch and Technology, von Buelow as well as Chancellor Schmidt were
in favour of the extension of 'district heating'
networks. They were particularly interested in the
fact that many jobs would be created and the scheme
would thus gain the support of the trade unions. No
decision was taken on whether to adopt a centralised
or a decentralised strategy. Some, like Haak,
favoured an 'island' decentral strategy of supplying
energy from local, neighbourhood power stations,
whilst others who had seats on the advisory and
administrative boards of the energy supply corporations favoured a more centralised approach. The
latter hoped to be able to adapt the planned nuclear
power stations to the use of 'district heating'.
    In a further effort to take up the challenge
posed by the ecology movement, Willy Brandt, as
chairman of the SPD, commissioned the Minister of
Transport, Volker Hauff, to prepare a report on the
'Ecological-political orientations of the SPD'.
Members of this commission included Alois Pfeiffer
from the DGB, Siegfried Martin, the vice-chairman
of the union for public service, transport and
traffic sectors, and representatives from the
ecological wing of the party (Johanno Strasser,
Klaus Traube, and Josef Leinen). Their report came
out strongly in favour of many of the arguments put
forward by the ecology movement. They acknowledged
that environmental destruction could cause 'world-
wide catastrophes'; ecological, economic and social
policy aims were regarded as 'equally' important;
and they all agreed that 'only jobs which are
reasonable from an ecological perspective are safe
in the future'. The commission suggested that the
SPD could regain the ground lost to the utopian
protest movement by becoming the 'party of hope'
and following the example of Ernst Bloch who was
'in love with success, not with failure'. The
report warns against an approach towards environmental issues which is founded on a narrow political
base of 'individual groups or Citizens' Initiatives'
or 'alternative lists'. These initiatives could,
according to the commission, 'from time to time'
become partners 'in an alliance with social-
democratic environmental policy'.(16) This statement brought up a theme which was taboo in some
regions because of the alliance with the FDP. Moreover, and again with little regard for liberal

sensitivities, the report called for clear powers of direction and control by the state.

The report listed some of the measures which were introduced by the Social-Liberal Alliance in order to improve the environment, although it also described the deterioration in several spheres. The initiatives towards 'district heating' were welcomed and there was a call for an expansion of industrial enterprises which provide equipment for the control of pollution.(17) The report declared that the extension of the road network was basically complete and was strongly in favour of greater use of transport by railway.(18) When I asked Anke Brunn, a member of the commission, whether this report represented the views of the majority of the party, she replied that it had been adopted unequivocally by the party executive committee.(19) The acceptance of the report was, at the very least, a recognition by the executive committee of the powerful tendency among party members to adopt many of the values and ideas of the ecology movement. A longer term aim was to regain the support of those layers of the population that sought radical reforms and an improvement in the 'quality of life'.

A major effort to integrate the supporters of the Green Movement into the SPD occurred in the 'new politics of understanding and dialogue' undertaken by the General Secretary of the SPD, Peter Glotz. When he was Senator for Science and Research in Berlin (1977-80), he developed the idea of dialogue and communication with groups and subcultures that opposed the state. To some extent he was following the practice of the Minister of the Interior, Gerhard Baum from the FDP, who had appealed successfully to some former terrorists, for example Horst Mahler, to become reintegrated into society. The basis for the action by Glotz rests on the recognition that the 'alternative to unconstrained agreement reached by talking - whether in the form of consensus or compromise - is violence'. He admits that the realists who rely on violence may turn out to be right, but thinks that it is worth making another effort to prove them wrong.(20) The new style of politics aimed at greater 'communication of people with each other'.(21)

When, in 1977, several German professors published the controversial 'Mescalero' text, written by some students who expressed their 'secret satisfaction' at the murder of the Federal Attorney General Siegfried Buback, Glotz undertook to carry out 'an exemplary public debate' with them because

of their 'vain opportunistic preparedness to sign
all kinds of resolutions'; he rebuked the professors
for publishing a text without adding any critical or
analytical commentary to it and wanted to deal with
them as 'opponents' and not as 'victims' over whom
he could exercise his powers.(22) In this and other
disputes he wanted to act as an intermediary or
'translator' of political cultures which were drift-
ing apart. He described his role as that of an
intermediary between those who, on the left, see
the state as a monolith and those, on the right, who
want the state to act in a monolithic manner.

At the same time Glotz was painfully aware of
the 'disappearing power of motivation of politics,
of established politics, including the social-
democratic type'. He felt that his party needed to
take a lead in offering people 'meaningful' aims and
commitments since there are many people 'who not
only want to live and work for their warm room for
their suits and for their car, but who seek over and
above that a transcendant meaning for their life'.(23)
Here Glotz was acknowledging the kind of criticism
of the system as expressed by the Beatniks in the
1950s. He argued that the SPD needed to integrate
the critical elements amongst the Greens in order to
ensure its own survival. Whilst recognising the
difficulties of communication between the established
culture and left-wing subcultures, he was convinced
that a large section of the younger generation could
be 'won over to the basic consensus of our Constitution', although there was a need for a 'great effort
in arguments' which was 'totally lacking' in the
Federal Republic.(24)

The central thrust of his political practice lay
in the attempt to bring closer the established
institutions and the protest movements. This was
particularly important to the SPD since a great distance had developed, during the conflict over
nuclear energy, between trade unions which sought to
secure jobs by supporting the expansion of nuclear
power stations and the environmentalists who stressed
the threat posed by such projects to the lives and
safety of the population. In addition, there was a
wide gap in the ideas about the way in which social
transformation should be organised; within the
ecology movement there was a strong aversion to
centralised and powerful organisations. Glotz
believed that young people could be integrated if
they came to understand that social development
could only be influenced by 'mass organisations'
which are anchored in certain 'enduring social

groups'; and that the SPD had to make it clear that these organisations 'cannot suddenly act according to the latest fashion and latest insights'.(25) In his opinion one of the most significant barriers to the introduction of new political issues into the SPD was the 'unavoidable conflict between interests, themes and (momentary) consciousness - the ethos - of the (diminishing) core groups of industrialism on the one hand, and the (growing) post-industrial middle classes on the other'.(26)

Whilst the majority of trade union members and their leadership remained pragmatic in their approach by accepting a few more jobs in the present and worrying about the long-term consequences of an expanded nuclear industry later, the main source of dissent to this attitude came from young trade unionists. For instance at the 1980 Youth Conference of the metalworkers' union, a majority voted against the use of nuclear energy.(27) Within the executive committee of the DGB their spokesperson on the economy, Alois Pfeiffer, echoed some of the arguments used by the ecology movement when he explained how measures to save energy could actually create more employment. Pfeiffer was also a member of the parliamentary commission of inquiry on future energy policy.(28)

Glotz made every effort to introduce the new themes, even though he did not go as far as the ecologists in seeking 'fundamental changes' since he believes that there is no realistic alternative to reformism and to 'antagonistic co-operation', a concept used to describe the relationship between 'big labour and big industry'.(29) He has pointed out that the huge increase in graduates between 1980 and 1990 will cause further antagonism because in the future the public service sector will be able to employ only a further 15 to 20 per cent of them rather than 66 per cent as it did at the time.(30) This could result in a much larger potential vote for groups like the Green Party if the protest movements do not accept 'antagonistic co-operation' as a solution.

Apart from the question of organisation, Glotz attempts to take up all the main issues that were raised by the ecology movement; he agrees with some of their criticisms of technocracy and calls for a more communicative style of politics: 'Social Democracy must ensure that in the eighties, politics is not restricted to administrative functions. It must reorganise the party into a living world, into a forum of communication for the formation of aware-

ness'.(31) He regards as one of the major errors of
the SPD after Bad Godeberg, its refusal to take up
spiritual and ethical questions in politics (32) and
feels that the working class movement needs to learn
again not to underestimate the significance of the
'ethical-political moment in history'.(33) He
reminds his readers that this 'unmarxist' thought
originates from Gramsci. Glotz thus directs his
attention to the theme of the 'loss of collective
identity' and the dimension of the world of life.
He argues that:

> The industrial societies have forfeited
> their collective identity through the
> loss of the criterion for progress.
> The cultural crisis which they are exper-
> iencing is more powerful in Germany due
> to the self-inflicted destruction of the
> national identity.(34)

The search for a new collective identity coincides
in West Germany with the end of the 'economic
miracle' which had offered to many an escape from
the need to recreate a national identity. Glotz
blames 'capitalist industrialism' for the loss of
old social connections and communities, and feels
that Social Democracy and the welfare state have
been criticised unfairly in this respect.(35) Yet
his insistence on the need for the party to recap-
ture the world of life is an admission of failures
in the past. In the concluding passages of Die
Beweglichkeit des Tankers Glotz outlines several
ways in which the SPD might reconquer the world of
life:

> At party conferences in the future there
> will be exhibitions in which the practical
> confidence-building work of the local party
> associations, factory groups and working
> groups will be presented. The most impress-
> ive will receive a prize (named after William
> Droeschner). A newly-founded 'Historical
> Commission' will provide suggestions to the
> organisation so that we do not neglect our
> history as we have done over the past
> decades.(36)

A review of the book by Glotz on the SPD and
the new social movements appeared in the Taz.(37)
The heading of the article read: 'Diaglotz or the
charm of a trap door'. This reflects the basic

mistrust of the 'dialogue' strategy since, although the analysis of the Left by Glotz is not disputed, his interpretation of events leads him to propose a reformist solution which is anathema to many within the ecology movement. However, the attempt by Glotz to reintroduce an element of idealism based on the new issues has ensured that many supporters of the Green Movement still look to the SPD for solutions to the problems which they have identified.

The efforts by the SPD to take up these issues became even more pronounced when Hans-Jochen Vogel took over from Helmut Schmidt as leader of the party. Vogel chose as his adviser on energy, environmental and research policy Professor Meyer-Abich, whose work has been widely appreciated in the ecology movement. He is strongly in favour of solar energy and measures towards the conservation of energy rather than nuclear energy. As an adviser   to the commission of inquiry on future energy needs he recommended the 'soft' rather than the 'hard' paths which were outlined in the report.(Table 5.1) The SPD electoral programme in 1983 stressed the need for sound environmental policies to such an extent that Antje Huber, a member of the party presidium, feared that these appeared to be more important than policies on the security of employment. Paradoxically, the chairman of the miners' and energy workers' union, Adolf Schmidt, protested when Vogel declared his preference for coal instead of nuclear power. The SPD would not however go as far as to accept the proposal by Meyer-Abich that the fast breeder nuclear reactor project at Kalkar should be brought to a standstill, although it did agree with him that no further public money should be spent on it. The SPD did, at least in its role as an opposition party, move a significant way towards the utopian aspirations of the ecology movement without adopting many of its ideological assumptions.

II Industrial and commercial interest groups

In the existing democratic system the role of co-ordinating policies on the supply of energy and the exploitiation of resources falls to the government and administrative apparatus. However, certain facts have already been established before any government begins its four-year term in office. Thus, when the Minister of Research and Technology, Hans Matthoefer, allocated (in 1977) four and a half

billion marks, out of a total of six and a half
billion, for research into nuclear energy, he explained that projects like the fast breeder reactor at
Kalkar had begun before he came into office and
therefore had to be continued even though this would
require vast sums of money.(38) Initially the
government gave its whole-hearted support to the
nuclear energy programme. None the less it would
be mistaken to assume that this led to a vast
'technocratic conspiracy'. Throughout 1982, for
example, there were continuous conflicts between the
state and the nuclear energy industry over the level
of contributions from public funds to the Kalkar
fast breeder project. Serious doubts were expressed
about the possibility of any financial gain at all
from the project. The second stage of the inquiry
into future energy policy resulted in a clear division of opinion between a minority of scientists who
were critical of the project and others who approved
of it.(39)
     In 1975, before the emergence of the ecology
movement, the Nuclear Research Centre in Juelich had
drawn up plans for the construction of 350 nuclear
power stations by the year 2000 which would be served
by 16 immense nuclear energy reprocessing plants.
The target for 2050 A.D. was 598 nuclear power stations and 23 reprocessing plants.(40) The aim was to
ensure a steady expansion of the market economy.
Following the opposition by the ecology movement,
these plans were scaled down to the proposed construction of only 33 nuclear power stations by the year
2000.(41) By 1982 serious doubts had been cast on
the economic viability of nuclear energy. One of
the main reasons for this was the success of the
challenge by the ecology movement which had demanded
higher levels of safety both in the construction of
nuclear power stations and the disposal of nuclear
waste. The courts had accepted the arguments of the
ecologists relative to the need for greater safety
levels. The ecologists were, however, not interested
in the economic viability of nuclear energy since
they were fundamentally opposed to it. In addition,
many of them failed to realise that in order to provide a coherent alternative concept for the supply
of energy, economic factors had to be taken into
consideration.
     The medium-term strategy of the Social-Liberal
Government did not show any marked changes in
priorities for future energy policy, despite the
report by the commission of inquiry on energy policy
which showed that it was not essential to rely on

Table 5.2   Investment in the energy research programme (1981-5)

Spheres of research and development	Recommended expenditure (millions of marks)	
	(1981)	(1982)
nuclear energy and reactor safety	567	635
thorium high temperature reactor	118	165
high temperature reactor	143	61
fast breeder reactor - SNR 300	233	362
other fast breeder reactors	142	220
nuclear research centres	674	630
coal vaporisation	25	672
coal liquification	71	163
heat from solar energy	23	19
electricity from solar energy	25	61
energy from biological masses	9	15
wind energy	48	29
geo-thermal energy	12	15
combined heat and power, district heating	49	68
new technology in power stations and heating systems	68	173

Source: Figures from Taz, 29 March 1982, p. 11.

nuclear energy. Table 5.2 shows the level of investment proposed in the Energy Research Programme for
the period 1981-5. The first column shows the sums
that had been proposed in 1981, and the second
column, the amended proposals which were made in
March 1982. Thus, although there occurred a massive
increase in investment in coal vaporisation and coal
liquification, the nuclear energy programme still
took first priority by a wide margin. Critics of
the programme pointed out that the thirteen ad hoc
committees and expert bodies in the Ministry of
Research and Technology were composed largely of
representatives from the nuclear energy lobby, whilst
institutes which are concerned with the development
of alternatives to existing forms of energy supply,
for instance the Oeko-Institut in Freiburg, receive
no support from the government.(42)
    Whilst all these odds seem to favour the
nuclear energy industry, the oppositional forces and
protest movements were able between June 1977 and
the end of 1981 to gain favourable verdicts in the
courts which completely stalled the nuclear energy
programme. These events prompted the following
remarks from the spokesperson of the SPD on the
economy, Wolfgang Roth, on how the ecological protest
was affecting the economy:

> In the Federal Republic of Germany, a highly
> populated and industrialised country, there
> obtrudes on us an unsolved problem more than
> in other countries. Without doubt, ecologi-
> cal fears and resistances have had a negative
> effect on economic growth. The BDI asserts,
> for example, that...investments of 100 bill-
> ion marks are blocked in the public and priv-
> ate sphere. This is a gigantic sum in the
> face of a total sum of investment of about
> 350 billion marks in the private and public
> spheres in 1981...I disagree with those who
> interpret these events as an anti-economic
> obstruction to investment...In truth it con-
> cerns a change in the structure of prefer-
> ences of the population or at least of cons-
> iderable sectors of the population. If one
> doesn't calculate these changes in the
> structure of needs, the danger of self-
> obstruction by the economy will increase.
> Traditional economic growth is increasingly
> getting into a psychological-ecological
> blind alley. An ecological crisis of confid-
> ence can become a barrier to growth. An
> economic-political strategy of the future
> must reconcile ecology and economy.(43)

These remarks were made in front of an audience that
included people from the banking industry. The initial response of commercial and industrial interests
to the 'ecological fears and resistances' had been
to interpret the efforts of the ecology movement as
an 'anti-economic obstruction to investment' and to
launch a campaign which appealed to the material
interests of the population. However, they also
adopted a more enlightened approach towards the
'ecological crisis of confidence' by investing in
spheres which promised a reconciliation between ecology and economy. I will now explain both these
strategies more fully.
      The main arguments used by the government agen-
cies and the nuclear energy industry were that the
security of employment and independence from the
Arab oil-producing countries could only be achieved
through a rapid expansion of nuclear power stations.
None the less the delay in the development of nuclear power and the absence of any shortage of energy
contributed to an increase in scepticism about the
benefits that might be derived from this form of
energy. The delay also allowed people time to be
influenced by the arguments of the ecologists. Data

Table 5.3 Attitudes to nuclear power (1976-1981)

| | September 1976 | | |
	Agree	Disagree	Undecided
in our country nuclear power stations are built too hastily and without enough experience	27	49	24
the population is not informed enough about the construction of nuclear power stations	60	22	18

	January 1977
nuclear power can help humanity very much but only if we learn to use it sensibly	60
nuclear power will probably cause damage to us because it is unlikely that we will learn to use it sensibly	18
nuclear power will certainly be very useful and advantageous to humanity one day	9
nuclear power will almost certainly lead to destruction because one day there will be a nuclear war	4
undecided	4

| | April 1980 and October 1981 (April 1980 in brackets) | | | |
	CDU/CSU	SPD/FDP	GREENS	TOTAL
we must build nuclear power stations if we want to maintain our prosperity	65(67)	46(53)	3(10)	52(56)
we must not build any more nuclear power stations – the danger is too great	34(32)	52(45)	96(88)	46(42)

Source: Figures from E.Nolle-Naumann (ed.), Allensbacher Jahrbuch der Demoskopie, (Allensbach, Institut fuer Demoskopie, 1977), Vol. VII, p. 184, and Der Spiegel, Nr. 50, 1981, p. 99.

from surveys carried out between 1976 and 1981 reveals an increase in scepticism about the development of nuclear energy.

In a survey conducted in September 1976 only 27 per cent of the population felt that nuclear power stations had been built too hastily and without sufficient experience. In January 1977 only 22 per cent were sceptical about the use of nuclear power, whereas 69 per cent had a more positive attitude. By April 1980 the sceptics comprised 42 per cent of the population and by October 1981 the figure had risen to 46 per cent although, according to a survey carried out by Emnid for the chemical industry, two-thirds of the population were in favour of nuclear energy in order to ensure a supply of energy independent of oil.(44) Among supporters of the SPD-FDP Alliance more than half were opposed to the construction of nuclear power stations.(Table 5.3) Whilst arguments about the security of employment and independence from the oil-producing countries in the Middle East were constantly repeated at a natio- nal level, different tactics were adopted to pers- uade people who lived in the vicinity of a planned nuclear reactor of the benefits of nuclear energy.

Local opposition to the building of potentially dangerous nuclear reactors arose partly because of a lack of truly isolated sites in the Federal Republic. At any rate, the opposition by local communities, especially in rural areas, gave a tremendous boost to the ecology movement which was based mainly in large cities. Those who determined to carry out plans for nuclear power thus often appealed to the immediate material interests of local populations and governing bodies in an attempt to stifle any opposition. In Gorleben one hundred million marks were offered to the local authorities in exchange for acceptance of a nuclear fuel reprocessing plant. This would enable local people to undertake and ben- efit from projects which they would only otherwise have fulfilled after many years.(45) Thus, when in July 1981 local political leaders agreed to the construction of depots for the intermediate storage of nuclear fuel rods and weak radioactive waste, the state of Lower Saxony and the Federation agreed to grant subsidies for fifty projects (including seven sports halls) in the area worth fifty million marks.(46) In Brokdorf the electricity supply industry sought to pacify the local population by building a swimming pool.(47) In Ahaus, North Rhine Westphalia, where a Citizens' Initiative had gained 25 per cent of the vote in communal elections, local dignitaries from the major parties agreed to the construction of a depot for the intermediate storage of radioactive fuel rods; the town now has a new shopping centre, a leisure centre and funds for various other projects. They have received 49 million marks from the state of North Rhine West- phalia, and will receive further renumeration whilst the plant is in operation.(48)

Although the nuclear energy industry had far greater material resources at its disposal than its

opponents it could not rely solely on the tactics
which I have just described in order to win support
for its aims. At any rate, it did not have the
resources which might be required to stifle the
opposition in large cities, and many members of local communities refused to accept any 'compensation'
which was offered in exchange for their tolerance of
new projects. A more subtle and effective approach
lay, therefore, in the adaptation by industrial and
commercial interest groups of many of the ecologists'
ideas within a new functional framework.

The interest shown by commercial and industrial
interest groups in alternative technology is not
directly linked to the emergence of the ecology
movement. None the less, it is related to the growing awareness of ecological issues throughout the
seventies and it has assumed a new urgency as the
public has become more sceptical or at least uncer-
tain about the uses of technology.(49) The capacity
of industrial interest groups to 'diversify' their
investments and to integrate new ideas can be shown
explicitly by the involvement of firms in the
Federal Association for Solar Energy. (Table 5.4)
The column on the extreme right of the table shows
the firms that are directly involved in the nuclear
energy industry. The main advantage gained by the
formation of such an association is that these firms
are in the best position to acquire the subsidies
which have been set aside by the Ministry of Research
and Technology for the development of solar energy.

Further evidence of the 'technisation and
monetarisation of ecological contexts' is provided
by Huber. He shows how the market economy can
adapt and expand on the basis of new and alternative
technologies, and thus invalidates one of the main
arguments of ecologists like Bahro, namely that the
capitalist system and modern science are not capable
of solving existing problems by discovering new
areas in which to expand.(50)

The development of micro-electronics is perhaps
the most significant since it is the 'symbol of an
industry that has conformed to ecology'.(51) The
silicon out of which the 'chips' are made is available in limitless quantities and micro-processors
contribute to savings in energy. They are also
becoming cheaper and thus available on a large
scale. The Federal Government has been spending
about a billion marks every year on information
technology, technical communication, electronics
and other key technologies.(52) Apart from the use
robots in factories, huge savings in time and

Table 5.4 Spheres of activity of firms in the Federal Union for Solar Energy

Names of firms	Collectors	Heat pumps	Preparation of hot water and heating	Temperature control	Energy storage	Solar generators	Solar power stations	Software/consulting	Investigations of economic viability	Building technology and materials	Steam turbines for power stations	FIRMS INVOLVED IN THE NUCLEAR ENERGY INDUSTRY
AEG		*				*	*					X
BBC	*	*	*	*	*			*				X
Bosch	*	*	*									X
Broetje	*	*	*						*			
Buderus	*	*	*	*	*							X
Dornier	*			*			*	*				X
Erno	*			*	*		*	*				X
Esser	*							*				
EVS	*	*	*			*	*	*	*	*		X
Flachglas								*		*		
Happel	*	*	*	*								
HEW							*	*				X
Hoechst	*	*	*		*					*		X
Kloeckner	*	*	*		*							X
Krupp	*	*	*									X
KKK											*	
Leybold						*						
MAN	*		*				*				*	X
MBB	*		*		*		*	*	*			X
Philips	*	*	*	*	*	*		*				X
Ruetgers	*		*					*		*		
Ruhrgas		*										X
RWE/ETS								*	*			X
Schaefer	*		*									
Siemens		*				*					*	X
Stiebel Eltron	*	*	*		*							
Thyssen	*		*	*								X
VDM	*		*							*		
Vereinigte Glaswerke	*					*				*		
Viessman	*	*	*	*								
VMH Multibeton	*	*	*		*			*	*	*		
Walo	*	*	*		*							

Source: <u>Taz</u>, 27 August 1980, p. 8.

energy can also be made in offices with the introduction of micro-electronic machinery; it is conceivable that most people will be able to work at home
and maintain contact with their office via a micro-
electronic communications network. 'Decentralisation' would thus be achieved on a huge scale.(53)
Plans to introduce cable television are at an advanced stage in the Federal Republic. Both this and
the colonisation of outer space provide further
opportunities for transcending the 'limits of growth!'
West German enterprises are involved in projects
which aim to produce new products to higher standards
in outer space.(54)
    Similar innovations are taking place in the
spheres of 'gene technology' and the development of
biological masses, although they are all controlled
by existing major enterprises. Progress in the
development of biological masses (which relies on
the renewability of plants) could, in the long term,
reduce the reliance for energy on coal, oil and gas.
(55) Here, as in other spheres, ecological ideas
can be manipulated or turned against their original
intention. In Brazil there are plans for the production of 300,000 barrels of diesel oil every year
from soya beans, peanuts and sunflower oil. The
refinement of cane sugar to produce cheaper petrol,
again in Brazil, is a further example of what some
ecologists would call the abuse of their ideas since
the process of distillation produces stinking and
poisonous wastes which are poured into rivers and
destroy huge expanses of the natural environment.(56)
There is a distinct possibility that farmers, instead
of planting food, will grow plants that can be used
to make cheaper petrol for those who can afford a
car. Similar steps are taking place in the research
and development of solar energy. Cells which are
needed to contain solar energy are likely to become
a thousand times cheaper over the next few years.
The cells can be located on a decentralised network;
control of the industry will remain, as I illustrated,
in the hands of huge centralised enterprises.
    These examples illustrate how new and alternat-
ive technologies which could have a less damaging
effect on the environment become adapted in a manner
that often contradicts 'ecological aims'. The
research and development, for instance of gene technology, has not taken enough into consideration the
possible damaging side-effects of certain biological
processes.(57) The rising cost of damage to the
environment has paved the way for a very lucrative
business in the disposal of waste. An industrial

remedy is prescribed for the damage caused by industrial interests. In the OECD countries the state and industry spend between 1.5 and 3 per cent of their gross national product on measures to protect the environment. Most, perhaps 90 per cent, of environmental protection in the industrial sphere is carried out because of directives from the state and not because of initiatives taken by enterprises. (58) A more sophisticated approach to these problems lies in the efforts to avoid environmental waste and damage. One of the best examples, as I have already pointed out, is the use of surplus heat from power stations and factories. A further stage in the effort to avoid high costs of the damage incurred by existing machinery lies in the introduction of a whole range of new materials, optical fibres and earthenware, like the heat-proof tiles used on the American space shuttle. Huge savings could be made, for example, in the cost of damage caused by rust. (59) Huber goes to some length to show how, on the basis of new technologies, a new super-industrial breakthrough could be financed.(60) He interprets the calls by politicians and economic planners for 'greater sacrifices from everyone' as an effort directed towards increasing profits for long-term investments.

uber had identified four main positions on the issue of 'ecology and economy': a regressive right-wing orientation towards 'ecological adaptation'; differentiated and 'selective' economic growth as a compromise between ecological aims and economic growth, supported by the Social-Liberal centre; ecological 'transformation' which aims at fundamental structural changes to the present system and is based on grass-roots democracy, supported by the ecological Left; and the super-industrial breakthrough based on some conformity to ecological principles, which is supported by the 'technocratic fraction' in all political groups.(61) Old political groups and positions are thus being reconstituted around environmentalism and the introduction of new technologies. The ecologists have thus aroused feelings which extend far beyond their own group of supporters about the destruction of nature, the search for personal and collective identity, and the defence of the world of life against the intrusion of 'technocratic' administrative and industrial forms of organisation. What they have lacked is a sense of being able to mediate between the established and the alternative groups. The major political parties and certain industrial interest groups have, to this

extent, shown much more awareness of the realistic
possibilities for mediation between and integration
of different groups in society.

NOTES

    1. Ronge, Grenzen der Natur, p. 22f.

    2. Ibid., p. 72f.

    3. Frankfurter Rundschau, 22 Jan. 1977.

    4. Ibid., 25 Jan. 1977.

    5. Sueddeutsche Zeitung, 11 March 1977.

    6. Der Spiegel, Nr. 50, 1979, p. 26.

    7. Ibid., Nr. 6, 1983, p. 50.

    8. P.Glotz, Die Beweglichkeit des Tankers (Bertelsmann,
Munich, 1982), p. 71.

    9. Deutscher Bundestag, Bericht der Enquete-Kommission:
Zuekunftige Kernenergiepolitik (Drucksache 8/4341, Bonn, 1980),
P. 7.

    10. Ibid., pp. 104-123.

    11. Ibid., pp. 143-4.

    12. Ibid., p. 140 and p. 142.

    13. Taz., 14 July 1980, p. 9

    14. 'District heating' on the use of waste heat takes
advantage of the fact that electricity generating stations are
only 30 to 35 per cent efficient, whilst the remainder of the
energy is wasted in the cooling water. A power station which
uses the waste heat, not only generates electricity in the
usual way, but additionally recovers most of the waste heat as
water at 70 to 90° C and uses this for 'district heating' in the
vicinity of the station. The overall efficiency of the generating station then increases to around 70 per cent.

    15. Taz, 20 March 1981, p. 12.

    16. SPD-Vorstand, Oekologiepolitische Orientierungen der
SPD (Bonn, Nov. 1981), p. 3ff.

    17. Ibid., p. 10.

    18. Ibid., p. 13.

    19. Interview carried out by the author with Anke Brunn,
SPD Member of the Berlin Senate, in May 1982.

    20. P.Glotz,'Staat und alternative Bewegungen' in
J.Habermas (ed.), Stichworte zur geistigen Situation der Zeit
(Suhrkamp, Frankfurt, 1979), Vol. 2, pp. 487-8.

    21. Glotz, Innenausstattung der Macht, p. 7.

    22. Ibid., p. 151.

    23. P.Glotz 'Dass die SPD Identitaetsprobleme hat, ist
ohne Zweifel richtig' in H.Gremliza and H.Hannover (eds.),
Die Linke: Bilanz und Perspektiven fuer die 80er Jahre (VSA,
Hamburg, 1980).

    24. Glotz, Innenausstattung der Macht, p. 184.

    25. Glotz, 'Dass die SPD Identitaetsprobleme hat'.

    26. Der Spiegel, Nr. 50, 1981, p. 106.

    27. Taz, 28 April 1980, p. 6.

28. Taz, 2 May 1980, p. 5.
29. Glotz, 'Dass die SPD Identitaetsprobleme hat'.
30. Glotz, Beweglichkeit des Tankers, p. 158.
31. Ibid., p. 55.
32. Ibid., p. 98.
33. Ibid., p. 101.
34. Ibid., p. 139.
35. Ibid., p. 88.
36. Ibid., p. 186.
37. Taz, 16 April 1982, p. 12.
38. Handelsblatt, 28 April 1977.
39. Taz, 22 March 1982, p. 4.
40. Taz, 8 April 1981, p. 11.
41. Taz, 13 Aug. 1980, p. 8.
42. Taz, 24 April 1981, p. 12.
43. Taz, 4 Feb. 1982, p. 11.
44. Taz, 8 Aug. 1980, p. 6.
45. Taz, 13 May 1980, p. 6.
46. Taz, 15 July 1980, p. 2.
47. Taz, 15 July 1980, p. 2.
48. Taz, 26 Sept. 1980, p. 6.
49. See the results of surveys in E.Nolle-Naumann (ed.), Allensbacher Jahrbuch der Demoskopie (Allensbach, Institut fuer Demoskopie, 1977), Vol. VII, pp. 182–3.
50. Bahro, Socialism and Survival, pp. 81–2 and p. 103.
51. Huber, Verlorene Unschuld, p. 210.
52. Ibid., p. 53.
53. Ibid., p. 60ff.
54. Ibid., p. 75.
55. Ibid., p. 82.
56. Ibid., p. 86.
57. Ibid., pp.80–1.
58. Ibid., pp. 104–5.
59. Ibid., pp. 108–9.
60. Ibid., p. 114f.
61. Ibid., p. 214ff.

Chapter Six

ALTERNATIVE MOVEMENT

The alternative movement covers a broad spectrum of political, social and economic activity, and reflects the whole range of themes and concepts which arise within the Green Movement. This is hardly surprising since all the various strands of the Green Movement were, to a greater or lesser degree, seeking to provide an alternative to the prevailing order. For instance the women's movement played a significant role in creating alternative communities and lifestyles; the Citizens' Initiatives which opposed the nuclear energy programme often based their activities on alternative concepts to industrial society; the various Green Parties formulated an alternative political programme; and the squatters' movement and youth protest throughout 1981 had, as a significant point of reference, the previous efforts of alternative groups to invent and experiment with new lifestyles.

The alternative groups sought initially to create a context for the fulfilment of their own aspirations away from 'established society'. However, the popularity of these groups among young people meant that they attracted much attention from established parties and institutions. Many groups realised that, although it had not been their original intention, they were inextricably involved in an attempt to construct their own utopia and were providing 'established society' with models for improving welfare services and facilitating social integration. The awareness of this fact prompted some groups, for instance in the squatters' movement, to take extreme measures in their subjectivist critique of 'technocratic' society. Others adopted a more pragmatic approach to the situation.

I Alternative projects as pioneers of welfare
   and other services

In 1980 it was estimated that in West Berlin and the
Federal Republic there existed around 11,500 projects
with about 80,000 active members. The circle of sympathisers and supporters was estimated at around
350,000 people.(1) Since then, the pressures of unemployment and the increase in the level of youth
protest, as expressed in the squatters' movement,
led to an even greater interest in these projects.
     The projects are mainly concerned with provid-
ing services for a particular subculture, although
a large percentage offer social, professional services to groups in the population that remain outside
this subculture. According to Huber (who has made
an estimate of the spheres of activity of the projects, Table 6.1) most of them are situated in the
'informal' sector of the economy. The main emphasis
of activity in the projects is in the spheres of
media, educational and publicity work; social, professional and leisure services; and political work.
This contrasts with the emphasis in the 'formal'
sector on industrial production, travel, transport
and trade as well as other services.(2)
     Huber is keen to emphasize the significance of
the informal sector which includes, in the Federal
Republic, 24 million private households. Thus, in
the entire economy there are thirteen times more
informal places of work than the 1.8 million large,
average and small factories and other places of
work in the formal sector.(3) According to Huber,
although the projects only constitute a. very small
percentage of the total places of work, they occupy
- in a qualitative sense - a central position
between the formal and informal sectors. So far
this position has been occupied mainly by the 'family
business' in the spheres of crafts, farming and
handiwork.(4) This might explain why the Christian
Democrats, once they had got into power in West
Berlin, showed great interest in the work of the
projects.
     The projects are managed by the ordinary members
and skills are acquired in an informal manner.
Investment in them is labour rather than capital
intensive. Three types of projects have been identified: firstly, professional projects in which
people are paid for their work (doctors' and lawyers'
collectives, bakeries and foodstores, centres which
offer advice in psycho-therapy, newspapers and

Table 6.1 Spheres of activity of projects in the alternative movement

Agricultural (4%)	-agriculture, gardening, animal rearing (4%)
Manufacturing trade (8%)	-printing press, composition (1%) -production and repair handicraft (e.g. bakers, joiners, etc.) (5%) -alternative technology enterprises (heating systems, sale of second-hand goods) (0.5%) - art handicraft (1.5%)
Traffic and trade (9%)	-transport (taxi, salvage collection, removals) (1.5%) -trade (food shops, coops, travel agencies, kiosks) (4.5%) -bookshops (3%)
Leisure infra- structure (9%)	-pubs, coffee houses, restaurants (4%) -meeting and holiday houses, centres for communication (4%) -cinemas, galleries (1%)
Information and publicity work (17%)	-media (film, video etc.) (3%) -graphic arts, photography, writing (1%) -magazines and other publications (9%) -publishing houses (4%)
Administrative services (5%)	-coordination and organisational projects (including advice and information) (5%)
Social, profess- ional services (22%)	-children (schools, parent-child groups, meeting places) (7%) -schools (adult education, free universities) (3%) -medical groups (including physiotherapy)(1%) -therapy, youth work, education (11%)
Culture (8%)	-art, sport, theatre (8%)
Political work (18%)	-Citizens' Initiatives (9%) -Citizens' Committees (e.g. on rents, discrimination of foreigners etc.) (8%) -party-like groups (the Greens, trade unions, and church groups) (1%)

Source: Figures based on J.Huber, Wer soll das alles aendern? (Rotbuch, Berlin, 1980), p. 28.

publishing houses); secondly, projects which rely on unpaid labour (parent-child groups, self-help therapy groups, environmentalist initiatives); and finally, projects which combine aspects of the first two types, to the extent that they provide goods and services to the wider market and for themselves and their own subsistence.(5) Two projects reflect the diversity of activities within the alternative move-

ment: the 'Factory for Culture, Sport and Handicrafts' (Fabrik fuer Sport, Kultur und Handwerk) in
Berlin and the 'Oeko-Institut' in Freiburg.

In June 1979 a group of people from the alternative 'scene' occupied a disused factory in the
Tempelhof district in West Berlin. After protracted
negotiations they agreed to pay a rent of four thousand marks a month to the municipal authorities in
order to lease the buildings which would otherwise
have been demolished. The site was named the
'Factory for Culture, Sport and Handicrafts', and by
1981 it offered a permanent home to sixty men, women
and children. With help from other supporters of
alternative projects and some small subsidies from
the state for certain projects, the occupants set up
workshops for carpentry, metal-work, glass-making
and pottery. Their bakery and small shops sell food
and handicrafts to the outside market. With help
from scientists at the Technical University of Berlin
they developed forms of alternative technology, for
instance combined heat and power energy. Every week
around four hundred people take part in leisure activities like theatre, pantomine, music instruction
and sport. Many young people acquire new skills by
working in the various workshops, for example in the
repair of bicycles. Various community projects offer
help to people with social and psychological problems.
All these activities take place on the site, and are
dependent on the financial and moral support of a
wide circle of sympathisers.

Whilst the above project attempts to put into
practice some of the ideas of the Green Movement on
communal living, the Oeko-Institut in Freiburg provides information on, and promotes research into,
alternative programmes (to the ones proposed by
established institutions) over a wide range of topics.
For instance, in a project which investigated environmental protection and employment policy, recommendations were made for more investment in environmental
protection; the development of 'ecologically-oriented
methods of production'; a reduction in the working
week; and the 'removal of alienation' from the process of work. The institute attracted mainly scientists and academics who wished to challenge the prevailing assumptions in economic and environmental
policies. It also held a more popular appeal for
supporters of the Green Movement who sought to
introduce 'democracy into science'. The institute
was thus able to overcome any financial difficulties
because of the regular contributions from around
3,500 members. It has also attempted to broaden its

basis for support by engaging trade unionists in
discussions on alternative policies on energy which
could lead to more jobs in the long term.(6)
    Undoubtedly the projects reach beyond the im-
mediate circle of sympathisers. An official in the
Ministry of Education expressed her interest in projects which sought to bring 'science to the people',
like the Wissenschaftsladen at the University of
Essen.(7) The aim of this project is to provide
scientific information to individuals and initiatives
that do not have commercial interests and are unable
to finance their own research work. The concept is
based on successful experiments carried out at the
University of Amsterdam and bears similarities to
the work of Legal and Advice Centres in Britain. A
great deal of the work involved in providing information to consumers, not only of material goods but
also of state services, was carried out by Citizens'
Initiatives in the Federal Republic.
    The absence of wide-ranging reforms, which had
originally been promised by the Social-Liberal
Alliance, ensured the survival of the Citizens'
Initiatives. One of the main reasons for their survival and for the emergence of alternative projects
was because the efforts to institutionalise the lack
of conflict in the economic-political sphere, (as
expressed in the 'concerted action' of the government, the trade unions and industrial interests)
prevented investment in areas of collective need
(namely, housing, public transport, education,
environmental protection and health). These areas
are often described as the sphere of reproduction.
The alternative groups were mainly concerned with
the fulfilment of human needs (for instance, community, friendship and creativity) in this sphere.
    In evidence submitted to a government commission
of inquiry on youth protest, a clergyman who was
closely familiar with the alternative movement said
that he regarded the projects, for example the ones
that emerged out of the squatting movement, as pioneer groups which were helping to democratise the
sphere of reproduction:

> What has transpired during this appropria-
> tion of houses is that we do not have the
> means to realise co-determination and self-
> determination in the sphere of housing and
> leisure...whilst the Citizens' Initiatives
> provide for hearings and protests, they do
> not have the power of co-determination.(8)

He argued that the illegal occupation of houses would
not have occured if the disposal of property, such
as old and empty buildings, had been settled in favour of those people who had a real need for accommodation. He went on to point out that there is an
unequal relationship between the owners of houses
and the tenants. Thus the partnership which is
'socially sanctioned in the sphere of production'
between employer and employee does not exist in the
sphere of reproduction. It does not enjoy the same
level of institutional support in the latter sphere.
     This lack of support has provided an opportun-
ity for alternative projects to act as pioneers of
new interest group formations in the sphere of reproduction. A report by the SPD Commission on Basic
Values compared the alternative movement to the working class movement in the late nineteenth century,
when it warned the working class movement of today
to pay greater heed to the 'problems and basic im-
pulses of the seventies and eighties' or otherwise
face the prospect of getting into the 'conservative
position of a social bureaucracy'. In particular
the commission felt that the following positive
aspects of the alternative movement and the 'change
in values' needed to be taken into consideration:
the will for autonomy as expressed in the critique
of any form of rule which was not legitimised; the
preparedness to take part in self-administered forms
of life and work; co-operative rather than authoritarian behaviour; an emphasis on the quality of life
rather than career and material success; and a
growing sensitivity about the destruction of the
'natural bases of life'.(9) Although the report
also criticised certain aspects of the alternative
movement, it did recognise the significance of the
movement in highlighting inadequacies in the system,
particularly in the sphere of reproduction. Similarly, the government commission of inquiry into youth
protest concluded that the protest movement was
concerned less with the problems of youth but rather
with problems relating to the whole of society.(10)
     As I have already stated, the alternative pro-
jects and initiatives survived and expanded as a
result of inadequate reforms in the sphere of reproduction. The main priority of government policy has
always been to secure adequate economic growth, to
secure an economic basis of legitimation in the
sphere of production. However, a growing awareness
has developed of the poverty of the public infrastructure, especially since negative trends in the
economy have become apparent. The welfare state has

been unable to deal with some of the problems of
modernisation which are publicised by the alternative movement. At the same time the alternative
movement has, to some extent without deliberate intention, begun to pioneer methods of dealing with
such problems and this has been recognised by the
state. The latter has observed how many individuals,
for instance drug addicts, alcoholics and people
with psychological problems, who could have been a
great burden on the resources of the welfare state,
find refuge and hope in alternative projects and
communities.

The interest within the alternative movement
for community medicine was reflected in two massive
conferences organised by various projects. The first
Health Conference took place between 14 and 18 May
1980 in Berlin and attracted around 10,000 people
who attended meetings and lectures on themes like
'health policy under National Socialism', 'nuclear
power stations and the occurrence of cancer among
children', yoga and the effects of spending cuts on
hospital services. The organisers of the conference
described it as an expression of 'the concern and
scepticism by members of the social professions
towards a society which pursues its economic and
political interests without consideration of individuals and their environment'. They went on to crit-
icise the existing health system because of its
anonimity and the stress and fear it causes to pati-
ents: 'The Health Conference does not offer ready-
made formulas; it discusses starting points for a
new designation of medical and social activity with
the aim of trying out models which do justice to the
problems'.(11) A similar conference took place in
Hamburg in October 1981 and was attended by about
16,000 people.(12) This conference was attended by
visitors from the SPD, which reflects the growing
political significance of this movement. Hence, in
March 1982 the Christian Democratic Senator of
Health, Social and Family Welfare in West Berlin
agreed to consider proposals for the conversion of
part of the Albrecht Achilles Hospital - which was
going to be closed down - for alternative groups
that were concerned with the provision of health
services and community medicine.

The cost of investment in an alternative project
is considerably less than in a typical factory or
other institution. According to a senior official
in the Ministry of Education and Science:

The creation of employment is by no means
limited to the sphere of education. The
alternative press, for example, creates work
for unemployed teachers; people want to
build, or set up and maintain, self-organised
youth centres which offer employment to
musicians, artists and social workers, even
if it does not necessarily offer an income;
alternative workshops for bicycle and car
repairs win new markets and pay taxes on profits; alternative doctors' and dentists'
practices as well as collectives for agri-
cultural produce, contribute to the creation
of surplus value and unburden the employment
market.(13)

The same official attributes to the projects the
role of 'signalling social developments' which must
be heeded by the state.(14) At the same time the
projects have realised how dependent they are on
financial support either from sympathisers or from
the state. Apart from recognising the social value
of some of the work carried out by the projects, the
state and the established political parties are
anxious to reverse the trend whereby a large number
of young people who support alternative groups
question the legitimacy of established institutions.

II Bases of support for alternative groups

Although most of the active support for alternative
groups has come from young, well-educated, middle-
class people, they have also attracted young people
from other social classes. The projects attract those
who wish to gain new experiences and who are generally dissatisfied with, and wish to opt out of,
competitive society (especially at school and university). Most people who are involved in the
projects feel that they have had 'enough' of the
meaninglessness of their situation and of what
society has to offer; the projects promise a new
perspective for those who wish to find friendship
and to overcome the alienation and complexity of the
outside world. For an increasing number of young
people, the projects present the only hope of any
employment at all.

In the Shell survey, 6 per cent of all respondents stated that they practised an alternative life-
style. This figure implies that, in 1981, around

540,000 young people in the Federal Republic practised an alternative life-style, since the survey drew
on a representative sample of the population of nine
million people who were between 15 and 24 years old.
Table 6.3 shows the overall level of support for
alternative life-styles and other protest movements.
The percentages on the left show the level of active
support or sympathy for particular life-styles or
habits. The other figures indicate the differences
in percentage values according to which particular
social groups and people with different levels of
education varied in their attitudes from the total
(percentage) level of support for a particular life-
style (given in the left-hand column). This table
shows that there is a greater level of support for
alternative life-styles among young women from the
middle and upper classes than for any other group.
None the less, the alternative groups are supported
in strength by young people from all social classes.
Sixty-two per cent of all young people actually live
like or sympathise with alternative groups. One of
the most striking features about the new protest
movements in comparison to those of the sixties is
the much more active role of women in them. The
support for protest groups and committed life-styles
rises from 32 per cent among those with a lower level
to 65 per cent among those with higher levels of
education. This is shown in Table 6.2. More than
85 per cent of all the young supporters of the Green
Party are either active supporters or sympathisers
of environmentalist and alternative protest groups.
Around 75 per cent of CDU and SPD supporters identify
with environmentalists; 45 per cent of CDU supporters
and 55 per cent of SPD supporters are attracted to
alternative groups, whilst the squatters enjoyed
the support of only about 20 per cent of CDU supporters. All these figures refer to the level of support from young people in the 15 to 24 age group.(15)

Table 6.2 Support for 'committed' and 'non-committal' life-
styles related to level of education (attained or likely to
be attained) (15-24 age group) (%)

Level of education	Supporters of...	
	committed groups	non-committal groups
intermediate	32	68
modern secondary	39	60
training school	41	59
grammar	62	38
university/higher education	65	35

Source: Shell Studie, (1981), Jugend 1981, Vol. 1, p. 502.

Table 6.3 Approval of various life-styles related to education, social class and sex (16–24 age group)

Actually live like this or sympathise with...	All Young People	Education						Class					
		Intermediate		Modern Secondary		Grammar		Lower		Middle		Upper Middle	
		Male	Female	Male	Female	Male	Female	Male	Female	Male	Female	Male	Female
Committed protest groups													
alternative groups	62%	-8	-6		+9	+5	+12			-9	+9		+7
environmentalists opponents of	81%	-7			+6	+8	+7	-7			+8	+8	
nuclear power	52%	-8		-5		+11	+13	-5		-5	+7	+7	
squatters	47%	-8	-10	+13		+13	+15	-5		+5	+6		+6
rock against the Right	26%	-7	-9			+17	+11			+7			+10
Non-committal groups													
football fans	35%	+15		+8	-14	-14	-20	+18	+14	-6	-11		-20
disco fans	34%		+17		-7	-5	-15				-5	-7	
army fans	14%	+5				-5	-5	+5		-6			-6

(This table only shows percentages which vary by five or more points from the figure in the left-hand column, which indicates the level of overall support for a particular life-style.)

Source: Figures from Shell Studie, (1981), Jugend 1981, Hamburg, Vol. 1, p. 497.

III The aspirations of young people as expressed by the squatters' movement

The occupation and renovation of empty houses by
young people in West Germany was closely linked to
their desire to overcome the isolation of urban life
and to form a community. The squatters of the 1980s
had either taken part in or been influenced by the
protest movement against nuclear energy and the
efforts by alternative groups to create their own
communities. The most specific examples of activity
by squatters were, however, provided by young people
in Switzerland who had taken to the streets in their
efforts to acquire 'autonomous' youth centres and
clubs. The first signs of similar activities in the
Federal Republic emerged in the town of Freiburg
near the Swiss border, when in June 1980 tens of
thousands of people took part in protests against
the eviction of squatters from a complex of buildings
which were going to be demolished.(16) The new
movement then spread and established itself in the
centre of East Germany, in West Berlin, where a
large proportion of alternative projects had already
come into existence.

Between December 1980 and July 1981 the number
of houses occupied by squatters in Berlin rose from
21 to 160. In December 1980 the eviction of squatters from certain houses led to a protest by four
hundred squatters and to street battles in which
more and more people became involved. Two hundred
demonstrators and seventy policemen suffered
injuries. In the following months there were more
riots and in September 1981 one person from a group
of squatters was killed, when he was run over by a
bus as he fled from the police. In 1981 many houses
and empty buildings were occupied by young people
right across the country; and they served as accommodation and space for them to carry out their own
life-style, in various forms of communal living and
in 'autonomous' youth centres.

The squatters became the focus of intense political debate and popular attention. In Berlin
alone it was estimated that between two and three
thousand people lived in the newly-occupied houses.
And beyond these houses many people identified in
some way with the squatters' way of life. The
Shell survey showed that active support for the
squatters came mainly from the 15 to 20 age group,
although the 21 to 24 age group expressed the
strongest sympathy for their activities. Support

for the squatters rose from 38 per cent among those
with a lower level, to 61 per cent among those with
a higher level of education among young people.
Activists in the movement tended to have a predominantly pessimistic view of the future.(17) The
squatters' protest attracted an increasing number of
young people from less privileged social backgrounds
because it adopted forms of protest which are also
used in a working-class milieu. In a similar manner
to the working-class subcultures, the squatters
focused on the world of material goods and on the
'subversive utilisation of the consumer culture' to
form their group style.(18)

The movement was not mainly concerned about the
lack of housing. In Frankfurt 75 per cent of the
squatters already had a fixed address.(19) A pilot
study for the Shell survey was carried out around
the time when the squatters' movement was at its
peak, and it showed that the main problems experienced by young people were the conflicts between generations (30 per cent), unemployment (26 per cent),
problems in relationships (21 per cent) and finding
an orientation in life(20 per cent).(20) Significantly, only 10 per cent referred to the lack of
housing and it featured comparatively low on the
list of problems. A similar pattern emerged when
young people were asked about problems of the future.(Table 6.4) Naturally, the generational conflict
appears less prominently on this list. The issue of
housing again features low in the list of problems.
Environmental problems, unemployment and 'alienation'
all feature prominently. Thus the generational
conflict, whilst it remains an important catalyst of
protest, gives way to a concern with new political
issues.

Nevertheless, the conflict among generations
was a central issue. For instance, the young
supporters of the Green Party - 86 per cent of whom
also supported the squatters - were the least likely to rely on their parents in helping them to
solve personal and financial problems.(Table 6.5)
This was particularly true of the squatters who
either sought or were forced to become independent
of their parents. Many of them were younger than
the generation of Spontis from the mid-seventies,
let alone the undogmatic Left from the sixties'
student movement. This led to new conflicts.

Many of their ideas and actions ran counter to
the beliefs of the undogmatic Left. Thus people in
the Federal Republic are often aware not only of
the gap between those who built the economic

Table 6.4 Problems for young people in the year 2000
(according to young people today) (%)

1. environmental pollution, environmental problems   38
2. unemployment   16
3. isolation, alienation, lack of rapport to surroundings 12
4. wars   9
5. technology which dominates everything   8
6. no meaningful leisure time   7
7. energy crisis   7
8. over-population   7
9. more constraints/authoritarian society   6
10. similar problems to the ones we have experienced so far 6
11. lack of housing   5
12. school/training   5
13. lack of orientation   4
14. drug problems   4
15. generational conflicts   4

(multiple choice; proportions under 4 per cent not included)

Source: Figures from Shell Studie, (1981), Jugend 1981,
Hamburg, Vol. 1, p. 381.

Table 6.5 Support from parents related to party-political
orientation (16-24 age group)(%)

Support from parents (often/sometimes)...	CDU/CSU (18%)	SPD (24%)	GREENS (20%)	NO PARTY (32%)
with personal problems	86	84	66	79
for major acquisitions	69	59	48	67
for purchase of household goods	44	43	33	36
with financial loans	70	63	61	66
with washing (clothes)	87	77	74	87
being able to eat at home	94	87	73	93

Source: Figures from Shell Studie, (1981), Jugend 1981,
Hamburg, Vol, 1, p. 674 and p. 677.

'miracle' and those who criticised it, namely the
student movement; many now perceive a gap between
the extra-parliamentary 'grandads' and the 'autonomists' of today. For some of the latter the writings
of Marcuse are now part of 'orthodoxy'.(21) Whilst
many left-wing groups that had spent several years
working in tenants' and district initiatives in
large cities began to express cautious solidarity
with the squatters (and even joined in the occupati-
ons), they soon realised that many of the young

squatters did not have a left-wing 'consciousness'.
The 'autonomists' of the 1980s found it necessary to
distance themselves from the older generation even
though they often shared the same accommodation.

Within the occupied houses there were conflicts
between the values and aims of different generations.
I was told of a house which offered lodging for a
mixture of people: on the one hand, people from the
1968 generation who had worked as architects, or
planners or painters and who were unemployed and, on
the other hand, young people with very different
perspectives.(22) None the less both generations
relied on each other for support. Some houses offered shelter to gangs of young people who had run away
from home or from welfare institutions. They identified mainly with the house they occupied and only
sought the support of radical groups when they were
threatened with eviction. Each house was different.
Many of the squatters were not prepared patiently
to analyse society, but preferred to act out their
ideas and live fully their personal desires and
dreams in so far as it was possible. Hence any unity
that emerged was full of contradictions. There was
often conflict between oppositional groups which had
carefully worked towards the creation of an alternative culture and community services, and the young
rebels. When the Taz expressed its scepticism
about the squatters' movement in October 1980, the
squatters' 'scene' in Berlin Kreuzberg decided to boy-
cott the newspaper and refuse to supply it with
information about its aims and activities.(23)

Further conflicts arose over the organisation
of daily tasks. In Bochum, the occupation of a disused factory by alternative groups was short-lived
because of contradictory attitudes. Some people
only wanted to confront the authorities and to imit-
ate the 'street-fighters' in Berlin. Others were
content to use the building without feeling responsible for it in any way. The small group of people
who carried out the daily tasks found that their
work was being undermined by the selfish attitude
of others.(24)

According to some squatters, a large section of
the Left had failed to understand that the new movement aimed at much more than the occupation of empty
houses: 'They did not understand that it was a real
attack on the state, on the ownership of land and
property'.(25) Despite the conflicts between the
young and the old Left, many of the squatters had
gone into the vacant houses with a left-wing
'consciousness'. Moreover, the only groups that

have engaged in a fruitful dialogue with the young
squatters come from the alternative and ecology
movements. The main barrier between the two generations was the desire of the younger one to resist
with violence the 'brutality by the state'.
Although the majority of young people are clearly
opposed to groups that use violence to further
their aims, about 3 per cent do support such methods.
(26) The majority within the alternative movement
do not support violence although there are no structures which enable them to overrule the minority
that does become involved in violent confrontations.
At any rate, they are generally not prepared to distance themselves from the minority because they feel
that the state is often equally responsible for
situations in which there is an eruption of violence.
None the less, the constant declarations of war on
the state by the minority have led to conflicts over
strategy and ideas.

According to a survey of about 2,000 people in
West Berlin and the Federal Republic, 86 per cent of
the population was in favour of a peaceful solution
to the conflict between the squatters and the authorities. Only 14 per cent were in favour of an
unconditonal eviction of the squatters. Fifteen per
cent were in favour of a legal agreement which would
allow the occupants to live in and administer the
houses themselves; 22 per cent felt that the squatters and people who were seeking accommodation
should be allowed to rent and administer the houses
themselves; and 45 per cent were simply in favour of
renting the houses to people who sought accommodation.
The public at large appeared less concerned with
the formal-legal aspects of the dispute than with
the issue of housing for those in need. The groups
which favoured a harder line against the squatters
were mainly old people, inhabitants of small towns
and villages, and men. People over 55 years of age
were particularly hostile to the squatters.(27)

Apart from the conflicts which were conditioned
by the gap between the generations, two particular
groups were hostile to the aims and practices of the
squatters: firstly, members of certain trade unions
and secondly, representatives of political parties
who emphasized the illegal nature of the squatters'
activities . In Berlin the building workers' union
organised a demonstration by its members against the
squatters because of the alleged threat to their
jobs posed by the squatters and the Christian
Democrats.(28) The latter apparently had plans to
reduce the level of public investment in the housing

sector. However, the threat posed by the squatters
to the employment prospects of the building workers
was in fact minimal since in Berlin there were still
around 10,000 vacant houses which could be made more
habitable if funds were made available to the building construction industry. A further point of conflict between the unions and the squatters was that
around thirty vacant houses which had been occupied
by squatters belonged to a trade union housing association, Neue Heimat. It was only through the
efforts of mediators like the chairman of the DGB in
Berlin, Pagels, that proposals were made to bridge
the gap between squatters and the housing association. Nevertheless the ill-feeling between the two
sides was further intensified by an appeal in the
Taz for tenants of the housing association to stop
paying their rent.

The other source of public hostility to the
squatters came from the staunch upholders of 'law
and order', especially in smaller towns and cities.
In Berlin even the CDU had modified some of its previous threats to use the police to solve the 'squatting problem'. In Duisburg, however, the Social
Democrat Town Clerk, Ebert, provided many people in
the protest movements with an excellent pretext for
rejecting offers of dialogue from the state. Ebert
wrote a letter to a priest who had tried to mediate
between the two sides, in which he compared the
squatters to aircraft hijackers who took hostages
for political purposes. Ebert admitted that the
squatters had used violence against objects and not
against people. However, he criticised the priest
for his 'far too light-hearted handling of this
serious moral and legal problem', which had been
posed by the activities of the squatters.(29) Yet
his own legalistic approach only hardened the resolve of the squatters not to discuss their demands
with the authorities. The idea of a rigid, oppress-
ive state and the repeated experiences of confrontation with the forces of law and order all served
to unite the squatters' and the other protest movements.

The squatters' movement offered to many people
who had little idea of what they wanted to do a
perspective and a shelter from the outside world
which they experienced as hostile and alien. When
asked what actually held things together in the
house she was living in, a squatter replied that,
apart from the commitment to repairing and renovat-
ing the house, there existed the possibility of
always being able to talk to people and to trust them:

> That is a kind of kinship or tribe relation-
> ship and at the same time a political group.
> It is very important for me that I can, on
> the one hand, for example in my position as
> a woman, separate myself and say I want to
> do that alone now, but at the same time know
> this neighbourliness and closeness of people
> whom I can trust exists around me. That it
> is up to me where I draw borders and where
> I can open them again.(30)

One of the major successes of the initiatives taken
by the squatters is that they have discovered a
life-style which, for a time at least, helps to deal
with the problem of isolation which many young people
experience in contemporary society. It is not
surprising to find that a large proportion of them,
even if they do not live as squatters, identify with
this life-style. The Shell survey showed that 79
per cent of all young people would like to live
together instead of being isolated.(31)
Many squatters believed that they had discovered
a form of organisation that could bridge the gap
between private life in a community and politics:

> If one is dissatisfied one moves out and
> moves on...this qualitatively new organis-
> ational structure is the 'secret' of the
> movement. Only on the basis of such a
> basic structure is the lack of hierarchical
> forms of organisation at all imaginable.(32)

In fact the Beatniks had tried out this style of
living without having to occupy empty houses. At
any rate, it did not take long for new forms of
hierarchy to emerge within the squatters' community.
Bernd Rabehl has pointed out that the loose movement was held together by 'cliques' and by charismatic leaders who knew how to exploit the uncertainty and discontent of younger members and who apparently embodied years of experience in 'revolutionary politics'.(33) The meetings of the central
Squatters' Council in Berlin did not resemble conventional political meetings. Often it was those
who talked loudest who had their say; it was not a
forum for theoreticians but for those who expressed
their arguments with 'power'.(34) These meetings
were often attended by around two hundred people.
Voting as such did not take place. Decisions were
only taken when everybody more or less agreed on a
plan for action, otherwise the matter was dropped.

However, people soon became dissatisfied with this very ineffective form of decision-making and the idea was conceived for the formation of councils for individual blocks of houses or flats. This made it easier to arrive at a consensus since people knew each other better and had more opportunities to express their views. The squatters thus begun to develop some concepts on a more local level.

Apart from the creation of district councils, the squatters in Berlin were held together by a network of working groups, meetings between the members of occupied houses, and handicraft and theatre groups. The central Squatters' Council continued to meet but became less significant.(35) The squatters were still able to respond quickly to any threats of eviction and to develop their own forms of expressive protest, but they did not succeed in developing structures which would ensure a progressive formation of opinions of the diverse individuals and communities.

They lacked clear and cohesive organisational structures; the basis for their unity lay in their common and deeply felt need for community and friendship. One squatter described how 'turbulent' his new life-style was, but added that the warmth he had experienced in this community had made him so strong that he would not change places with anyone. He felt that he had extracted a 'better life' out of a 'wretched culture', and that any effort by the authorities to destroy the squatters' 'last dreams and freedoms' would face fierce opposition.(36) The squatters tended to understand the social problems of industrialisation not in historical and economic terms but as a sign of the overall decay of civilisation into emptiness and war. The peace movement thus provided them with a perfect vehicle for them to extend their subjectivist critique of 'technocratic' society.

NOTES

1. J.Huber, <u>Wer soll das alles aendern?</u> (Rotbuch, Berlin, 1980), pp. 29-30.

2. Ibid., p. 33.

3. Ibid., p. 39.

4. Ibid., p. 40.

5. Ibid., pp. 41-2.

6. <u>Taz</u>, 10 March 1982, p. 11.

7. Interview carried out by the author with Gisela Marsen-Storz at the Ministry of Education and Science in Bonn, in May 1982.

8. Deutscher Bundestag, Stenographisches Protokoll der 12 Sitzung der Enquete-Kommission, Jugendprotest im demokratischen Staat am 08.02.82 (Schoeneberg, Berlin, 1982), pp.108-9.

9. Der Spiegel, Nr. 5, 1982, pp.20-1.

10. Deutscher Bundestag, Zwischenbericht der Enquete-Kommission, Jugendprotest im demokratischen Staat (Drucksache 9/1607, Bonn,1982), p. 6.

11. Taz, 14 May 1980, p. 2.

12. Taz, 5 Oct. 1981, p. 3.

13. K-J.Luther, Die Bedeutung alternativer Projekte aus bildungspolitischer Sicht (revised version of an unpublished paper which was presented to the 'Fachtagung 1981 der Deutschen Vereinigung fuer politische Wissenschaft', Essen), p. 12.

14. Ibid., p. 8.

15. Shell Studie, Jugend 1981, Vol. 1, p. 686.

16. Taz, 12 June 1980, p. 12, and 16 June 1980, p. 2.

17. Shell Studie, Jugend 1981, Vol. 3, p. 78.

18. Ibid., Vol. 1, p. 484.

19. Taz, 2 April 1981, p. 6. The figures were provided by the President of the police in Frankfurt, Gemmer.

20. Shell Studie, Jugend 1981, Vol. 1, p. 662.

21. W.Spindler, 'Bist du dabei in Brokdorf?' in Kursbuch 65, (Berlin, 1981), p. 120.

22. Interview carried out by the author with Professor Bernd Rabehl, Free University of Berlin, January 1982.

23. Taz-Journal, Sachschaden. Haeuser und andere Kaempfe, Nr. 3, (Berlin, 1981), p. 8ff.

24. Ibid., p. 59f.

25. Taz, 19 June 1981, p. 11.

26. Shell Studie, Jugend 1981, Vol. 3, p. 82.

27. Taz, 19 March 1982, p. 16, refers to a survey carried out by Infratest for Prof. Peter Grottian (FU, Berlin).

28. Taz, 20 April 1982, p. 3.

29. Taz, 19 May 1981, p. 3.

30. Haerlin, 'Von Haus zu Haus', pp. 19-20.

31. Shell Studie, Jugend 1981, Vol. 1, p. 472.

32. Haerlin, 'Von Haus zu Haus', p. 23.

33. Rabehl Interview, January 1982.

34. Haerlin, 'Von Haus zu Haus', p. 22.

35. Taz-Journal, Sachschaden, p. 73f.

36. Taz, 20 April 1982, p. 3.

Chapter Seven

PEACE MOVEMENT

The issue of peace had aroused great public interest
and secured support for the Ostpolitik of the Social-
Liberal Alliance in the early 1970s. Willy Brandt
had brought to a climax an initiative which was
begun by the Christian Democrats under Erhard to
improve relations with the East European neighbours
of the Federal Republic. There followed a period
in which progress in this sphere was consolidated
and public interest was diverted by other issues.
Thus when Chancellor Schmidt discovered a 'gap' in
the defences of NATO in 1977 and proposed the placement of new missiles in the countries belonging to
the alliance, and when the dual-track decision was
actually taken in 1979 to introduce Cruise and Pershing missiles, there was little public outcry. In
the sphere of 'peace politics', the Social Democrats
enjoyed widespread even though 'passive' support.
However, the dual-track decision immediately inspired
initiatives all over Western Europe, and especially
in Scandinavia, to oppose it. Groups from Scandinavia soon established contact with internationalist,
church, left-wing and pacifist groups in the Federal
Republic, which for many years had been conducting
peace and anti-militarist campaigns at the grass
roots. The Green Movement offered a sound base of
support for these initiatives. The peace movement
was destined to bring together all these initiatives
as well as groups and individuals from established
political parties and organisations. It also
brought to the surface latent feelings of nationalism and anti-Americanism, and offered another outlet for the expression of utopian and fundamentalist
ideas.

I Bases of support

The peace movement extended considerably the bases
of support for the Green Movement and gave added
strength to the participatory, as opposed to the
governmental, elements within the SPD. In a survey
carried out for Der Spiegel (representative sample:
2,150 people) in October 1981, a majority of the
respondents were opposed to the decision by the
United States to go ahead with the production of the
neutron bomb. This majority comprised mainly supporters of the SPD, the FDP and the Green Party.
(Table 7.1) Voters were also asked what they
thought of the NATO dual-track decision to place a
new range of nuclear missiles in the country. Although 36 per cent were in favour of this decision
and 22 per cent opposed to it, 30 per cent were undecided. The figures in brackets (Table 7.2) show
the results of a similar survey carried out in January 1983 during the campaign for the Federal Elections. Whilst in 1981 the opposition to the new
missiles tended to cut across party lines, to the
extent that around 20 per cent of the supporters of
the three established parties were opposed to the
dual-track decision, the atmosphere surrounding the
1983 Federal Elections led to a greater polarisation of views, especially in the dramatic shift of
CDU/CSU voters from 38 per cent to 51 per cent, and
of FDP voters from 35 per cent to 51 per cent, in
favour of the dual-track decision. In October 1981
almost half of the population thought that the
peace movement was basically good, even though only
9 per cent were prepared to take an active part in
it.(Table 7.3) At the same time around a third of
CDU/CSU voters and well over half of the voters of
the other major parties were sympathetic towards it.

Table 7.1 Attitudes to the neutron bomb (%)

	Total	CDU/CSU	SPD	FDP	GREENS
opposed to it	54	41	·62	55	95
in favour of it	45	57	37	45	5

Source: Figures from Der Spiegel, Nr. 48, 1981, p. 59.

Table 7.2   Attitudes to the NATO dual-track decision (%)

	Total	CDU/CSU	SPD	FDP	GREENS
opposed to it	21(22)	18(13)	22(27)	23(13)	60(67)
in favour of it	36(38)	38(51)	37(26)	35(51)	17(15)
undecided	30(28)				
indifferent	12(11)				

(figures in brackets relate to January 1983, the others relate to October 1981.)

Source: Figures from Der Spiegel, Nr. 48, 1981, and Nr. 6, 1983, p. 90.

Table 7.3   Attitudes to the peace movement (%)

	Total	CDU/CSU	SPD	FDP	GREENS
think that the peace movement is basically good, but will not take part in it	39	31	47	55	16
will perhaps, definitely, or already do take part in it	9	4	10	9	70

Source: Figures from Der Spiegel, Nr. 48, 1981, p. 63.

(i) The Green Movement

The initiative taken by some Scandinavian women to collect signatures in support of a 'petition for peace' - in Denmark alone, over 100,000 people had signed such an appeal - inspired women in West Germany to form a 'Women's Initiative for Peace' (Anstiftung der Frauen zum Frieden - AFF) Initially the AFF was supported by women from the Green Movement, including feminists; however, it soon attracted members of other groups, for instance church groups, and other people who did not identify particularly strongly with the policies of particular parties and whose main commitment had so far been to their family. The core of this group consisted of about fourty women aged between 22 and 70 who shared a middle-class background. By May 1980 they had gathered 80,000 signatures for their 'petition for peace'. Thus, despite the small size of the core group, it was able to reach out to many other people who felt as strongly as they did about the threat

of nuclear war. The commitment and symbolic importance of this group characterises the fact that,
within the Green Movement, many women have either
been offered or been able to fight for greater participation and the formation of a new identity. The
AFF was one of the earliest decentralised initiatives
which was formed in response to the NATO dual-track
decision in 1979.

It could be argued that the commitment of women
in the peace movement is related to the burden of
responsibility that many of them feel about bringing
a child into a world whose future existence depends
on the success or failure of the threat of nuclear
war. In addition, since women are more inclined
than men to express openly fears and emotions, they
may be more prepared to articulate the fear that
people have of nuclear war. In West Germany this
feeling was accentuated because of proposals by the
government that women should also be enlisted to do
military service. I am not suggesting that because
women are more inclined than men to express their
fears and emotions, they do not engage in rational
argument; it is simply that the issue of peace and
nuclear weapons has, in all Western countries, gained
powerful support among women, and that in their role
as mothers or grandmothers many of them have expressed deep concern about the future of their children
and grandchildren. (In Britain the protest by
30,000 women at Greenham Common Airforce Base in
December 1982 was perhaps the most vivid expression
of these characteristics.)

The moral opposition by groups of women to the
deployment of nuclear weapons was matched by groups
within the church. Ever since the 1950s church
groups had opposed the re-armament of Germany, and
had campaigned for peace. For instance an organisation called Aktion Suehnezeichen/Friedensdienste
(ASF) was founded in 1958 to enable West Germans to
travel to West European countries as well as Poland,
Israel and the United States to carry out voluntary
work for 'peace and reconciliation' with nationalit-
ies that had faced the terror of the Nazi regime.
Over the past two decades more than 8,000 volunteers
have been engaged in these activities.(1) Organisations like the ASF influenced the Ostpolitik in the
1960s and early 1970s. Its influence, in a similar
manner to the 'Women's Initiative for Peace',
extended far beyond its own membership of two hundred
people.(2) Around 30 per cent of its funds come
from the Evangelical Church, the remainder from
voluntary organisations and contributions.(3)

Since 1974 the ASF has organised peace festivals and since 1980 - in response to the NATO dual-track decision - it has extended its activities by calling for 'peace weeks' all over the Federal Republic. Thus in 1980 more than 300 initiatives or alliances were formed all over the country and they took part in activities to celebrate 'peace weeks'. Between 15 and 21 November 1981 similar events were organised in 400 different locations. The provincial synod of the Evangelical Church in West Berlin (Brandenburg) declared that the aim of the 'peace weeks' was to encourage people in the following manner:

> to discuss questions, to attempt to do new things and to overcome the widespread scepticism about the combination of religious faith and work for peace...What we desire is that among us there arises a new trust in the activity of God for peace, which encourages people to take imaginative and consequential steps towards practical work for peace.(4)

This aim was partially realised when groups within the Evangelical Church managed to convert the nineteenth German Evangelical Congress in June 1981 into a massive display of the desire for peace and nuclear disarmament. They had assessed correctly that members of the church were more likely to respond favourably to initiatives for peace than to the protest against nuclear energy, and they referred to the statement by the Ecumencial Council of Churches in 1975 that initiatives should be taken by the Churches so that people can live without the protection of weapons.(5) On 18 June 140,000 people attended the congress in Hamburg; they included the Minister of Defence and the Federal Chancellor. The bishop of Hamburg, Woelber, who acted as host of the congress, stressed that those who had organised it were not involved in the appeal for a rally for peace on 20 June. None the less, about 80,000 people took part in this rally which offered an opportunity for co-operation between christian, pacifist and radical opponents of the policy by the government on nuclear weapons. Inspired by the success of this rally, the ASF - under the motto 'all political contradictions must be integrated' - worked out an appeal for a demonstration in Bonn with environmentalist groups, the Green Party, the Jusos and many other groups.(6) The ASF thus became the main carrier of an appeal signed by 777 regional and local, national and international groups and

organisations; they all declared their support for
the rally in Bonn (October 1981) which was attended
by 300,000 people.

The emergence of the peace movement offered an
opportunity to the Green Party to present itself as
the representative of more than just a single-issue
organisation and to relate the question of nuclear
energy to nuclear weapons. At the same time, within
the decentral initiatives of the ecology movement
there was a shift of emphasis from opposition to
nuclear energy towards anti-militarism and peace.
For several years members of both the Green Party
and the BBU had been trying to direct the attention
of the movement against nuclear energy towards the
issues of nuclear weapons and militarism. In October
1979 the BBU and the 'German Peace Society'(DFG-VK),
the oldest exptra-parliamentary organisation in this
sphere, met to discuss the possibility of joint
action. Decentral initiatives were planned and
carried out in September 1980, and in the following
month about 10,000 supporters from both movements
joined forces in a demonstration against the storage
of weapons in the Emsland region around Lingen.

It is interesting to note that the DFG-VK, with
its membership of around 20,000, represents the
traditional wing of the peace movement and that one
fraction within it is fairly close to the German
Communist Party. However, the DFG-VK, although it
remains the oldest organisation that has survived
from the peace movement of the 1950s, has not attracted into its ranks the majority of supporters of
the new peace movement. The survey carried out for
Der Spiegel revealed a strong correlation between
support for the peace and ecology movements. Eighty
per cent of the supporters of the peace movement
were opposed to the construction of nuclear power
stations, whilst a similar percentage of the opponents of this movement felt that nuclear power stations were necessary.(7)

The Taz played an important role in coordinat-
ing the activities of the diverse strands of the
peace movement. Not only did it offer up-to-date
reports on the ill-timed, clumsy and even provocat-
ive statements and policies of the Reagan Administration in the United States in relation to the neutron bomb, the new range of nuclear missiles, and the
remarks about the possibility of nuclear war limited
to Europe, it also enabled even the smallest peace
groups in rural areas to feel that they were part of
a broader movement. The Taz also published details
about the location of nuclear weapons all over the

Federal Republic; this led to the fear, expressed by
the CDU, that military bases would assume the same
significance for the peace movement as nuclear power
stations had done for the movement against nuclear
energy. This is of course precisely what did happen
for example in the widespread protests which involved
more than half a million people over Easter 1983.
A detailed map of all the known sites of nuclear
weapons was produced in June 1981 by the newspaper.
(8) The Taz was able to make full use of the experience of an ex-intelligence officer and military
commander in the United States Army, W.Arkin, as an
informant.(9)

An editor in the Taz compared the election of
President Reagan 'by the American people' to that
of Hitler by the Germans since they thereby permitted the greatest military and arms budget in history.
He also accused all 'Yanks', not only the supporters
of the President, of taking part in the 'genocide
in Vietnam' and of supporting the preparation for a
nuclear war in Europe. The editorial concluded:
'We are not anti-American. We like the Indians in
the United States and respect the Coloured people
and the Puerto Ricans. But: Yankee go home'.(10)
Several letters were published from readers who
were critical of the attitudes expressed by this
editor. None the less, the tone of the article
undoubtedly appealed to more militant groups within
the Green Movement, particularly those that had
become involved in violent protests against celebr-
ations to commemorate the 25th anniversary of the
Federal Army.

Ever since the formation of the Federal Army
rituals and ceremonies had taken place several
times a year during which new recruits were publicly
sworn in to military service. In 1980, in order to
commemorate the 25th anniversary of the acceptance
of the Federal Republic into NATO, the government
decided to play a more prominent role in these
ceremonies. Thus at the opening one in Bremen (May
1980) the guests of honour included the Federal
President, the Minister of Defence and the Mayor of
Bremen. The attempt by politicians to turn these
ceremonies into a display of loyalty to NATO
increased the polarisation of opinion around the
issue of peace and nuclear weapons. In Bremen a
minority of about 500 demonstrators - out of an
overall number of 10,000 - forced their way into
the stadium where the ceremonies were being held.
The riot that ensued was a signal for further
violent confrontations between young people and the

police in several other towns and cities, notably in
Hannover and Stuttgart.

These protests served as an important model for
young people who were dissatisfied with their situation and who sought to overcome their declining
position in society and their search for identity
by occupying vacant houses. Militant squatters
became committed to the 'struggle for peace', which
took on a far from peaceful appearance especially
when the American Foreign Minister, Alexander Haig,
came to visit Berlin in September 1981. Between
30,000 and 80,000 people took part in a protest
against American policies.(11) Some banners proclaimed, 'we like Americans, but not the neutron
bomb' and others, 'Haig must live so that we can
die'. Around 2,000 demonstrators then set about
confronting the police and in the ensuing riots
around 200 people from both sides were injured.
Similar riots accompanied the visit by President
Reagan in June 1982. As one newspaper pointed out
after the visit by Haig to Berlin, 'the times when
in Berlin a whole city cheered an American President, are gone'.

Although most supporters of the peace movement
did not approve of the violence which arose in the
conflicts between squatters and police, most of them
sympathised with the squatters. In the _Spiegel_
survey 70 per cent were in favour of the occupation
of vacant houses by young people and 28 per cent
were opposed to them. However, among the opponents
of the peace movement, 88 per cent were opposed to
the squatters.(12)

The peace movement secured the support of young
people in all the major political parties and trade
unions, especially among those with a higher level
of education. Among young people aged between 18
and 29 nearly 25 per cent were prepared to take an
active part in the peace movement, and about a
further 30 per cent were in favour of it.(13) It
is striking that 41 per cent of those who were less
than 36 years of age and had a higher level of education were prepared to take an active part in the
peace movement.(14) These figures suggest that
there is a strong element of conflict between an old
and a new elite rather than between generations.
None the less, the experiences of two different
generations did appear to influence attitudes towards
the withdrawal of American troops from Germany.
Whilst only 12 per cent of the population would have
welcomed the withdrawal of American troops from the
Federal Republic, most of the people who nurtured

Table 7.4 Support within the peace movement for the withdrawal of American troops (%)

Born after 1941					Born before 1941		
age groups...							
18-21	22-25	26-29	30-39		40-49	50-64	65+
22	26	11	15		11	10	8

Source: Figures from Der Spiegel, Nr. 49, 1981, p. 101.

this idea were born during or after the last war.
(Table 7.4) Among conscientious objectors to military service 61 per cent were potential active
supporters of the peace movement, and a further 18
per cent sympathised with it.(15) Over the past few
years about 55,000 young people have, every year,
submitted objections to carrying out military service.
     The youth section of the trade union movement
was strongly in favour of the peace movement. This
position was not shared by the union leadership.
Several unions voted against their youth sections
when the latter declared their intention to take
part in the mass rally in Bonn (October 1981). This
view was shared by the federal executive committee
of the DGB. None the less, for the first time since
the emergence of the Green Movement, a significant
number of trade unionists expressed their support
for one of its major aims. Similarly the youth
organisations within the three established parties
all took part in peace rallies which were directed
against the policies of their own parties. The
youth wing of the CDU was highly critical of the
party leader when he accused the participants at the
Bonn rally of forming a 'people's front', or Volks-
front, a term which is normally associated with
broad alliances which are strongly influenced by
Communists.(16) I will now assess the response of
establihed groups and their supporters to the peace
movement by referring, above all, to the trade
unions and the Social Democratic Party.

(ii) Established Groups

As I have already suggested, most of the initial
support for the peace movement within the trade
unions came from younger members. In March 1981
the youth section of the public service, transport
and traffic union declared its opposition to the

introduction of new nuclear missiles and the neutron
bomb, and was therefore reprimanded by the leadership of this union. In the following month the youth
section of the DGB supported the idea of a 'nuclear
free zone' in Europe. Whilst some trade unions, for
example the chemical workers' union, emphatically
declared their support for the NATO dual-track decision, the trade union congresses of the railway
workers and of the print and paper workers opposed
it. In July 1981 the chairman of the metalworkers'
union wrote that it was questionable whether further
armament did not in fact increase the threat of
nuclear war when compared to other solutions.(17)
      The leadership of the DGB appeared to have
launched a new initiative against the peace movement
in August 1981 when it issued a joint statement with
the Federal Army and declared its official support
for the latter in its role as a defender of the
Constitutional State and as the protector of 'the
freedom of political and social self-fulfilment'.
This was certainly a historic statement in the light
of the previous opposition by the trade unions to
the re-armament of the Federal Republic in the 1950s.
Whilst the joint statement recognises that a citizen
may have reasons of conscience for refusing to per-
form military service, it states that 'in general
military service the citizen fulfils his duties
towards the community'.(18) This event served only
to alienate further the Green Movement from the
trade unions, and this was clearly the intention of
the trade union leadership. The DGB was uneasy
about the dynamic situation which had arisen as a
result of the activities of the peace movement,
especially after the events in Hamburg (June 1981)
and the prospect of an even larger protest in Bonn
in October. It simply forbade its youth wing to
take part in the rally on the grounds that the trade
unions represented an independent force with eight
million members.
      In addition, as a direct counter to the so-
called Krefelder Appell, a petition for peace which
was initiated by groups in the peace movement, the
DGB launched its own petition, the Dattelner Appell,
which urged people to support the NATO dual-track
decision as well as further negotiations with the
Eastern Block. The Krefelder Appell expressed opposition to the policy of the Federal Government on
nuclear weapons. The close ties between the SPD
Government and the trade unions meant that the trade
union leadership was reluctant to take an independent stance. Instead it described the petition as

part of 'communist propaganda'. Although this was
partly an allusion to the involvement of communist
groups in initiating the petition, it also reflected
the extent to which Helmut Schmidt had succeeded in
co-opting the trade union leadership whilst he was
Chancellor. However, one prominent member of the
trade unions, Georg Benz, from the executive committee of the metalworkers' union, accepted an invita-
tion to address the rally in Bonn. He spoke not as
a member of his union but as an 'individual person',
thus formally complying to a directive issued by the
leadership of the DGB. There were stirrings of
revolt on the shop floor. The works council of a
firm in Oberdingen where three thousand people were
employed in the production of electrical appliances,
wrote to the DGB and complained about its decision
not to support the rally in Bonn.(19) In reply to
all his critics, Oskar Vetter, as leader of the DGB,
declared that:

> We cannot follow those who say better red
> than dead! If that kind of pacifism were
> to be carried out, then there would be no
> struggle against exploitation and suppress-
> ion; commitment to the liberation movements
> in the Third World would no longer be poss-
> ible. Should we then turn the slogan into:
> better exploited than dead?(20)

This did not deter trade unionists in Cologne
who decided to form their own trade union block at
the Bonn rally. By mid-September over three hundred
trade union organs at various levels declared their
support for the rally; the youth section of the DGB
in Berlin lent its official support to it.(21) In
Hannover sympathies among trade unionists for the
rally were so powerful that a compromise was achieved between the DGB and its local members: the latter
would be allowed to march under the banner 'DGB -
Hannover district', whilst the demonstration would
be described as 'one out of many possibilities to
make clear the position of the union on security
and peace'.(22) Support was also evident among
teachers and academics, print and paper workers, and
people employed in the manufacture of ceramics,
paper and chemicals. Apparently, within the executive committee of the DGB, the unions representing
workers in the chemical, mining, energy and construction industries had all tried without success to
pass a motion in support of the rally. One of the
main reasons for this was the presence of a large

number of christian pacifists in these unions.(23)
It was estimated that around 100,000 trade unionists
took part in the Bonn rally, since groups and individuals from trade unions had chartered more than
two thousand buses to attend the rally.(24) The
massive support for the peace movement was also
reflected by the fact that the Dattelner Appell had
been signed by about 700,000 people, whilst the
Krefelder Appell had been signed by around 2 million
people including many trade unionists.

The Dattelner Appell had been welcomed by
Chancellor Schmidt since it stressed that the military capability of the Soviet Union was superior to
that of the West. The appeal was launched by prominent trade unionists, Social Democrats and even a
Christian Democrat professor. The main founder was
Horst Niggemeier, the press spokesman for the mine-
workers' union, who was regarded by the producers of
Green Movement ideology as the typical example of
how trade union leaders had become corrupted by power.
(25)

Despite the slow pace at which organisations
like the trade unions and the SPD can adjust to the
demands of the Green Movement, their capacity to
take up new issues has often been underestimated by
the latter. The SPD, was ultimately in the best
position to listen to the demands of the campaigners
for peace since, although it was partly responsible
for asking for the new range of nuclear missiles, it
had in the past secured progress in the spheres of
peace and detente.

As I have indicated, a majority of ordinary
members of the SPD either felt that the peace movement was basically good or wanted to take an active
part in it. At the party congress in December 1979
a large minority of delegates were opposed to the
NATO dual-track decision. As Rolf Zundel pointed
out, for the first time in a decade the party was
forced to make decisions on the issue of peace:
'The Social Democrats are tortured by the awareness
that a core element of Social Democratic Government
policy which has so far not been damaged, can easily
be badly affected: detente.'(26) After the congress
in which the Left suffered a series of defeats, the
'Parliamentary Left' was formed within the party
and tried to develop a unified policy towards disarmament and the plans for further armament. In
March 1982 a group around the Frankfurt Circle prepared alternative proposals to those of the party
executive committee, calling for a moratorium or at

least a delay in the deployment of the new missiles.
(27) This was partly in response to the campaign by
the party executive committee which aimed to counter
the feeling that, at a local level, the membership
might oppose the peace policy of the leadership at
the 1982 party congress(28); and partly to show the
extra-parliamentary movement that it could rely on
the support of this group of around 40 to 50 Members
of Parliament. Provisionally, the matter was shelved
at the party congress.

The role that has befallen the SPD as the opposition party and the withdrawal of Helmut Schmidt as
candidate for Chancellor has strengthened the hand
of those who wish to give more attention to the
demands of the peace movement. Even before the withdrawal of Schmidt, both he and Willy Brandt had
warned people not to condemn in a hurry the peace
movement since it also contained a positive 'national element'. It would also be unfair to overlook
the difficulty of Schmidt's position. Whilst he did
not share Brandt's enthusiasm about the movement, he
was highly critical of the Reagan Administration for
a series of tactless remarks, for instance about the
possibility of a limited nuclear war in Europe, and
for its decision - without prior consultation of its
European allies - to go ahead with the production of
the neutron bomb which would only be used in Europe
in the event of war. Chancellor Schmidt did, however,
prefer a more cautious approach and he was distressed
to find that 50 Members of Parliament from the SPD
wished to take part in the Bonn rally, and that one
of them, Erhard Eppler, would actually make a speech
there.

One of the MPs who did take part in the rally,
Hermann Scheer, explained his views on the arms race:
he acknowledged that the Soviet Union may be fearful
of being surrounded by enemies and may not have
aggressive aims; however, he questioned the intention of the Superpower to modernise its potential in
the form of the SS-20 missiles, even though a policy
of detente had been implemented successfully by
Brandt. In reply to the sceptics who do not see
much value in present negotiations between the Superpowers, he emphasized that they were necessary
since negotiations had to be carried out to prevent
the spread, not only of existing weapons, but also
of 'systems which do not yet exist', for instance
satellites and laser weapons.(29)

The statements by Scheer were made in front of
a large audience which was strongly in favour of the
peace movement. Much of what he said was greeted

with only mild applause and occasionally with derision. However, the same audience was not blindly opposed to the SPD if one judges from the reception that was given, at the same meeting, to Erhard Eppler who had been highly critical of the policies of the party leadership. Eppler was applauded warmly when he expressed his scepticism about the usefulness of arms control negotiations; he stressed that at any rate no negotiations would have taken place without pressure applied by the peace movement. Not surprisingly, Eppler was admired by many members of the peace movement who had become detached from the SPD.

Yet Eppler had isolated himself from the centres of power within the SPD, and efforts towards dialogue with members of the peace movement came largely from people like Peter Glotz who were in a better position to attempt the integration of the diverse factions within the party over this issue. For instance in August 1981, Glotz organised a forum in which about sixty Social Democrats and representatives of the peace movement could discuss their different attitudes on how to bring about peace. The participants included the Minister of Defence as well as Rudolf Bahro and Petra Kelly from the Green Party.(30) It may turn out to be one of the ironies of this relationship between the SPD and the Green Movement that once the latter had posed a serious challenge to the policy of the SPD on peace, the path was paved for an increase in support for the peace movement from the supporters of established groups, and that this, at the same time, facilitated the ultimate integration of most of the supporters of the Green Movement into the SPD.

The issue of peace and nuclear weapons led to a greater polarisation of views among supporters of the SPD and the CDU. When people were asked how they would act if the United States deployed new missiles in the Federal Republic, twice as many SPD (38 per cent) than CDU/CSU voters (19 per cent) said they would either sign a protest petition, or take part in demonstrations, or join a Citizens' Initiative which opposed the deployment.(31) Similarly a higher proportion of SPD (47 per cent) than CDU/CSU voters (36 per cent) agreed that if the Federal Government held a different view to the United States on how to react to the Soviet Union, it should not conform to its Superpower ally.(32) In addition, twice as many SPD voters favoured the withdrawal of American troops from the Federal Republic in comparison to CDU/CSU voters: of the 12 per cent of all voters who wished to witness such

a withdrawal, 7 per cent were from the CDU/CSU and
15 per cent from the SPD.
　　It is thus not surprising to learn that the SPD,
especially following the withdrawal of Schmidt as
their candidate for Chancellor, sought to make the
dual-track decision on new missiles in Germany 'unnecessary'. The General Secretary of the party,
Glotz, has shown great sympathy for the aim of the
peace movement to oppose the placement of such
weapons(33), and the Greens became increasingly
fearful that Hans-Jochen Vogel would adopt a policy
that could wrest the initiative on this issue from
them. The SPD could still become the strongest base
of support for the peace movement. Moreover, as the
Hamburg state election (December 1982) showed, the
unpopularity of the new alliance between the CDU/CSU
and the FDP among supporters of the peace movement,
enhanced the chances of a return to power of the SPD.
This was one of the main reasons why the SPD tried
to turn the 1983 Federal Elections into a referendum
on nuclear weapons. Another reason, of course, was
the need for the new Chancellor-candidate, Vogel,
to establish himself as a prominent figure in
'peace politics' both at a national and an international level.

II　Anti - Americanism and nationalism

Attitudes towards the Reagan Administration and its
ability to solve global problems have varied according to the party-political orientation of voters. In
October 1981 about 31 per cent of the respondents
in the Spiegel survey stated that they had experienced a decrease in faith in the ability of the United
States to solve problems since President Reagan had
come into office; 27 per cent had greater faith,
and 41 per cent felt the same as they had done previously over this issue. The greatest decrease in
faith had occurred among supporters of the SPD (37
per cent), the Greens (77 per cent) and the FDP (41
per cent).(34)　Between October 1981 and January
1983 the percentage of those people that trusted the
United States to deal with world problems fell from
62 per cent to 43 per cent.(35)　However, this
should not be confused with widespread anti-American
sentiment. Surveys over the past two decades have
shown that around half of the population 'likes'
Americans, around 20 per cent don't like them and
the remainder are either undecided or hold no

particular views.(36)

I have already pointed out that SPD voters are much less willing than CDU voters to see the Federal Government complying to the wishes of the United States on various issues. Not surprisingly, 81 per cent of the active supporters, and 52 per cent of the sympathisers of the peace movement believe that if the government holds a different view to the United States on how to react to the Soviet Union, it should not conform to the wishes of its Superpower ally.(37)

The charge has frequently been levelled at the peace movement that it is either manipulated by or playing into the hands of the Soviet Union. It is thus particularly interesting to compare attitudes of both the critics and the supporters of the movement towards the two Superpowers. On the whole the level of trust towards them varies drastically between supporters and opponents of the peace movement. Around 30 per cent of the opponents and critics of the peace movement believed that the United States was aiming at military superiority, whereas 80 per cent felt that this was the intention of the Soviet Union. Among activists within the peace movement, 66 per cent feel that the United States, and 58 per cent that the Soviet Union, are aiming for military superiority.(38) It is not surprising that among activists and sympathisers of the peace movement there is a greater suspicion of the Western rather than the Eastern Superpower since their campaign is directed at the immediate 'threat' posed by the former in their own country. Some observers have been critical of this tendency by the peace campaigners not to take into consideration sufficiently the potential of force and the power structures within the Soviet Union.(39) Over the issue of the withdrawal of American troops from the Federal Republic, 62 per cent of the respondents said they would regret to see it happen, and 12 per cent, they would welcome it. Fifty-six per cent of the supporters of the Green Party would have welcomed the withdrawal of the troops.(40)

Apart from certain groups within the Green Movement, most supporters of the peace movement are not anti-American, even though opposition to the United States forms a significant issue which helps to unite the diverse groups within it. To this extent the peace campaign has occasionally assumed the form of an 'anti-colonial' struggle, and has contributed to a renewed interest in the question of German nationality and sovereignty.

147

At the Bonn rally in October 1981 the Evangelical pastor Heinrich Albertz raised the issue of the status of the Federal Republic in relation to the United States, in the light of the NATO dual-track decision, the neutron bomb and the arms policy of the Soviet Union:

> Everyone knows that according to the latest level of armaments and the strategical plans, both parts of Germany will be a shooting ground for the Superpowers. And we are in a position of total dependence, without total sovereignty, without a peace treaty in a divided country...I am asking all this as a German, if you like, as a German patriot. Why should we always leave the national interests to the Right?(41)

He felt that the interests of the United States and Europe were no longer the same. Whilst older people like Albertz are acutely aware of the historical events that led to the division of Germany, some members of the younger generation regard the military presence of the United States as the 'colonisation' of the Federal Republic. Petra Kelly reproached Helmut Schmidt for giving up the struggle for peace and turning the country into 'the outlying nuclear colony of the United States and NATO'.(42) A young spokesman for conscientious objectors to military service told the same rally that any pacifist who refused to conform to a policy of further armament was 'perhaps more of a patriot' than those who sought 'to deliver our country into a nuclear holocaust'.(43)

Nearly all the speakers at this rally emphasized that they were not anti-American but were opposed to specific American policies. However, the fact that the opposition was directed against the policies of a foreign power facilitated the re-discovery of a national identity which has remained one of the unresolved issues of post-war German history. On the issue of nuclear weapons the CDU/CSU has identified closely with the policies of the United States. This prompted Heinrich Boell to remark ironically that the Christian Democrats in the Federal Parliament were even less critical of American policies than ordinary Americans.(44) The theme of German nationalism was also raised by Helmut Gollwitzer, a prominent member of the peace movement, in letter to Der Spiegel in which he wrote that, 'No German can accept this unconditional subjection of the interests

of our people to foreign interests, this surrender-
ing of power over the existence of a people to a
foreign government'.(45) According to Professor
Ulrich Albrecht, a vice-president of the Free University of Berlin, the unclear constitutional situation meant that 'in strict legal terms, the United
States could station anything they like here;
strictly speaking in the pressure of events, they
wouldn't have to ask us'.(46) Thus the SPD began to
consider how a peace treaty might be made with the
allies in order to clarify the complex legal situation and status of the Federal Republic.

Many people within the peace movement wished to
overcome the reluctance of the Left to politicise
the theme of nationalism because of its feeling of
guilt and dissatisfaction over events in the recent
history of the country. The ironic statement by the
Spontis that 'Germans should leave Germany and then
there will be peace' echoes this dissatisfaction
with the German political culture.

Recently new initiatives have emerged which not
only question the history and the military strategic
role of the Federal Republic but which look across
the border to East Germany. The president of the
German Writers' Union, Bernt Engelmann, launched an
appeal from the writers of Europe calling for the
abandonment of the new weapons systems and for real
disarmament, and for people to join 'across fronti-
ers and different social systems' in order to work
for peace 'so that Europe does not become the atomic
battlefield of a new and final world war'.(47) The
appeal was signed by writers all over Western Europe
as well as several Soviet and East German writers.
Within East Germany there is a growing discussion
among church groups about the threat of nuclear
weapons which is independent of the officially
sanctioned calls for peace. Above all, some young
people discussed the possibility of 'social work for
peace' as an alternative to military service. The
proposal for an alternative to military service provoked a sympathetic response from elsewhere: the
synod of the Saxon Regional Church offered cautious
support to around 800 people who wished to put into
practice this alternative, and 2,000 signed a docu-
ment which supported the idea of 'social work for
peace'.(48) This demand later gained the support of
five out of eight regional bodies of the Evangelical
Church in East Germany. They questioned the idea
that peace could be achieved by military strength
and called for calculated steps towards disarmament
in consultation with their allies and for

'defensive' rather than 'threatening' systems of defence. The demand for an alternative to military service was rejected cautiously by the authorities. When young people in East Germany wore a badge which showed a blacksmith hammering a sword to make it into a plough, they were strongly reproached and forbidden to wear it.(49) The symbol was adopted by many people in the West German peace movement who sought to promote discussions over the question of German unity and independence of European nations from both Superpowers.

III Utopian proposals and fundamental questions

When nuclear weapons were first introduced in West Germany they were feared much less than the 'Russian threat'. Lately, however, neutrality has re-emerged as an issue. Thirty-five per cent of the respondents in the Spiegel survey were in favour of neutrality as it is practised in Austria. Sixty-three per cent were opposed to the idea.(50) There has always been a strong potential for the idea of neutrality and the re-unification of Germany. 'Neutralists' can be found in all the main political parties. What distinguishes the present discussion over neutrality from previous debates is the attempt by peace researchers, including advisers to military establishments, to draw up alternative defence strategies, since some people within these circles believe that the idea of 'mutually assured destruction' is being surpassed, as a deterrent, by technological innovations in the production of weapons. They point out that a Cruise missile based in West Germany could reach Moscow within a few minutes, thus allowing virtually no time for a reply to be given to any warning issued by either side. The neutron bomb is regarded as the symbol of a development in which the distinction between conventional and nuclear weapons cannot be made easily. The accuracy of intercontinental ballistic missiles which enables them to land within a few hundred yards of a distant target and the effectiveness with which, for example, the United States can locate Soviet submarines all over the globe, are regarded as an increasing threat because each side may tend to believe that if it launches the 'first strike' it might escape the full impact of the opponent's armed might.
        Fears about these changes have been expressed by, firstly, peace researchers, for instance Dr.Horst

Afheldt at the Starnberg Max-Planck Institute;
secondly, people all over Europe who were increasingly disturbed by the statements of the Reagan Administration about the possibility of a nuclear war
restricted to their continent; and thirdly, supporters of the Green Movement who have pointed out that
the control over nuclear weapons is not only in the
hands of a foreign power but also beyond any effective democratic control by the population. The concept of a technocratic 'nuclear state' which had
been adopted by the campaigners against nuclear
energy was now used to interpret the control and
secrecy that surrounds nuclear weapons bases. In
the light of these developments and changes in perception the search for alterntives has become more
significant.

Among the alternatives that have been proposed,
are: firstly, a non-nuclear defence capability, that
is, one that excludes both long-distance nuclear
rockets which attract destructive counter-attacks
and self-destructive tactical weapons which would
normally be intended for the home battle-front;
secondly, a strategy which would be based unambigu-
ously on defence and not directed at opposing territory, and would include modern anti-tank, anti-
craft and anti-rocket weapons; thirdly, a decentralised system of defence instead of huge military
centres which would attract massive retaliation;
fourthly, 'social' defensive measures, including
non-military forms of popular resistance and technical sabotage, which would make any occupation appear
fruitless; and finally, the introduction of measures
for civil defence (based on the contentious assumption that the enemy would not use nuclear weapons) as
a boost to morale. Some supporters of the peace
movement feel that the introduction of these measures
would undermine the justifications used by the
Soviet Union to place troops in East Germany.(51)

Some peace researchers like Afheldt have introduced concepts which might be applied specifically
to the West German Army, for instance the conversion
of the army into a defensive, decentralised and
technically well-equipped guerilla force. However,
his ideas were not well-received by decision-makers
in the army. None the less, some groups within the
peace movement regard them as a viable first step
towards the reduction of the threat of war and the
arms race, especially in view of the crucial role
which befalls the Federal Republic in American
military strategy.(52)

Another proposal by supporters of the peace

movement has been to convert the arms industry from
military to civilian production. Although there is
little evidence of widespread support for this idea
some works councils, for instance at the Bremen
Vulcan Wharf, have begun to think along these lines.
At the Blohm und Voss shipyard in Hamburg a working
group was formed and put forward specific proposals,
for example the design of a machine to dehydrate
bananas, and turn them into banana powder. This
would help Third World countries to save a large
part of their crop since 80 per cent is often destroyed by the warm climate. This working group comp-
ised only about twenty-five people who met regularly
to discuss these issues.(53) Supporters of the
peace movement were encouraged by a statement issued
by the congress of the metalworkers' union in 1980,
whose membership included 90 per cent of all workers who depended on the arms industry: this trade
union spoke out against the export of arms and
called instead for the 'preparation of the gradual
conversion from military to civilian production
on the basis of highly developed technologies'.(54)
It is unlikely, however, that similar proposals
would be accepted on a wider scale in country which
has become one of the leading exporters of weapons
in the world.
     One of the main characteristics of the Green
Movement is its desire for fundamental changes.
This attitude has been reinforced by the involvement
of members of the Protestant Church in the peace
movement. As I pointed out earlier, groups within
the Church exercised a powerful influence on the
formation of an alliance by hundreds of groups in
support of the rally in Bonn in October 1981. In
their appeal to this event they called for a
'nuclear-free Europe in which nuclear weapons are
neither produced, nor stored, nor used'.(55) Some
of their fundamental demands are undoubtedly utopian
and it is useful, in this context, to adopt the distinction made by Karl Mannheim between ideology and
utopia. Thus the demand for the total abolition of
nuclear weapons is utopian to the extent that it is
'situationally transcendant'.(56) It is not ideological since the human race has, until this century,
been able to secure peace without threatening the
(nuclear) destruction of the entire world, and by
the use of 'conventional' weapons. Mannheim himself
has written that certain demands are not ideological
'in the measure and in so far as they succeed through
counteractivity in transforming the existing historical reality into one more in accord with their own

conceptions'.(57)

The involvement of members of the Protestant Church in the peace movement today echoes the manner in which one of its earliest intellectual inspirers, Martin Luther, succeeded in 'transforming the existing historical reality' and fundamentally called into question the authority of the Roman Church. The opening speech at the Bonn rally in October 1981 was made by the Protestant pastor Heinrich Albertz in which he read out a list of questions which, in his opinion required an answer:

> Is it true that today a war in Europe means the destruction of our country and of all life? Is it true that defence is only possible at the cost of the destruction of all that which we have just built up? Is it also true that in an emergency no German can decide whether and when and which nuclear weapons are used? If all that is true, and I fear that no one can prove the contrary, what kind of security can the Superpowers offer the Federal Republic? Yes, naturally and deliberately I speak of the other side. Because in no other country in the world does war imply that one part of a people to which we still apparently belong, should kill off the other part as its first victim. These questions need to be asked. These questions have so far remained unanswered. We will not remain quiet until they are answered.(58)

Albertz and other prominent members of the Church impart a huge responsibility on the peace movement, namely to make people aware of the discrepancy between the millions of people who live on the border of starvation and the massive expenditure on arms throughout the world. It is not surprising that the ethical dimension of this discrepancy and the ethical problems posed by the threat of nuclear annihilation (as a basis for peace policy) should preoccupy members of the Church.

There is also a close link between the concern with fundamental questions and an apocalyptic vision of the world. It is interesting to note that among the Jews in the early Christian era, apocalyptic writing was highly popular, and it has emerged repeatedly throughout history in times of uncertainty, trouble and moral insecurity. The most famous piece of apocalyptic writing can be found in the Book of Revelations in the New Testament, and according to one theologian it should be understood as a 'tract of the times' which was written 'to increase the hope and determination of the Church on earth in a period of disturbance and bitter persecution'.(59) It is debatable whether the peace movement can be compared to the early Christian Church. However, in the minds of the activists within the movement they are living in a similar situation of disturbance and persecution. To this extent, their utopianism cannot easily be distinguished from ideology (in the manner described by Mannheim).

The peace movement has attracted a broad spectrum of political and ideological tendencies. The strongest elements are those based on a socialist and liberal tradition, although libertarianism and cultural pessimism also play a significant role. Same people have accused the movement of being subberted by Communists; however, even reports from the state security services have indicated that although Communists formed an activist minority there was no likelihood that they could impose their aims on it. (60) The intellectual inspirers of the Green Movement often regard it as a 'movement for survival which is broader than the working-class movement'(61) In reality most of the active support comes from well-educated, young, middle-class groups. None the less, the strength of support for the movement, particularly among trade unionists, has forced the SPD, especially in its role as an opposition party, to allow certain utopian ideas to re-emerge within it.

Even if large sections of the active supporters become disillusioned by the lack of fulfilment of their ideas, the issues they have raised will continue to play a significant role in West German politics. However remote or close the threat of nuclear war lies, people's lives are continually affected by the vast expenditure on arms and by the arguments which are used to justify this. To its credit the peace movement has reminded politicians of the urgent need to negotiate and work towards a reduction in nuclear weapons. The danger of its activity is that it may too often lapse into ideological distortions of the real situation and generate a polarisation of society which can only contradict the aim of taking steps towards disarmament. In addition, an exagerrated utopian view of the world will undermine the credibility of the movement, which seeks to take up the responsibility of the future of humanity. A fanatical belief in the peaceful nature of human beings can lead to disillusionment with non-violence when this quality is not manifested in human activity. Many activists in the movement point to the success of Mahatma Gandhi and Martin Luther King without giving due consideration to the context in which the activities of these two men took place, and to the powerful element of charismatic individualism which they had in common with each other. The fears and hopes of supporters of the peace movement are not born solely of an idealistic interpretation and perception of the world. The fear of unemployment, which is felt particularly strongly by those with a higher level of education,has contributed to a radicalisation of this layer of the population. This fear, as much as any doubts about the values of an affluent society and its materialism, has been channelled into 'peace politics'. The common denominator of the activities of the peace movement remains the opposition to the deployment of a new series of missiles in Western Europe. To some extent the basis for unity of the diverse groups remains very narrow; none the less, the potential of this issue to politicise broad layers of the population has grown immensely over the last few years.

NOTES

1. Aktion Suehnezeichen/Friedensdienste, Bonn 10.10.81 (Lamuv, Berlin, 1981), p. 200.

2. Bartolf, Etwas fuer den Frieden tun, p. 10.

3. C.Bartolf, Frieden schaffen ohne Waffen (unpublished seminar paper, Berlin, March 1982), pp. 2-3.

4. Ibid., p. 6.

5. Taz, 3 June 1981, p. 11.

6. Aktion Suehnezeichen, Bonn 10.10.81, p. 16.

7. Der Spiegel, Nr. 50, 1981, p. 99.

8. Taz, 18 June 1981.

9. Taz, 9 Oct. 1981, p. 4.

10. Taz, 25 May 1982, p. 9.

11. The lower figure was provided by the police, the higher one by the organisers of the rally.

12. Der Spiegel, Nr. 50, 1981, p. 99.

13. Ibid., Nr. 48, 1981, p. 63.

14. Ibid.

15. Ibid., p. 97.

16. Sueddeutsche Zeitung, 14 Oct. 1981.

17. Taz, 23 July 1981, p. 11.

18. Taz, 11 August 1981, p. 11.

19. Taz, 1 Sept. 1981, p. 11.

20. Taz, 3 Sept. 1981, p. 5, (speech by Vetter in Dortmund on 'Anti-war Day').

21. Taz, 18 Sept. 1981, p. 15.

22. Taz, 21 Sept. 1981, p. 5.
23. Letter from the Federal Secretary of the youth section of the union for print and paperworkers, in Taz, 22 Oct. 1981.
24. Taz, 13 Oct. 1981, p. 11.
25. Taz, 7 Oct. 1981, p. 5.
26. Die Zeit, 7 Dec. 1979.
27. Sueddeutsche Zeitung, 8 March 1982, and 17 March 1982.
28. Ibid., 17 Feb. 1982.
29. H.Scheer at a meeting organised by the E.F.Schumacher Gesellschaft in Munich, 2 Oct. 1981.
30. Taz, 31 Aug. 1981, p. 7.
31. Der Spiegel, Nr. 49, 1981, p. 106.
32. Ibid., p. 101.
33. Guardian, 29 Nov. 1982.
34. Der Spiegel, Nr. 48, 1981, p. 61.
35. Ibid., Nr. 6, 1983, p. 90.
36. W.von Bredow, 'Zusammensetzung und Ziele der Friedens-bewegung' in aus Politik und Zeitgeschichte, B24/82, p. 12.
37. Der Spiegel, Nr. 49, 1981, p. 101.
38. Ibid.
39. G.Schmid, 'Zur Soziologie der Friedensbewegung und des Jugendprotests' in aus Politik und Zeitgeschichte, B24/82, p.18.
40. Der Spiegel, Nr. 49, 1981, p. 103.
41. Aktion Suehnezeichen, Bonn 10.10.81, p. 82.
42. Ibid., p. 146.
43. Ibid., p. 135.
44. Ibid., p. 159.
45. Quoted in Taz, 9 Oct. 1981, pp. 10-11.
46. Guardian, 13 Oct. 1981, p. 15.
47. Ibid.
48. Taz, 23 Oct. 1981, p. 9.
49. Taz, 6 April 1982, p. 9.
50. Der Spiegel, Nr. 49, 1981, p. 94.
51. R.Bahro, 'Selbstmord fuer unsere Sicherheit' in Bremer Nachrichten, 23 March 1981, and quoted in Taz, 15 April 1981, p. 6.
52. Taz, 5 Aug. 1981, p. 9.
53. Taz, 9 Oct. 1981.
54. Taz, 31 July 1981, p. 9.
55. Aktion Suehnezeichen, Bonn 10.10.81, p. 7.
56. K.Mannheim, Ideology and Utopia (Routledge and Kegan Paul, London, 1979), p. 185.
57. Ibid., p. 176.
58. Aktion Suehnezeichen, Bonn 10.10.81, pp. 81-2.
59. A.Jones (ed.) The Jerusalem Bible (Darton, Longman and Todd, London, 1968), p. 320 (New Testament).
60. Schmid, 'Soziologie der Friedensbewegung', p. 17.
61. Aktion Suehnezeichen, Bonn 10.10.81, p. 138.

Chapter Eight

THE GREEN PARTY

This chapter examines the historic events surrounding the formation of a national Green Party which
occurred after the wave of protest against nuclear
power stations. These events provide an opportunity
to assess the manner in which a social movement
searches for new structures to ensure the continuity
of its aims. In the Green and Alternative parties
heterogeneous groups in the population that had
campaigned at a local level sought to guarantee the
continuity and success of the movement. The appearance of homogeneity at a local level and the absence
of more central organisations to further their protest, influenced many activists to try and form a
national Green Party. In addition, the formation of
a party appealed to supporters of the SPD who were
disappointed with the policies of the Social-Liberal
Government and who sought to introduce a greater
level of participation through party-political activity and not only through loosely-structured social
movement organisations.
    Once the Green Party had been formed, traditio-
nal political divisions between left- and right-wing
groups led to a series of debates and controversies
from which there emerged policies of a predominantly
left-wing complexion. None the less, there developed a conflict between those who were 'fundamentally'
concerned about the realisation of the aims and
ideas expressed by the Green Movement and those who
adopted a more pragmatic, radical approach to the
solution of various problems and towards the existing structures. This meant that the Green Party did
not assume the role of a central organisation which
represented the entire Green Movement. Other
umbrella organisations and the alternative press,
notably the Taz, made certain that the various
strands of the movement retained their autonomy.

The Green Party

The Green Party does, however, provide an important
structure for the movement, especially when the
momentum of its campaigning activity and 'spontaneity' shows signs of fatigue, and when its 'magical'
appeal begins to wear thin.

I   From mass movement to mass organisation

As I showed in Chapter Four a variety of groups and
individuals sought to organise the mass movement
against nuclear energy into various political parties
which scored successes in a series of state elections.   In October 1979 environmentalists met at
Offenbach to discuss the possibility of integrating
their ideas and social bases of support in a common
programme and organisation.   Over 1,000 delegates
attended this congress, including radical environmentalists from large cities like Berlin and Hamburg.
The latter were invited only as 'guests' and did not
have the right to vote at this congress.
      The first major controversy was sparked off by
a proposal which aimed to ban 'dual membership' in
the new party.   'Authentic' environmentalists like
the 'ecological' farmer Baldur Springmann, who had
proposed the motion, wanted to set themselves at a
clear distance from dogmatic communist groups that
had become involved in the campaign against nuclear
energy.   Herbert Gruhl, the former Christian Democrat MP, tended to support this proposal, but for
the first and by no means the last time he was
defeated over a major issue.   The Greens, although
they did not identify with the dogmatic communist
groups, wished to uphold the principle of freedom
for minorities to express their views.   For the
moment at least the issue of tolerance of dual
membership in both the Green Party and any other
political organisationswas resolved in a formal
manner.   This was an essential precondition for
unity to emerge among the diverse groups which met
at this congress.
      The delegates were wary of upsetting the pre-
carious balance between traditional conservative and
radical democratic elements, and they therefore
avoided any detailed discussions over a Green Programme.   After much debate they agreed that the party
would pursue 'ecological, social, grass-roots democratic and non-violent'policies.   These general aims
reflected the main principles which had determined
the activities of Citizens' Initiatives, although

trade unionists who attended the congress were not
entirely satisfied with this single clause which
summed up the aims of a Green Party.(1)
    A speech by Rudolf Bahro proved to be one of
the highlights of the meeting. He called for a
broad alliance 'for the emancipation of human beings'
and stressed that environmentalists and socialists
needed to learn from each other and join forces.
He called on socialists to abandon their narrow base
of a 'working class and trade union movement of the
traditional kind' and to take part in a 'psychological revolution' which was directed against the
capitalist mode of consumption.(2) He also declared
that he was in agreement with the assessment by
Gruhl of the catastrophic effects of industrialisation on the environment, even though they had both
arrived at similar conclusions from different
directions. Thus there was sufficient agreement
among the delegates at Offenbach to want to meet
again in Karlsruhe in January 1980.
    Between October 1979 and January 1980 member-
ship of the 'other political association', the
Greens, rose from 3,000 to 10,000. The new members
were represented by about 1,000 delegates at Karlsruhe. Again, the congress was split over the issue
of dual membership. Five-hundred-and-fourty-eight
delegates voted for, 414 against the banning of dual
membership. Delegates from Berlin, Hamburg, Hessen
and North Rhine Westphalia had voted against the
motion. Gruhl and Hasenclever (Baden-Wuerttemberg)
and Dinne (Bremen) were pleased with the vote; however, no applause could be heard since most people
did not want any 'vanquished'.
    Hasenclever, chairman of the Greens in Baden-
Wuerttemberg, explained that they did not want
'chaos and lack of concepts' and that people who
relied on violence would not be accepted into the
party. He added that the prospects of success for
the Greens in the forthcoming state elections in
Baden-Wuerttemberg were excellent.(3) Olaf Dinne,
who had been elected into the Bremen Parliament,
supported Hasenclever and justified the ban on dual
membership by referring to the psychology of voters
in the Federal Republic, who would want little to do
with a party that included members of communist
groups in its ranks. Left-wing ecologists found
that such an attitude contradicted the claim by the
Greens to be an 'alternative' to other parties and
organisations. It was clear that a compromise was
necessary if a united force was to emerge out of
this congress. Whilst some delegates criticised

the 'dissidents' for imagining that a party like the
Greens could exist without restrictions of membership qualification, others made offers of reconciliation. Hasenclever, for example, proposed that a
variety of working groups should be formed within
the party and their membership should include a wide
spectrum ranging from Christians to Communists.(4)
At any rate the motion on dual membership was modified by a majority of the congress: individual
regional or state groups would be free to formulate
their own statutes and thus, during an unspecified
period of transition, decide for themselves how to
tackle the problem of dual membership.

The new party statutes tried to show how the
Greens would be different to other organisations.
Large majorities voted in favour of structures which
would permit the Greens to be more open to social
movements. The formation of a federal executive
committee, composed of representatives from the
various states, was regarded as a protective measure
against over-centralisation. Paragraph 10 of the
statute aimed to secure the 'autonomy' of all groups
down to the lowest level. Posts in the executive
committee could not be held in conjunction with a
mandate in the European, State or Federal Parliaments.
It would require a two-thirds majority to allow any
exceptions to this rule. For the executive committee a 'rotating system' was devised, whereby half of
its members could be re-elected after a year in
office; re-election would only be permitted once.
Once again, it would require a two-thirds majority
vote by the assembly to allow any exceptions to this.
The executive would comprise seventeen members, and
women were supposed to be equally represented at all
levels.(5)

An attempt by Gruhl to have a programme hurriedly
accepted without much discussion was defeated; the
preamble on which the conservative, reformist and
socialist forces agreed upon, sealed an historic
occasion, the formation of a new party:

> The aim of the Green Alternative is to over-
> come social conditions, in which the short-
> term emphasis on economic growth, which only
> benefits part of the entire population, takes
> precedence over the ecological, social and
> democratic needs for life of humanity.(6)

In his speech at this founding congress, Bahro
stressed that the destiny of the party would 'depend
decisively on the level of its internal communication

and tolerance' since it had to unite 'elements from
heterogeneous origins'. Yet the events following
this congress did not portend well for the broad
alliance. At the end of January there was a bitter
dispute in Baden-Wuerttemberg between committed pro-
abortionists and others over the existing law on
abortion (paragraph 218). Initially a majority had
voted for the abolition of this law. However,
Hasenclever asked for the vote to be re-counted and
took the opportunity to warn the delegates that if
this motion were to be passed many conservative
members would leave the party. On the next count
the vote was reversed, much to the dismay and anger
of those who opposed the existing law on abortion.
They walked out of the meeting, but remained in the
party to try and reverse the vote at a more opportune
moment.(7)

On a regional level the Green Party reflected
the strength of the different factions in each area.
In Rhineland Palatinate for example, much more liberal and left-wing statutes were adopted, whilst in
Baden-Wuerttemberg the efforts by Hasenclever not to
frigthen away conservative voters culminated in a
success when, in the state elections in mid-March,
the Greens secured enough votes to enter, for the
first time, a parliament in a large state. Many
conservative voters had switched their vote from the
CDU to the Greens.

Following this success the Greens met at Saarbruecken in March 1980 to debate the formulation of
a party programme. The disucssion over an economic
programme ended in resounding victories for the Left
and the withdrawal of Gruhl as a candidate for the
executive committee. None the less, it was the
Centre-Left, represented by Petra Kelly, Norbert
Mann and August Haussleiter, rather than the far
Left that gained the majority in the elections to
the executive committee.

Gruhl withdrew his candidature following the
defeat of his proposals for economic policy and the
triumph of a list of demands which, in his opinion,
contradicted the attempt to save the natural environment from destruction, since they could only be
fulfilled if there was much more economic growth.
The economic demands included the following: a just
distribution of incomes in a system of production
based on needs and not on the realisation of profit;
the disentanglement of large enterprises into graspable units which are administered by the workers;
the introduction of a 35-hour working week without
a reduction in wages and without an increase in the

level of production; longer periods for training and
apprenticeships; a total ban on the export of nuclear
technology; a halt to the operation, construction
and planning of all nuclear power projects with the
aim of decentralising the supply of energy; and the
use of solar and wind power. Gruhl accused some of
the Greens of leading people to strive for more
power, prestige and property rather than upholding
spiritual values, and of having too much faith in
technology and technocratic solutions: 'This way of
thinking is linked with a great belief that anything
can be achieved and everything be put in order much,
much better than hitherto, with the introduction of
new laws, new organisations and new institutions'.
(8) He felt that in reality we find ourselves in a
world where it is only a question of preventing the
worst; and he was disappointed that the Greens had
undertaken a 'competition with promises, a competition that is mastered much better by the old parties'.
    According to Gruhl the polarisation over these
issues was not occurring between Left and Right but
between the supporters of materialist and spiritual
values. In fact traditional political divisions
appeared to determine conflicts not only over economic but also over social policy and foreign policy.
Some conservative ecologists were highly displeased
at the preoccupation of the congress with the rights
of women and of minorities; Baldur Springmann complained that the Greens had become a party that was
'mainly concerned with the rights of women and of
sexual minorities'.(9) Among other things he was
probably referring to the dispute over the law on
abortion. On this issue three alternative proposals
(with twenty-six amendments) were presented to the
delegates. A show of hands among the delegates
indicated that a majority were in favour of totally
rejecting paragraph 218; however, a compromise
solution was accepted, namely, that if pregnant
women who underwent an abortion were going to be
brought to court, then so too must the men who had
made them pregnant. There were no compromises over
the formulation of a foreign policy. Within a short
space of time a list of left-wing demands decorated
with ecological niceties was approved: the dissolution of the military blocks in East and West; an
end to the exploitation of raw materials in the
Third World by the industrialised countries; the
right to self-determination and to a decentralised,
ecological economy in the Third World countries; and
unilateral nuclear disarmament of the Federal Republic. The adoption of these policies accentuated the

polarisation between Left and Right. Thus, no sooner had the Green Party attempted to organise the utopian aspirations of the ecology movement, when it was accused by some of its own supporters of practising democratic centralism and using majority voting to impose binding decisions.(10)

II Internal conflicts and failure at the 1980 Federal Elections

The split between conservative and left-wing members was most striking in Schleswig-Holstein where the Saarbruecken Programme was accepted by a majority of only one vote. Moreover, in Baden-Wuerttemberg, more radical-democratic positions were accepted in what was considered to be a more conservative regional group. Three left-wing people were elected on to the executive committee which comprised fifteen people, including eight women. Here the Greens had fulfilled their promise by gaining over 5 per cent of the vote in the state elections. Following this success, they were not admitted as a 'fraction'since they did not have the required minimum of eight delegates. The Greens only occupied six out of the 124 seats in the parliament. However, they were granted all the rights of parliamentary initiative, in particular the right to introduce major inquiries, to call for immediate debates on important issues, and to present details of possible legislation. They also received a seat in the Council of Elders, payment for two scientific advisers and substantial amounts of money for office and other expenses. A sound infrastructure for the support of the Green Party and the extra-parliamentary movement was being established in one of the largest states in the Federal Republic.
    Yet despite their success in Baden-Wuerttemberg, there followed a series of disappointing results when in the state elections in the Saar (April) and in North Rhine Westphalia (May) the Greens only secured 2.9 per cent and 3 per cent of the vote respectively. Whilst they only had a small group of supporters in the Saar, the result was disappointing since this is an area which is seriously affected by the deterioration of the environment. It is interesting to note that in this state the SPD had come out in opposition to nuclear energy.(11) The result of the elections in North Rhine Westphalia supplied 'proof' to conservative members of the party that

their doubts about the Saarbruecken Programme were justified and the public had turned away from the Greens because of the unrealistic economic and social policies. Perhaps more significantly there was a marked contrast to previous elections in the amount of support from young people for the Greens. Whilst 10 per cent of them voted for the Greens, 50 per cent voted for the Social Democrats. The SPD had reacted swiftly to the success of the Greens in Baden-Wuerttemberg and its machinery for publicity had also been set in motion because of the forthboming Federal Elections (October 1980). A key issue in the Federal Elections was the personality of Franz-Josef Strauss who had been nominated by the Christian Democrats to contest the election. The SPD reminded young people of the threat posed by the Greens, to the extent that, if they secured sufficient votes, they could make it easier for Strauss to get into power.

The insecure basis of unity for the party was mirrored, on the Right, by the continued existence of Gruhl's old party, the Gruene Aktion Zukunft (GAZ), and on the Left, by the many alternative lists like the one in Tuebingen which supported the Greens but retained its autonomy as an independent organisation. In the communal elections in Baden-Wuerttemberg, the Greens and the alternative Bunte Liste competed separately in towns like Freiburg, even though there were no significant programmatic differences between the two groups.(12) Meanwhile members of GAZ met and decided not to dissolve their party, and to determine its future existence after the next congress of the Greens in Dortmund, where they hoped to amend some of the policies that had been agreed upon in Saarbruecken. At their meeting they complained that the word 'family' did not appear in the Saarbruecken Programme, and that the introduction of the 35-hour working week would cause problems with leisure time.(13) After the GAZ congress there emerged a definite split in Schleswig-Holstein where about 150 members left the Green Party because of the left-wing policies of the executive committee.(14) This represented a clear failure of the attempts to unite conservatives and radical left-wing groups. None the less, it would be misleading to suggest that the Left and the Right formed coherent groups and were themselves not divided, for instance over the extent to which they should make compromises during the election campaign, and once they had secured seats in parliaments.

So far, the Greens had not been able to present a coherent answer to the following question: how far could an ecologically-oriented economic policy be carried out in conjunciton with the preservation of jobs and the improvement of working conditions? A debate over this question was taking place only among certain intellectual circles and the columns of the Taz.(15) In addition, there was little time for such discussions to take place since the Federal Elections were going to be held in the same year as the Greens were founded as a party. They were thus drawn into the realm of 'high politics' even before they had either fully committed themselves or at least gained much experience in this sphere. Yet another conference was convened in Dortmund (June 1980) to clarify certain programmatic issues. Prior to the conference, the party executive committee declared that it aimed to prevent Strauss getting into power and, at the same time, did not regard the Social-Liberal coalition as a lesser evil. It rejected the claim made by some people that an economic policy guided by ecological principles would endanger the security of employment. However, it did not offer specific proposals and confined itself to statements like 'ecological politics means that we recognise ourselves and our environment as part of nature' and 'we are dependent on the natural bases of life if we wish to live'.(16) The executive committee went on to announce that although trade unions had 'given up' the struggle to change the conditions of production, the Greens would support grass-roots initiatives within them.

At the Dortmund Conference the Greens agreed on a platform which would enable both the Left and the Right of the party to unite in the forthcoming elections. A motion condemning fascism was proposed by the Alternative List from Berlin but was then modified into a resolution which criticised both capitalism and 'real existing socialism' in Eastern Europe. Greater emphasis was laid on ecological aspects of economic policy. However, the conflict over this issue threatened to destroy the fragile basis for unity when groups from Schleswig-Holstein and Bremen called for the replacement of the Saarbruecken Programme by the more 'ecological' Electoral Programme. When the majority of delegates rejected this proposal, the group from Bremen called a press conference and declared that it could no longer, 'under these conditions', take part in the Federal Elections, since the Saarbruecken Programme had not passed the test of the state elections in North Rhine Westphalia. Gruhl declared his support for this group of dissidents but resolved not to take any further action until GAZ had met to discuss the matter. When Gruhl did stand for election to the executive committee he failed to gain enough support, and many delegates were surprised that he got as many as 371 votes. An editorial in the Taz praised the delegates for renouncing 'prominent figures' and 'tactical calculations' in favour of a 'relationship to the grass roots', and for their attempt to become a political force 'without bending to the dominant structures of the media and consciousness'.(17) On this occasion the Taz, one of the filters of opinion within the Green Movement, approved of the development of the Green Party; it had endorsed emphatically the idea of the 'charisma of the group' rather than the 'charisma of individual personalities'.

One of these charismatic personalities was Olaf Dinne from Bremen, who repeatedly angered the alternative Left. When a narrow majority in Bremen(52:46) decided to participate in the Federal Elections, Dinne announced that he would work in an alliance with 'purely ecological circles' around Gruhl and Springmann.(18) The latter had plans to form an 'Ecological Federation' independent of the Greens. Dinne was therefore criticised by Bahro for seeing things too much in terms of electoral and power strategies instead of an ideological process which undermines party borders.(19) This critique by Bahro suggests that the early success of the Greens in Bremen may have distorted the assessment by the movement of its best strategy - at least at this early stage.

The executive committee of the Greens appeared to share Bahro's view that they should concentrate on ideological processes rather than on trying to overcome the 5 per cent electoral hurdle in the Federal Elections. Dieter Burgmann, from the executive committee, declared that 'percentage figures are not what counts' and that the main aim was 'not to get into parliament but to introduce changes'. Petra Kelly explained that a national Green Party allowed them to make topical certain themes which could not be considered at a regional level, for instance the role of NATO.(20) Moreover, most supporters of the Green Movement had not got used to the idea of competing for power at national elections. Others, disillusioned with 'democratic centralist tendencies' (Heinz Brandt) within the Greens, called on the public to vote for the SPD in order to prevent

Strauss from getting into power.(21)

Regional differences also accounted for conflicts within the Green Party during the election campaign. For instance in Hamburg there was much greater emphasis than in other areas on the problems of marginal groups and alternative subcultures. This led to criticism from members of the party with a trade union background who stressed that the underprivileged and those who worked in factories still faced serious social problems; and who sought to maintain the support of Gruhl and Dinne.(22) The Greens in Hamburg replied that they were not primarily motivated by electoral considerations. Their leading candidate, Corny Littmann, drew a distinction between personalitites like Gruhl, Dinne and Springmann who pursued an 'individualist form of politics' and those who were concerned with the group of 'ordinary members'. The latter, he claimed, had allowed themselves to be duped by individual charismatic figures:

> To some extent, the fact that the ordinary
> party members allowed these people to make
> statements on behalf of the party had a
> self-destructive effect. We were all so
> naive and credulous and did not expect these
> people to turn against the party if they
> did not get a majority for their policies.(23)

It is thus not the charisma of individual figures but rather of the 'group of ordinary members' which is a major force of motivation within the Green Party at this stage of its development. Yet the sanctity of the 'group of ordinary members' served the purpose of certain factions within the party to discredit their political opponents. The idea of the charisma of the group does not prevent individual members of the group from becoming the representatives of it. There is little doubt that most people who support the idea of the importance of the group rather than of individual prominent figures are sincere in this belief. This sincerity does not reduce the amount of conflict within the Green Party which, in its state of inexperience, failed badly at the Federal Elections, not only to gain votes but even to make certain themes topical.

The widespread support for the Greens in the state elections vanished at the Federal Elections. The Greens had been unable to formulate credible alternatives in two significant spheres: foreign or 'peace' policy and economic policy. Overall they

only received about 1.5 per cent of the total vote.
In Baden-Wuerttemberg, for instance, they had gained
more than 5 per cent in the state elections, whilst
they only secured 1.8 per cent at the Federal Elections. In North Rhine Westphalia their share of the
vote dropped from 3 per cent to 1.2 per cent, and
in Bremen from 5 per cent to 2.7 per cent. Two of
the main reasons for this loss of support were the
controversies at a regional level and the failure
to unite in a convincing manner traditional conservative positions with radical socialist ones. The
polarisation between Schmidt and Strauss prompted
many people to vote for either of the major parties
rather than 'waste' their vote on the Greens who had
little prospect of getting into power or of forming
a coalition with another party. The poor result may
also be related to the phenomenon which is familiar
in Britain, of people who are willing to support a
minor party in a by-election but then rally to the
major parties at a national election. Nevertheless
this does not explain fully the fact that, within a
few weeks of their defeat, 30 per cent of the population thought that the Greens ought to be represented
in parliament. The membership of the party continued to rise and by December 1980 they had 19,000
members.(24) Far from being a spent force the Green
Party, in the period after the Federal Elections,
emerged much stronger. This is related, above all,
to two factors: firstly, the politicisation of the
issue of peace and nuclear weapons on West German
soil, and secondly, the solid progress which Green
and Alternative parties had made in convincing the
public of their seriousness of purpose and sense of
responsibility at a communal level. The first
factor signalled a new phase in the capacity of the
Greens to make topical a significant issue; and the
second factor had ensured that, despite any setback
in a Federal Election, the Greens had secured a
reliable base of support in certain regions where
there was much disaffection with the established
parties.

III Success at a communal level

The issues which attracted the support of people at
a communal level and which secured votes for Green
and Alternative Lists included the following: 1) the
opposition to nuclear energy and to other major projects which were regarded as a threat to the environ-

168

ment; 2) criticism of local policies of modernisation and restoration, particularly in the sphere of housing; 3) efforts to improve facilities for young people and to encourage alternative cultural activities; 4) the criticism of party patronage, especially by the SPD, in large towns and cities; 5) the support for the rights of women and minority groups.(25)

The results of the communal elections that followed the 1980 Elections show that when the Greens and other environmentalist groups campaign against certain projects and for the 'living world' or 'world of life' on a local level they are capable of gaining a significant proportion of the vote. As in the European Elections in 1979, the best results were achieved in areas where local opposition to specific projects was combined with the support of young, well-educated protestors from nearby university towns and cities. Moreover, they increased their vote in some areas over a period of several years. In the Hessian communal elections (March 1981) the support for the Greens in Ruesselheim rose from 5.6 per cent to 16.5 per cent; and in Darmstadt from 8 per cent to 10 per cent. In nearly all the major towns and cities in Hessen they gained more than 5 per cent of the vote. In the communes around Frankfurt Airport they reached 25 per cent in Moerfelden-Walldorf and in Buettelborn, 16 per cent in Ruesselheim, 15 per cent in Kelsterbach and 13 per cent in Gross-Gernau.

In the communal elections in Lower Saxony (September 1981) nearly 1,000 local councillors and about 130 members of local parliaments were elected as representatives of the Green Movement. Overall the Greens and other environmentalist groups gained 6 per cent of the vote, whilst the CDU gained an absolute majority (50.1 per cent) and the SPD suffered heavy losses, from 45 per cent (in the previous communal elections) to 37 per cent. Again, local opposition to specific projects in rural areas combined with support from urban protest groups led to successes for the environmentalists. In the area around Gorleben they achieved the following results: Luechow-Dannenberg, 18 per cent; Trebel, 42 per cent; Gartow, 23 per cent; and in Friesland, Wittmund and Ammerland they increased their share of the vote in comparison to previous elections. In Friesland, for example, their share of the vote rose from 7.4 per cent to 11.3 per cent. Out of the 13 electoral districts, the Greens were represented in nine.(26) In the communal elections in Schleswig-Holstein (March 1982) the Greens gained 5.5 per cent of the

overall vote, the SPD dropped from 40.5 per cent to
36.8 per cent, the CDU rose from 49.2 per cent to
50.1 per cent and the FDP rose from 6.3 per cent to
6.8 per cent. In all large towns and cities the
Greens acquired between 5 per cent and 10 per cent.

In all these elections the Green and Alternative
Lists gained votes especially from the SPD, although
they made gains at the expense of the three big
parties in rural areas where there was a particular
project which was perceived as a threat to the
'world of life'. The increasing appeal of the Greens
for members and supporters of the SPD and FDP was
also encouraged by the predominance of left-wing
positions within the new party especially in relation to environmentalism, peace politics and the
emphasis on participatory politics. There was bitter
disappointment at the failure of the SPD to take a
lead over these issues.

The participation by the Left within the Green
Party in communal politics signals a shift away from
the traditional mistrust of parliamentary practices
and mainstream politics by sections of the extra-
parliametary movements. The commitment to politics
on a communal level is regarded as an opportunity to
deal with the needs of the population especially in
the sphere of reproduction. These needs include the
desire 'for sufficient and humane living space, for
educational and health care, for possibilities for
relaxation and communication, for local means of
travel and shopping facilities, for the preservation
and improvement of the environment'.(27) Involvement in communal politics offers an opportunity to
'integrate' the various groups within the Green
Movement, for example women's groups, environmentalist groups, alternative and media projects, groups
concerned with the welfare of guest workers and
their children, and groups working in the sphere of
community medicine.(28) This kind of integration is
not regarded as co-optation but as the 'creation of
a larger context' which has long-term aims. Above
all, political commitment to local politics is
regarded as an opportunity to influence people on
issues which the national media cannot 'manipulate'
in the usual manner. The local press is not regarded as a threat since it 'could not, even if it
wanted to, manipulate people's consciousness in a
corresponding manner'. The alternative Left feels
that, because it has more active supporters than
the established parties, it can more easily and
effectively conduct 'politics on a small scale'
where people are 'more important than the media in

spreading demands and ideas'.(29) Undoubtedly,
communal politics do not offer enough scope to more
talented politicians and the Left thus feels that at
this level it can rely on the fact that 'one is
confronted by fairly stupid opponents'.(30)

This section of the Left has clearly been
inspired by the philosophy of the Spontis rather
than Marxist theory. It bemoans the lack of imagination and spontaneity within the Left. It believes
that at a local level it can more easily present
'concrete utopias' - a term used by Ernst Bloch -
for instance in town planning, housing policy and
'human' communication.(31)

Reports on the activities of these groups at
a communal level indicate that much communication
does take place between the local population and the
new initiatives, especially when the former feel
that specific interests have been neglected by the
established parties. In Eimsbuettel, Hamburg, the
alternative Bunte Liste was approached by a variety
of social groups which sought help over a wide range
of issues. The population in Eimsbuettel comprised
around 200,000 people. In this district, co-
peration took place between the Bunte Liste and
groups of people who were 'directly affected' by
planning decisions which threatened their living
and recreational space.(32) There are indications
of a new emphasis by the Green Party to communicate
its policies to the population rather than simply to
present the 'correct' ideological position and of
a willingness to carry out discussions with the
public. This had been a feature of the campaign
against nuclear energy when, in thousands of neighbourhoods, discussions took place between activists
and ordinary citizens over the dangers of nuclear
power stations.

There is a genuine desire among people who work
in communal politics to gain knowledge and expertise
since it appears to be the level on which grass-
roots democracy can best be fulfilled within the
parliamentary system. This is particularly important
because the newly-elected parliamentarians are highly
sensitive about criticisms that allude to a loss of
contact with the grass roots and with the Citizens'
Initiatives. Delegates are therefore anxious to
to stress the advantages of work in the local
parliaments, for instance: access to information
which might serve the extra-parliamentary movement;
improved contact with the media; and more financial
resources which can be used to finance 'the flow of
information between the parliamentary fraction and

the grass roots and Citizens' Initiatives'.(33)
	Among the main disadvantages experienced by the
Green Parties was the lack of power and influence at
a local level since communal parliaments act more as
administrative organs of control rather than bodies
which take important policy decisions. Thus, when
the Green List in Moerfelden-Walldorf gained 25 per
cent of the vote in the Hessian communal elections,
it did not hesitate to call for greater 'decentral-
isation' and for 'autonomy' of the commune; to propose that the supply of electricity should come from
a smaller local power station rather than from the
massive nuclear power station at Biblis; and to suggest that intermediate and small-scale business
should be encouraged in the locality in order to
reduce the reliance on the city of Frankfurt.(34)
	The main preoccupation of the environmentalists
in this commune, however, was to prevent the extension of Frankfurt Airport. To achieve this aim, it
supported the idea of a plebiscite among the population of Hessen. This idea forms part of a belief in
communal 'direct democracy' and is also propagated
by the Greens outside the boundaries of Hessen. In
Bavaria, for example, the Greens supported a campaign
to introduce plebiscites to decide on controversial
issues like the planned airport at Edinger-Moss near
Munich.(35) In Baden-Wuerttemberg proposals were
made in the state parliament in favour of greater
participation by local communities in decision-
making processes (Buergerentscheide).(36) These
populist demands for an increase in the powers of
communal organs and for plebiscitary rule form part
of an effort to 'remain close' to the ordinary citizens, to the Citizens' Initiatives since, despite
all good intentions, a gap has developed between
some who have taken up positions in parliaments and
local councils and others who are working at the
grass roots.
	The gap between elected representatives and
supporters from heterogeneous groups has, to some
extent, been bridged by the idea that they are all
defending specific communities, or the 'world of
life', against technocracy and the 'arrogance of
power'. Thus in Moerfelden-Walldorf the Green List
campaigned 'against the arrogance of power - for an
environment worth living in'. According to a member
of the Greens in the area, this slogan formed the
core of the electoral alliance and 'hit upon the
mood of the population'.(37) The leading candidates
of the Greens in that area were a farmer, a veterin-
ary surgeon, followed by more farmers, teachers,

post office officials and schoolchildren.(38) Here,
as in many other areas, the local branches of the
established parties were also opposed to specific
local projects which were regarded as a threat to
the environment. Yet the Greens were regarded as
more consistent and lacking in contradictions over
this theme. This was not surprising since they had
nowhere been called upon to show how the defence of
the world of life can be carried out in specific
political practice.

Members and supporters of the Greens do try and
differentiate between what they desire and what is
possible in practice. Thus, one of their leading
delegates, Norbert Kostede, accepts that 'if communal politics wants to be successful, it must set itself limits', since he tends towards the view that
the scale and complexity of social problems is
increasing, whilst the political resources needed to
solve them are becoming more and more scarce. However, he soon shifts his attention to the favourite
theme of the protest movement, namely the efforts to
rescue the world of life in the city. He suggests
that an alternative communal policy should be based
on co-operation with 'influential projects' which
are supported by urban protest groups and Citizens'
Initiatives; they would help to bring about 'self-
organisation and self-administration' in communal
politics and to organise 'plebiscitary elements'.
This would all form part of an effort to overcome
the 'apocalypse of the city' which is characterised
by the adoption of nuclear technology in densely-
populated areas, the 'usual suicide' of private
transport, the 'brutality' of underground railways
and the 'individual isolation' experienced by residents of the city.(39) Another supporter of the
Greens uses similar imagery to describe the 'situation in Frankfurt', where people have been 'driven
out' of the city centre by 'large banks, huge
department stores and offices for administration'.
(40) The defence of the world of life against a
centralised, technocratic and 'inhuman' administration (which, at the time, was equated with the
Social-Liberal Alliance) is one of the most significant issues that mobilises the population to support
the Greens.

In response to this wave of support, many within the party have tried to work out realistic concepts for alternative policies at a communal level.(41)
Yet in order to maintain the support of the new
movements, they reproduce and embellish certain
images about the existing social structures and

institutions and about the damage to the world of
life which has been caused by 'industrial civilisation'. Thus they are more lucid in their critique of
the deterioration of the urban environment, especially large cities, rather than of the relations in
the sphere of production. Those who become involved
in the routine work in parliaments and in local
administrative organs appear to realise that the
only way to improve social conditions, to prevent
any further destruction of communities, is to provide workable, modest alternatives. They often find
it difficult to reconcile this insight with the
belief of many activists and other participants in
the Green Movement that the entire system 'stinks'
and that it is totally corrupt.

IV The uneasy rapport between fundamentalist,
    utopian and pragmatic tendencies

The creation of a Green Party organisation brought
to the surface some of the contradictions which
remained hidden as long as the Green Movement was
only a mass social movement. The range of themes
and concepts that had helped to unify the mass movements, particularly the search for fundamental and
utopian alternatives to technocratic society, shaped
the formation of different factions within the party.
        I have already alluded to the leftward shift
within the Green Party and the dissatisfaction which
was expressed by Gruhl and others with the economic
demands that were made at the Saarbruecken congress.
In the 1981 communal elections in Lower Saxony,
supporters of Gruhl stood against candidates of the
Green Party in a number of communes. They were unable to secure many votes, whilst the official Green
Party was able to attract a respectable number of
voters. Gruhl's GAZ party and several other groups
went on to found the Oekologisch-demokratische
Partei (Ecological Democratic Party). None the less,
the criticism by Gruhl of some of the Greens'
demands was taken up repeatedly by some members in
Bremen. They belong to what I will describe as the
pragmatic tendency that rejects utopian demands, and
therefore came into conflict with other sections of
the party.
        Although the Green List in Bremen dissociated
itself from the Green Party at the 1980 Federal
Elections, the dispute is important because it highlights the difficulties which arise in attempts to

reconcile practical reforms with utopian and fundamentalist concepts. The two other tendencies within
the party can be described as the Spontis who
wish to form a 'fundamental opposition' based on
support from the grass roots and Citizens' Initiatives; and the radical reformists who put forward
'concrete utopian alternatives'. The uneasy rapport
between these tendencies can be assessed in relation
to: the attempts to combine grass-roots democracy
and professional politics; social and economic policies; and parliamentary democracy, peace politics
and the monopoly of violence by the state.

(i) Grass-roots democracy and professional politics

In the 1978 state elections in Hamburg the Bunte
Liste understood itself as an 'alliance of Citizens'
Initiatives and grass roots initiatives'. It resolved that its activity in the communal parliaments
would be determined by 'the aims and activities'
of these groups.(42) Yet after two and a half years
of work in the Eimsbuettel district parliament some
delegates described how difficult it was for grass-
roots democracy to work in practice because the
ordinary supporters of the party did not attend
'voters' meetings' in sufficient numbers.(43) Others
reflected on the naivety of their initial approach,
founded on the belief that they could cope with work
in a parliament simply by propagating the 'aims and
activities' of their bases of support.(44) Instead
they had to face situations in which it was difficult to reconcile the aims of different Citizens'
Initiatives which had their own particular interests.
For instance in Eimsbuettel, two Citizens' Initiatives were formed when plans were announced to reduce
the volume of traffic on a particular road. One
initiative, composed of residents from that road,
supported these plans; the other, which comprised the
residents from a nearby road, opposed them because
the traffic would partly be diverted on to 'their'
road.(45) This led to the following insight: there
was a need for the formulation of plausible concepts
and concrete proposals for city and traffic planning
to encourage local public transport. At any rate,
once it had been elected into the local parliament,
the advice and help of the Bunte Liste was sought by
a variety of social groups, and not only those from
grass-roots initiatives.(46) Thus it began to adopt
a more pragmatic radical reformist approach.
    In Hamburg, however, there was - at least init-
ially, a strong tendency in favour of fundamentalist

opposition rather than radical reformism. Both in
1980 (during the Federal Elections)(47) and in 1982
(during the state elections) in Hamburg, the Greens
and the Green Alterntive List (GAL) declared that
they were the 'parliamentary arm of the grass-roots
movements'. To avoid the danger of 'alienation
from the extra-parliamentary movement' and from its
own base of support the GAL declared in 1982 that
they would be allowed the 'maximum possibilities to
influence and participate in the formation of opinions within the GAL'.(48) The Bunte Liste in Bielefeld criticised the abstract nature of the idea that
the Greens could act as the 'parliamentary arm of
grass-roots initiatives and Citizens' Initiatives'.
(49) It admitted that without these initiatives the
Bunte Liste could not have won an election. However,
it presents a more sober assessment of the relationship to the initiatives after two years of work in
the city parliament:

> the Bunte Liste was forced very quickly to
> work out its own position on a series of
> important communal-political issues and, to
> a certain extent, to practise 'representat-
> ive' politics by becoming the executor of
> the interests of those who are directly
> affected. Ideological purity would only
> have been preserved if one did not have an
> opinion on many important questions and had
> given up nearly all political initiatives.(50)

The same author argues that those who are directly
affected by planning and other decisions, for example
old people, are not always capable of taking action
and that a Green List was 'inevitably more' than
'the addition of the individual interests' of the
various initiatives. This tendency towards pragmatic
radical reformism arose whenever the Greens entered
parliaments.
    In addition, the Greens have shown a keen inte-
rest in learning about the institutions they have
entered and the bureaucratic apparatus. In several
instances, they have developed a working relationship with the SPD and have secured some concessions.
At the same time, they have attempted to uphold some
of the principles of the broader movement from which
they gain their support, for instance by making it
difficult for individuals to accumulate power and
offices. Members of Parliament are expected to
keep only a small part of their salaries for themselves and to channel the rest of the money into the

party for various projects and initiatives.

One method of trying to ensure that leading figures do not dominate the party is to apply the 'principle of rotation' which requires delegates to give up their seat in a parliament after two years. In Baden-Wuerttemberg, the first large state in which the Greens were represented in a parliament, the delegates argued successfully that this was an impractical measure since, over a two-year period, a great deal of useful knowledge and experience had been acquired, and that it was therefore not sensible to replace them. Similarly, at the party congress in Hagen (November 1982) members of the executive committee like Petra Kelly and Dieter Burgmann argued that because of their experience and knowledge they should be allowed to retain their posts until the Federal Elections in March 1983. On this occasion the ordinary party members were not prepared to accept a contravention of the principles of grassroots democracy. This showed the scepticism with which party activists view those who work for the party. As soon as someone does distinguish either himself or herself in their work for the party, that person becomes vulnerable to the charge of being greedy for power. The fact that individuals like Petra Kelly are regarded as prominent figures by the media and the population at large is often seen as a threat to the sanctity of the group.

Many people realise that a strict adherence to the principles of grass-roots democracy is not possible if the Greens are to assume the responsibility of taking and influencing decisions in politics. A member of the party in the state parliament in Baden-Wuerttemberg declared that 'whoever wants to change existing conditions, must develop a relationship to power'.(51) Others stressed that the Greens had to accept the idea of delegation of power(52), and of the need for qualified people to deal with the complex institutional and bureaucratic apparatus.(53) The lack of consensus over these issues can finally be illustrated by the varying attitudes to the question of an 'imperative mandate', whereby a delegate must give up his or her seat in a parliament if called upon to do so by the grass-roots membership. The GAL in Hamburg declared that its MPs would be bound by this principle so that they could be controlled effectively by the members.(54) However, in Baden-Wuerttemberg a parliamentary delegate of the Greens dismissed such 'dreams' of an imperative mandate since most people were not interested in continual political activity, and explained that

this was 'really the reason why the lofty principles
of grass-roots democracy clash with reality'.(55)
The same person argued that it was hardly possible
for ordinary members to pursue their delegates all
over a large state like Baden-Wuerttemberg in order
to ensure that they were upholding party policies
and that even in large towns and cities only a select
number of people can take part regularly in such an
exercise.

(ii)   Economic and social policies

The Green Party has experienced the greatest difficulty in reaching agreement on economic and social
policies, and this has prevented it from broadening
the bases of its support. The conflict over these
issues among the heterogeneous founding groups of
the party led to the withdrawal of conservative elements. In Bremen, the Green List was split when
Olaf Dinne angered alternative groups by rejecting
their demand for one million marks to finance their
own 'communication centre' in the Ostertor district.
Dinne felt that state subsidies would only encourage
economic growth which the Greens had originally set
out to oppose.(56) He made the distinction between
the 'consumptive' and 'investive' parts of the budget
and was opposed to the latter since it would stimul-
ate economic growth.(57) In addition, he was
opposed to the new 'communication centre' since it
would, in his opinion, turn the district into a
ghetto for students and guest workers. Therefore he
supported a conservative Citizens' Initiative that
wanted to clean up that district to prevent it from
turning into a slum. He reproached the alternative
groups for making 'egoistic' demands and failing to
try and achieve a broad alliance with conservative
groups based on an opposition to the deterioration
of the environment and to economic growth. Above
all, Dinne felt that the Green Party had made excessive demands for the expansion of welfare services
which could only be financed by more economic growth,
and that this would alienate the middle-class supporters of the Green Movement.(58)
     When the Greens met to discuss the possibility
of formulating a coherent economic policy in June
1982, pragmatic, radical-reformist and fundamentalist tendencies could not agree on a common approach.
The delegates from Berlin explained why they had
published a short-term 'employment programme', since
it had been necessary to formulate some specific
alternatives for the public. The Greens from Hessen

repudiated this concept with the argument that they did not wish to 'repair the capitalist system', even though they went on to approve a short-term 'employment programme' themselves once they had entered the state parliament. Delegates from Hamburg, Hessen and North Rhine Westphalia acknowledged that their aim to 'socialise' large enterprises and bring them under self-management by the workers might only be fulfilled in the distant future; none the less, these demands featured prominently in their respective programmes. In contrast, the Greens from Baden-Wuerttemberg were in favour of a more liberal economic system and proclaimed the right to private property of all kinds as set out in the Federal Constitution.(59) Others, like Bahro, desire both fundamental changes and concrete utopian alternatives, but are critical of the demands which could imply an increase in economic growth since this would lead to a further deterioration of the environment. However, he had not antagonised the alternative scene in the manner of Dinne because he had been much more careful to play down his role as an intellectual inspirer and charismatic leader of the movements, despite the attempts by the press to identify him as a leading figure. Bahro as well as others who find themsleves in a similar position repeatedly emphasize the importance of the 'group' and of 'collective leadership'.

Bahro, who was elected on to the executive committee of the party in November 1982, has accused some delegates of being far too 'reformist' and of nurturing the 'illusion which is spread by Erhard Eppler, namely that ecology and economy - the existing economic system - can in some way be reconciled'. (60) Some delegates have in fact proposed that environmentalist aims can be reconciled with economic growth in particular spheres. Thus the idea of 'qualitative growth' has been favoured both by some groups within the Green Party and environmentalists within the SPD like Erhard Eppler. These groups tend, as I showed in an earlier chapter, to have great faith in technology to solve existing problems and to set us on the path to utopia.

The GAL in Hamburg has proposed that new power stations could be built 'according to the latest technology' to reduce noise, poisonous fumes and dust.(61) It called for 'an immediate programme to clean the air by the introduction of the most modern technology for environmental protection'.(62) The reduction of noise in machinery, at its source, is regarded as 'largely unproblematic from the techni-

cal point of view'.(63) The leading candidate of
the Greens in Hamburg in the 1980 Federal Elections
felt that 'if there was really intensive research'
in the sphere of alternative energy, it would only
be 'a question of a few years before one had found
such carriers of energy'.(64)

The Greens point out that existing technology
is dominated by the interests of large-scale centralised enterprises and there is a lack of social
control over the economic process.(65) Instead of
proposing a specific alternative they call on working people to 'work out their own path'. This is
hardly surprising since the Greens have found it
difficult to define 'social usefulness'. The aim
of the GAL in the sphere of production is to introduce a 'conscious planning of needs'. This would,
in theory, occur democratically since workers would
be able to decide on their own working conditions
and on the types of product that are 'socially useful'. The producers would consult the consumers
about their needs.(66) This does imply that they
are in favour of 'co-operative' ideas and practices.
The Hamburg electricity supply industry would be
controlled and directed politically by the local
population. New housing projects would only be permitted if the owners agreed to link them up to decentral forms of electricity supply.(67) We are
given few hints about how these utopian demands and
plans can be realised without the emergence of a
massive bureaucratic apparatus.

To support their proposals for a 35-hour working week without a reduction in wages and for an
expansion of welfare services (including an increase
in unemployment benefit) the Greens have made some
pragmatic radical suggestions. In Hamburg for
instance, the GAL hoped to finance these and other
measures by increasing taxes on profits and on those
with high incomes; reducing subsidies for the expansion of the harbour and the airport; refusing to
build a new headquarters and various smaller stations
for the police; and intensifying efforts to prosecute tax-evaders, particularly in the sphere of
business.(68) It is striking, however, that they
should call for greater efforts to uncover tax-
evasion and to 'criminalise all property speculation'
(69), whilst at the same time opposing plans to
improve the efficiency of the Hamburg police. This
reflects, once again, the difficulties encountered
by the Greens in their efforts to reconcile pragmatic reforms with the assumptions that underlie some
of their fundamentalist attitudes and utopian ideas.

(iii) Parliamentary democracy, peace politics and
      the monopoly of violence by the state

The Green Party was formed on the basis of the
strength of the ecology movement; however, the emergence of a powerful peace movement enabled it to
argue that it was concerned with more than just a
single issue. The close co-operation between the
Greens and the ecology movement was extended into
the peace movement. Within countless initiatives
there was a switch from a campaign against nuclear
power stations to one against nuclear weapons. The
executive committee of the party, aware of its inability to politicise the issue of peace, on its own
terms, in the 1980 elections, was quick to seize the
opportunity offered by the growing campaign against
the placement of more nuclear missiles in West Germany.
      The demand for unilateral nuclear disarmament
had been accepted by the Saarbruecken congress at a
time when there appeared little prospect of a widespread campaign against nuclear weapons. In February
1981 the executive committee of the party presented
a detailed programme of activities for that year.
At a congress in October 1981 the Greens formulated
a peace manifesto, although this did not prevent
differences of opinion between radical pacifists and
pragmatic reformers from rising to the surface.(70)
In Baden-Wuerttemberg the Greens supported concepts
like 'social defence' and the abandonment of 'first-
strike' weapons, but there was no unified policy on
how to bring about the reduction of nuclear weapons.
Nevertheless there was a growing tendency to modify
claims for immediate unilateral disarmament and
withdrawal from NATO. The programme of the GAL in
Hamburg (1982) called for a 'process' of withdrawal
from NATO, and 'step-by-step' disbandment of the
armed forces.(71)
      Unanimity existed, however, over the total re-
jection of the Pershing and Cruise missiles. The
Greens were also unambiguous in their rejection of
Soviet medium-range missiles and called on both East
and West to disarm. When Brezschnew visited Bonn
in November 1981 the Greens supported a protest in
support of disarmament and greater political freedom
in Eastern Europe. Similarly, when Reagan visited
West Berlin the Alternative List supported a protest
rally against the United States government, although
it soon found itself in an awkward position because
the demonstration had been banned by the authorities.
      When violence resulted from this demonstration

the Alternative List was blamed for it, even though
it did not condone violence. None the less, it had
refused to distance itself from the violent demonstrators since it believed that the police and the
authorities were as much to blame for the violence
on the streets.(72) In some regions the Greens
would have distanced themselves from the violent
demonstrations in an unequivocal manner. In Berlin,
the potential for conflict and the strength of the
militant squatters prevented agreement over this
issue.

Support for the squatters' movement by the
Greens was not confined to Berlin. In the Baden-
Wuerttemberg state parliament they were the only
party to support people who were evicted from the
Schwarzwaldhof in Freiburg, a disused building which
had been occupied by squatters in June 1980.(73)
Nevertheless, Berlin did become the bastion of the
squatters' movement, and as one journalist from the
Taz pointed out, 'the few hundred activists of the
Alternative List are perhaps to a greater extent
than anywhere else only a small part of the protest
movement'. He commented that arduous discussions
had revealed that part of the AlternativeList was
not prepared to go along with every 'twist and turn'
in the squatters' movement and was therefore demand-
ing a more critical attitude towards it. However,
another group within the Alternative List, namely
those who had been influenced by the ideas of the
Spontis, called this an act of betrayal.(74) When
violence did arise, the Alterntive List was not prepared to distance itself from the demonstrators for
the reasons mentioned earlier. This posed problems
for it during the 1981 elections to the Berlin
Senate. The fundamentalist wing of the party was
less concerned with exercising direct influence in
parliament but expected 'some fun occasionally, and
now and again, the chance to be able to go to the
public with certain political issues'. However, the
current of political events forced the Alternative
List to think in terms of practical political
alternatives and the massive tendency to abstain
from elections, as on previous occasions, was not
even present in the squatters' movement.(75)

In an interview in Der Spiegel Petra Kelly dis-
agreed strongly with the interviewer who suggested
that parliamentary democracy implies the ability to
enter coalitions and make compromises; she felt that
parliamentary democracy had to accept a 'fundamentalist anti-war party' and an 'ecological non-violent
party' which does not enter any coalition.(76)

She explained that for her parliaments were like a 'market place' in which she could bring in her views and come out with information. She felt that the centres of power were not located in parliament, and that it was more important to work at the grass roots:

> Parliament is not the place where decisions are made about further armament. The decisions have already been programmed elsewhere, like in the arms lobby..the most important thing is to work at the grass roots, to build ecological houses, sun collectors, together with women, to build self-help centres and to practise social defence - and to link that with parliamentary methods.(77)

The involvement of the grass roots does not prevent the establishment of certain power structures, which are often essential if the Greens are to develop their own political identity. There exists great uncertainty over the extent to which the party does or should actually 'represent' the diverse strands of the Green Movement. In Hamburg, the GAL and the SPD could not achieve a compromise over the issues raised by the squatters. The GAL refused to accept that the state should be able to evict and prosecute people who occupied vacant houses illegally. A similar attitude prevailed in Berlin. It is thus not surprising to find that at the Hagen congress in November 1982 the Greens did not, as they had originally intended, issue a statement on their policy on the use of violence and the monopoly of violence by the state. In fact, the speakers who rejected any proposals that the party should distance itself, for example, from the violence around Frankfurt Airport, gained much applause.(78)

In Baden-Wuerttemberg some Green delegates have accepted unequivocally the monopoly of violence by the state, and the need to work within parliamentary democracy since it is the only 'open' system in existence.(79) Here the Greens had established a good rapport with all the established parties. In Berlin, the Alternative List was initially frightened of 'contact' with the SPD, yet within a few weeks of its entry into the Berlin Senate it no longer harboured this fear.(80) Differences of opinion over the value of work in parliaments still prevail among the Greens. As I showed in an earlier chapter, attempts to bridge the gap between these

differences, between uncompromising, fundamentalist
attitudes, utopian demands and pragmatic, radical
reforms, are a distinctive feature of the debates
within the party and the Green Movement. The out-
come of these debates has been crucial in determin-
ing the extent of co-operation between the Greens
and the Social Democrats.

Support for the Greens among young people comes
from all layers of the population, although the
activists are mainly middle-class. The Shell survey
showed that only 6 per cent of young people who
supported the Greens in 1981 were members of the
network of groups and organisations which form part
of the alternative subculture.(81) This reflects
the lack of interest in organised forms of political
or general group activity. In local elections, the
Greens have attracted the support of broader layers
of the population, and where rural elements have
combined with urban protest groups in opposition to
specific projects, they have secured a substantial
proportion of the vote. None the less, many people
have discovered that the Greens, although they pose
certain fundamental questions and represent many of
the aspirations of the protest movements, may be in-
capable of providing practical alternatives to the
existing society. This is particularly true of
their proposals in relation to the sphere of production. In other areas they have made a convincing
appeal for the reassessment of certain policies.
They have articulated the feeling of despair and
loss of identity that was expressed by the supporters
of the Green Movement and have thereby posed a
threat to the electoral bases of support for the
Social Democratic Party.

NOTES

1. Frankfurter Rundschau, 7 Nov. 1979 and 17 Dec. 1979.
2. Bahro, Socialism and Survival, pp.20-1.
3. Taz, 14 Jan. 1980, p. 1.
4. Taz, 14 Jan. 1980, p. 2.
5. Taz, 15 Jan. 1980, p. 2.
6. Taz, 15 Jan. 1980, p. 2.
7. Taz, 28 Jan. 1980, p. 11.
8. Taz, 25 March 1980, p. 4.
9. Taz, 24 March 1980, p. 2.
10. Heinz Brandt in Taz, 26 March 1980, p. 2.
11. Taz, 29 April 1980, p. 2.
12. Taz, 20 June 1980, p. 12.
13. Taz, 20 May 1980, p. 5.
14. Taz, 4 June 1980, p. 4.

15. Taz, 9 June 1980, p. 4, and in a series of articles throughout that year.

16. Taz, 19 June 1980, p. 4.

17. Taz, 23 June 1980 and 24 June 1980.

18. Taz, 17 July 1980, p. 2 and 16.

19. Taz, 23 July 1980, p. 3.

20. Taz, 7 Aug. 1980, p. 4.

21. Heinz Brandt in Taz, 29 July 1980, p. 12.

22. Taz, 18 July 1980, p. 6.

23. Interview carried out by the author with Corny Littmann, leading candidate of the Green Party in Hamburg in the 1980 Federal Elections, September 1980.

24. Taz, 5 Dec. 1980, p. 2.

25. Bunte Liste Bielefeld/Bielefelder Stadtblatt, Alternativen in der Kommunalpolitik. Kongress am 14-15 Nov. 1980 (Bielefeld, 1980), p. 20.

26. Taz, 29 Sept. 1981, p. 3.

27. Bunte Liste, Alternativen in der Kommunalpolitik, p.20.

28. Ibid.

29. Ibid., p. 21.

30. Ibid.

31. Ibid., p. 22.

32. E.Hoplitschek, 'Die Alternativen und die Macht - die parlamentarischen Erfahrungen der AL Berlin' in R.Schiller-Dickhut et al., Alternative Stadtpolitik, pp. 138-9.

33. Bunte Liste, Alternativen in der Kommunalpolitik, p.99.

34. Taz, 4 May 1981, p. 6.

35. Taz, 20 May 1981, p. 5.

36. Kretschmann, 'Die Gruenen im Landtag von Baden-Wuerttemberg', p. 107.

37. N.Winkler, 'Gruene Buergerliste fuer Demokratie und Umweltschutz in Moerfelden-Walldorf' in R.Schiller-Dickhut et al., Alternative Stadtpolitik, p. 69.

38. Taz, 19 March 1981, p. 3.

39. Norbert Kostede, 'Oekologische Linke und Konservative im Streit um die Stadt' in Taz, 23 June 1981, p. 9.

40. Taz, 13 Nov. 1980, p. 4.

41. See Bunte Liste, Alternativen in der Kommunalpolitik, p. 35ff. for examples of plans for an alternative traffic system in Bielefeld.

42. Langer and Link, 'Ueber den Umgang mit Defiziten linker Politik in Hamburg', pp. 129-30.

43. Bunte Liste, Alternativen in der Kommunalpolitik, pp. 8-9.

44. Langer and Link, 'Ueber den Umgang mit Defiziten linker Politik in Hamburg', p. 130.

45. Ibid., p. 138.

46. Ibid.

47. Oxmox, Die Gruenen (K.Schulz, Hamburg, 1980), p. 11.

48. GAL Hamburg, Beschluesse zur Parlamentsarbeit (Hamburg, 1982), p. 10.

49. Boch et al., 'Die alternative Wahlbewegung und die Kommunalpolitik', p. 33.

50. Ibid., pp. 34-5.

51. Kretschmann, 'Die Gruenen im Landtag von Baden-Wuerttemberg', p. 107.

52. Hoplitschek, 'Die Alternativen und die Macht - die parlamentarischen Erfahrungen der AL Berlin', p. 152f.

53. Langer and Link, 'Ueber den Umgang mit Defiziten linker Politik in Hamburg', p. 136f.

54. GAL Hamburg, Beschluesse zur Parlamentsarbeit, p. 10.

55. Kretschmann, 'Die Gruenen im Landtag von Baden-Wuerttemberg', p. 109.

56. Taz, 28 Sept. 1981, p. 3.

57. Taz, 20 March 1980, p. 4.

58. Taz, 18 Jan. 1982, p. 6.

59. Taz, 22 June 1982, p. 11.

60. Taz, 15 March 1982, p. 7.

61. GAL Hamburg, Programm, p. 13.

62. Ibid., p. 17.

63. Ibid.

64. Oxmox, Die Gruenen, p. 58.

65. Taz, 15 March 1982, p. 11.

66. GAL Hamburg, Programm, p. 8.

67. Ibid., p. 13.

68. Ibid., pp. 10-11.

69. Ibid., p. 32.

70. Taz, 6 Oct. 1981, p. 5.

71. GAL Hamburg, Programm, p. 5.

72. Taz, 14 June 1982, p. 4.

73. Taz, 19 March 1981, p. 4.

74. Taz, 7 May 1981, p. 5.

75. Taz, 28 April 1981, p. 5.

76. Der Spiegel, Nr. 24, 1982, p. 47ff.

77. Ibid.

78. Frankfurter Allgemeine Zeitung, 15 Nov. 1982, p. 5.

79. W.Kretschmann in Der Spiegel, Nr. 42, 1982, p. 134.

80. Taz, 29 June 1981, p. 3.

81. Shell Studie, Jugend 1981, Vol. 1, p. 686.

Chapter Nine

THE SOCIAL DEMOCRATS UNDER THREAT

The clearest expression of the growing support for
the Green Movement after the 1980 Federal Elections
was the success of the Green Party in communal and
state elections. This culminated in the 1983
Federal Elections when more than 5 per cent of the
electorate ensured that for the first time in the
history of the Federal Republic a Green Party, with
twenty-seven delegates, would voice the demands of
the extra-parliamentary protest movements within the
Federal Parliament. None the less, efforts by the
Social Democrats to integrate the party-political
wing of the Green Movement had begun long before the
1983 elections.

I Communal and state elections

Following the communal elections in Bielefeld (September 1979) the Bunte Liste entered the city parliament in which the SPD, although it was the most
powerful fraction, did not have a majority and did
not form a coalition with either the FDP or the CDU.
Instead, the Social Democrats wished to form alliances and majorities on a changeable basis of support. Thus when the CDU and FDP opposed the budget
put forward by them, the opportunity arose for a
bargain to be struck between the SPD and the Bunte
Liste since the latter had shown a willingness to
become immersed in the detailed work and tasks of
parliamentary activity. The budget was passed with
the support of the Bunte Liste, even though it meant
that projects like the extension of a motorway would
now have enough financial support. In exchange for
this, the SPD agreed to provide more money for cycle
routes and for youth centres; to prevent the de-

struction of houses in an area improvement scheme;
to draw up an experts' dossier on energy needs; and
to increase the funds available to an autonomous
'women's house'. Co-operation between the two
parties also occurred in the spheres of youth and
educational policies, although there were no attempts
to form a coalition.(1)

In Kassel, the Greens helped the SPD into power
in the city parliament. They did not form a coalition but developed a 'working relationship'. The
SPD supported the Greens in their opposition to the
construction of a nuclear reprocessing plant in
Hessen. By doing this they were contradicting the
policy of the leader of the SPD in that state. The
SPD agreed to commission an experts' report on the
effects of a nuclear fuel reprocessing plant on the
lives of the population in Kassel, to introduce a
cycle route in the city centre, to work out an energy
concept for the city and to extend the scope of public transport.(2) It is interesting to note that
this working relationship was threatened by two
issues: the protection of the environment and tenants'
rights, both of which were related to the sphere of
reproduction and to the 'world of life'. Thus when
the SPD, with the assistance of the CDU and FDP,
voted in favour of a large project to extend a railway line for fast trains, the Greens criticised the
fact that local residents would be burdened by the
noise, and more recreational space would be destroyed
to the detriment of the local population.(3) In
Marburg, close co-operation between the SPD and the
Greens was brought to a halt when a member of the
Greens in the city parliament angered the established
parties by taking part in a demonstration against
Boerner, the Minister President of Hessen who was in
favour of plans to build the West Runway at Frankfurt Airport.(4) Party activists in Marburg and
Kassel had expressed their strong disapproval of any
co-operation with the SPD. None the less, these
early efforts towards co-operation became increasingly significant as the Green and Alternative Lists
went from strength to strength in state elections all
over the Federal Republic.

The results of these elections indicated the
concretisation of moves towards a detachment from
the main political parties by a significant minority
within the electorate, namely by well-educated,
young people who share a highly critical and often
pessimistic view of society. The efforts by the SPD
to gauge the possibilities for co-operation with
this new force increased with each new state

Table 9.1   Summary of results in state elections (1981–1982)

			GREENS	SPD	FDP	CDU/CSU
May	1981	Berlin	7.2 (3.7)	38.4	8.1	47.9
March	1982	Lower Saxony	6.5 (3.9)	36.5	5.9	50.7
June	1982	Hamburg	7.7 (4.5)	42.8	4.8	43.2
Sept.	1982	Hessen	8.0 (2.0)	42.8	3.1	45.6
Oct.	1982	Bavaria	4.4 (1.8)	31.5	3.4	59.0

(Figures in brackets indicate the results of the 1979 elections in Berlin and of the 1978 state elections in various states.)

election.(Table 9.1) Early in 1981, surveys had shown that the Alternative List in Berlin might hold the balance of power in the Berlin Senate following any elections. Although the 'threat' to the main parties did not materialise, the prospect of such a situation led to a variety of initiatives by the SPD to enter discussions with the Alternative List. Thus a congress entitled 'Berlin in the year 2000', which was organised by the Jusos at the Technical University in Berlin, allowed prominent spokespersons of the SPD (Peter Glotz, Anke Brunn, Olaf Sund) who were all in favour of a better relationship to the new movements, to enter informal discussions with members of the Alternative List in a public forum.(5) The SPD also attempted to attract some of the potential voters of the new party by adopting popular demands by Citizens' Initiatives like the opposition to a huge motorway project.(6)

The Taz, one of the main filters of opinion and coordinators of action within the Green Movement, was able to take up offers to interview leading figures within the Social Democratic Party. One editor suspected that the newspaper had become the potential carrier of 'Social Democratic dialogue':

> The poison of dialogue is having its effect;
> both sides are getting closer. They, as
> Social Democrats, shiver with good reason
> because of our votes; we shiver in secret,
> but very much, at the prospect of the CDU
> getting into power. We allow the SPD a
> voyeuristic glance into the new youth move-
> ment. We put into words what the scene
> allegedly cannot express. We are levelling
> the path for understanding, mediation,
> integration. We are already almost the
> institutionalised form of dialogue.(7)

These comments appeared on the same day as the publication of an interview with the Federal Minister of Research and Technology, von Buelow; the interview had been carried out in the offices of the Taz in Berlin.

Within the Alternative List there emerged two main standpoints towards a possible future minority SPD Government in West Berlin: the Sponti members rejected any form of help or 'tolerance' towards such a government, whilst the radical reformists who had some experience of working in purely political organisations would have liked to co-operate with a minority SPD Government under certain conditions. A general assembly of 1,500 members of the Alternative List revealed a clear 50:50 split over this issue. (8)

Despite the failure of the SPD to form a minority government after the elections in West Berlin (May 1981), many opportunities for co-operation arose at a district level. The election result meant that the Alternative List was entitled to take over responsibility for at least one administrative department in each district; however, since it was in a minority, it faced the prospect of only being in charge of the relatively uninfluential posts of city councillor responsible for health. In Kreuzberg, where the Alternative List was dominated by those who wished to co-operate with the SPD, it agreed to help the latter to gain various posts in the city council in exchange for the more influential post of city councillor responsible for buildings. The decision was condemned by the Alternative List in Wilmersdorf, Schoeneberg and Tiergarten, where no attempt had been made to co-operate with the SPD at this level.(9) Significantly, the Alternative List in Kreuzberg had already been represented in the district parliament for two years and gained recognition for its work there. In the words of the chairman of the SPD in Kreuzberg, Walter Mompert: 'I have been pleasantly surprised up to now, by the way the Alternative List has tried to relate to concrete issues. The trust relates above all to the stability of the contents of their political positions'.(10)

In the Berlin Senate there was no official co-operation between the two sides, yet on an informal level there occurred a great deal of mutual assistance and exchange of information. Two members of the Alternative List in the Senate, Micha Wendt and Peter Finger, both came from the SPD. A year after the Alternative List had entered the Senate, the CDU and SPD were impressed by the hard work which had been

performed by members of the new party and by their
business-like attitude towards their new responsibilities. The CDU was also becoming worried about the
numerous occasions on which the Alternative List and
the SPD voted together. In addition, the 'Kreuzberg
Model' was regarded as a serious experiment for
future co-operation. The main stumbling block to
official co-operation was the issue of violence and
the refusal by the Alternative List to condemn out-
rightly the riots that accompanied some demonstrations.(11) Prominent members of the party began to
insist that it should be more careful about which
demonstrations it supported, since they felt that
some of the 'autonomists and professional street-
fighters' clearly wanted riots and consciously
sought confrontation with the police.(12)

The state elections in Lower Saxony confirmed
the trend whereby the SPD, more than any other party,
was losing the support of many of its former voters
to the Greens. None the less, because the CDU gained
an absolute majority, the Greens had to wait until
the Hamburg state elections to move into a key position in state politics. In Hamburg the FDP secured
less than 5 per cent of the vote and thus no seats
in parliament. The Greens, however, gained 9 seats
and held the balance between the SPD with 55 seats
and the CDU with 56 seats. Prior to the election,
the Greens had laid down certain conditions before
they would tolerate a minority government by the SPD.
The two sides sat down to fifty hours of negotiations over a period of eight days, but the talks
failed to produce any compromise. Whilst possibilities emerged of an agreement over the issues of the
control of environmental pollution and the cleaning
of the River Elbe, neither side was able to compromise on the following issues: the expansion of the
harbour and consequent destruction of century-old
villages on the Elbe; nuclear energy from the Stade
and Brunsbuettel power stations; and the monopoly of
violence by the state. The Greens were opposed to
the expansion of the harbour; they wanted a total
renunciation of nuclear power; and they felt that
squatters should be neither evicted nor prosecuted
when they occupied vacant property.(13) Whilst the
leader of the SPD, Dohnanyi, blamed the Greens for
the failure of the talks to produce a practical
agreement, the leader of the Greens, Ebermann,
declared that the ability of the Greens to compromise
had not been put to the test and this was only the
'first round'.(14)

The failure of these talks led to an unpreced-

The Social Democrats under threat

Table 9.2 Attitudes to co-operation between the Greens and the SPD among voters of different parties (%)

Question: Do you think that the Greens and the SPD should work together when such a possibility arises or would you reject any such co-operation?

Spring 1982

	Total	CDU/CSU	SPD	FDP	GREENS
they should work together	40	24	55	45	70
they should not work together	54	69	38	53	28

September 1982

	Total	CDU/CSU	SPD	FDP	GREENS
they should work together	34	17	49	32	72
they should not work together	61	78	46	66	27

Question: If the SPD and the Greens gained enough votes in the Hessen state elections to be able to form a government, should they try and form a coalition, or should they reject this from the start?

September 1982

	Total	CDU/CSU	SPD	FDP	GREENS
they should try	30	12	45	28	69
they should not try	65	84	50	71	31

Source: Figures from Der Spiegel, Nr. 16, 1982, p. 28 and Nr. 35, 1982, p. 58.

ented event. For the first time in the existence of the Federal Republic, new state elections had to be called within a short period of time to try and create a stable government in a state. The Greens were becoming worried that the new voters they had attracted, were largely in favour of an alliance with the SPD. Prior to the elections in June 1982, 57 per cent of the Green voters in Hamburg supported the idea of a coalition with the SPD, 17 per cent, a coalition with SPD and FDP and 5 per cent, a coalition with the CDU. Similar figures emerged in a survey carried out before the state elections in Lower Saxony.(15) In two surveys carried out in Spring and in September 1982 around 70 per cent of the respondents who supported the Greens were in favour of co-operation with the SPD. Among supporters of the SPD, around half were in favour of co-operation with the Greens.(Table 9.2)

In Autumn 1982 the Federal Social-Liberal Government collapsed and there emerged a new alliance between the Christian Democrats and the Liberals.

A survey carried out at the time revealed that voters
of the Greens were far from indifferent to this
change; 77 per cent regretted the change and only
7 per cent welcomed it.(16) Out of the entire electorate, 14 per cent were in favour of a coalition
government between the SPD and the Greens if there
emerged only a minority government after the 1983
Federal Elections; only 11 per cent were in favour
of a coalition between the SPD and the FDP, whilst
30 per cent favoured a coalition between the Christian Democrats and the Free Democrats.
       The failure of negotiations between the Greens
and the SPD in Hamburg was not regarded as a major
setback but as a stage in a long-term process of
negotiations and compromise. Before the Hessen
elections very few people saw much prospect of similar dicussions in the event of an analogous balance
of power emerging out of this contest. However, the
Greens went on to secure 8 per cent of the vote and
9 seats in the state parliament. The SPD and CDU
secured 49 and 52 seats respectively, and the FDP
gained only 3 per cent of the vote and no seats at
all. This shock result gave the impression that the
Free Democrats were in rapid decline and it stimul-
ated discussions over the possibility of a new
'majority on the Left' which would comprise the SPD
and the Greens. In Hessen the Greens had gained
between 6 per cent and 10 per cent of the vote in
most of the 55 electoral districts; in only five
districts did they fail to get more than 5 per cent.
(17) The leader of the SPD in Hessen, Boerner,
decided to send a delegation to Hamburg where they
might learn something from their colleagues about
their experiences with the Greens. Boerner, who was
regarded as a hard-line pragmatist, became less
forceful in his demands for the expansion of the
programme for nuclear power stations, although the
controversy over the extension of Frankfurt Airport
remained a major stumbling block to any negotiations.
       The SPD was allowed several months' breathing
space because the Greens lent their support to a
short-term budget, which included immediate measures
to combat unemployment, a small programme for environmental protection, 1.5 million marks for housing
adapted to the needs of the disabled and 9.5 million
for investment in energy conservation. However, the
SPD called for new elections in autumn 1983 because
the Greens were not prepared to vote for a long-term
budget, which would imply a continuation of the
reliance on nuclear energy. The Greens also wanted
to bring to an end any further major road-building

projects and to make huge savings on police expenditure.(18)

II   The 1983 Federal Elections

The Greens began to find themselves in an awkward situation. Although many activists were opposed to co-operation with the established parties, many of their ordinary supporters, especially those who had come from the SPD, wanted to see an alliance between the two parties at some stage. Petra Kelly tended to echo the view of the party activists when she stated that she feared that the Greens would 'suddenly get 13 per cent' of the vote and become a party which 'seeks only to gain power': 'It would be better if we only get 6 or 7 per cent and remain uncompromising in our basic demands; better that, than to put forward ministers'.(19) This perspective was not shared by the newly-elected chairperson of the party, Rainer Trampert, who felt that if the Greens did hold the balance of power after the 1983 Federal Elections, they should negotiate with the SPD. The switch from Kelly to Trampert was significant. Trampert wanted, in the same manner as many Social Democrats, to unite 'ecology' and 'economy'. According to one report around that time:

> Pragmatists and reformist politicians are
> increasingly influencing the picture of the
> party; ecological utopians and supporters
> of a fundamental opposition are on the
> retreat. There is an increasing doubt as
> to whether it makes sense to hold onto
> hitherto highly-esteemed principles such
> as grass-roots democracy, rotation of
> parliamentary delegates and a control of
> salaries.(20)

These views were echoed by another member of the executive committee of the party, Ernst Hoplitschek, who spoke of an 'increasingly imaginary grass roots'. He added that true grass-roots democracy could only function if the grass roots had faith in their own representatives and that this was rarely the case with the Greens.(21)
     The Greens became increasingly aware that if they abstained from making decisions within parliaments, they could make it easier for the CDU to consolidate its power. The SPD was not slow in point-

ing this out. Willy Brandt observed astutely that
after the Greens had been in several parliaments,
some of them were increasingly asking themselves:
'What shall we do with such exalted principles, if
we allow the opportunity to escape, to exercise some
influence?'(22) Once the SPD found itself in opposition, Brandt sought to form a 'majority on the Left'
which would include the Greens. The early electoral
strategy of the SPD was to focus on the issue of
peace and nuclear missiles. Their candidate for
Chancellor, Vogel, labelled Chancellor Kohl from the
CDU as the 'rocket Chancellor' and said that he
would do his utmost to make the deployment of the
missiles unnecessary. However, the Greens insisted
that any alliance with the SPD could only be formed
on the basis of an uncompromising rejection of nuclear missiles and nuclear energy. According to
Trampert, these were issues of 'survival' over which
there could be no compromises.(23) Thus, only a few
weeks before the Federal Elections, the SPD declared
that it was no longer prepared to negotiate with the
Greens even if the latter held the balance of power
in Parliament. It was an acknowledgement of the
failure of its strategy to form a 'majority on the
Left' rather than of the Centre.

Issues raised by the protest movements played a
significant part in the 1983 Federal Elections.
Opinion polls showed that 56 per cent of the population regarded unemployment and 32 per cent, the deployment of nuclear weapons as important electoral
issues.(24) Although the ideas of the Greens on how
to tackle these problems were widely dismissed as
unrealistic, they still influenced the statements
and electoral programmes of the major parties. Thus,
even the CDU cautiously stated in its electoral programme that economic growth was 'not an end in itself', and the economy had to take into account
human needs and the natural foundations of life.
The leader of the SPD, Vogel, declared that although
he was not opposed to economic growth, it was unrealistic to imagine that it could wipe away unemployment since this would require a doubling of
the gross national product by the year 1992. Such
a solution, he added, would lead to a severe reduction in the quality of life.(25) Moreover, the
Greens have called consistently for a shorter working week and for early retirement; the SPD wants to
do the same, and the Centre-Right Coalition Government had considered similar plans. The main difference lay in the demand by the Greens that a shorter
working week should be linked neither to a reduction

in wages nor to an increase in productivity.

The most significant basis for co-operation between the SPD and the Greens was created by the supporters of the peace and ecology movements, who came from both parties. In October 1981,38 per cent of SPD voters were probably involved in some form of protest activity against the policy of the Social-Liberal Government to accept a new range of missiles. (26) At the same time, 22 per cent of SPD voters were opposed to the NATO dual-track decision, whilst 37 per cent were in favour of it; by January 1983 the balance had shifted to 27 per cent against, and 26 per cent in favour of the placement of the new missiles. Well over half of SPD voters had opposed the policy of Helmut Schmidt's Government on nuclear energy. At the Federal Elections in 1983 the Greens were able to present themselves as the party of the peace movement. The attempts by the SPD to turn the election campaign into a referendum on nuclear miss-iles in West Germany improved the chances of the Greens at the polls. In addition, the efforts by the leadership of the SPD to win back supporters from the Greens probably alienated some voters at the Centre who were fearful of adventurous policies.

The main breakthrough of the elections was the entry of the Green Party into the Federal Parliament. It gained 5.6 per cent of the vote which meant that the CDU/CSU, with 48.8 per cent, had to rely on the FDP in order to form a government. Both the FDP (6.9 per cent) and the SPD (38.2 per cent) had lost many votes to the Greens. For the first time in post-war history, a party to the left of the SPD had, with 27 seats, entered the Federal Parliament. Fifty per cent of the Greens' candidates in the elec-tions were less than 35 years old; this contrasts with 7 per cent, from the SPD, 12 per cent, from the CDU/CSU and 11 per cent, from the FDP. However, there was little overall difference between the socio-economic background of candidates of the Green Party and other parties.(27) Most of them were public servants, including teachers, and professional people. The new MPs from the Green Party were required by their own party to give up their post after two years in office, in accordance with the 'principle of rotation', although proposals were submitted which would allow them to stay on as 'advisers' to new delegates. The Green parliamentar-ians soon modified the 'principle of rotation' when they decided that any delegate who could obtain the support of seventy per cent of other members of the party would be allowed to serve a full four-year

term. According to one delegate this was already
leading to a massive competitive struggle between
the parliamentary delegates.(28) Women are supposed
to be equally represented at all levels, and in the
Federal Parliament 40 per cent of the Greens' delegates are women.

The results of the election were greeted with
mixed feelings by some members of the party. Rainer
Trampert felt that, apart from the success of the
Greens the result was a 'catastrophe' because of the
resounding victory of the Centre-Right Coalition.
The electoral success of the Greens appeared to
strengthen the hand of those delegates who wished to
spend less time on 'fundamental opposition' and more
on providing practical alternatives in co-operation
with the Social Democrats. However, the 'fundament-
alists' were far from being a spent force, especially
since the reformist concept of a 'majority on the
Left' was not realised during the election campaign.

The Greens attracted many Social Democrat and
Free Democrat voters in large towns and cities. They
did not, in contrast to local elections, gain many
votes in small towns and villages where there was
powerful opposition to specific projects. This
confirms the predominance of the left-wing ecologists
within the party and, at the same time, the failure
to rally the support of traditional conservative
voters. The efforts by the SPD to incorporate the
issues raised by the protest movements, in order to
keep the Greens out of the Federal Parliament, may
have led many of its traditional supporters to vote
for the CDU. For example, in North Rhine Westphalia
the CDU gained 45.8 per cent of the vote and became
the most powerful party, even though the SPD held
an absolute majority in the state parliament of this
traditional stronghold. About 1.5 million people
who voted for the Social Democrats in 1980 supported
the CDU/CSU in 1983. Another reason for this swing
in the vote was, of course, the concern of many
voters about the rising level of unemployment. The
Greens offered stiff competition to the established
parties in gaining the support of young, first-time
voters. They collected 23 per cent of these votes,
whilst the SPD and the CDU/CSU obtained 37 per cent
and 23 per cent respectively.(29)

The Greens are likely to ensure that the other
parties do not become complacent over certain issues,
and there is a chance that they, rather than the SPD,
will capture the imagination of the public as the
opposition party which 'truly' opposes the policies
of the government on nuclear missiles, nuclear

energy and civil rights. Social Democrat members of
the Berlin Senate have already experienced how a
large number of people regard the Alternative List
as the 'real' opposition in the city. The campaign
by the Greens against 'acid-rain', which has already
destroyed or damaged 7.7 per cent of all forests in
West Germany, also became an issue in the Federal
Elections.(30) In 1982 the CDU had criticised the
Liberal Minister of the Interior, Baum, for
'exaggerating' the effects of 'acid-rain' on the
destruction of forests.(31) However, during the
1983 election campaign, Chancellor Kohl announced
plans to invest £3.3 billion in an attempt to curb
industrial pollution. Previously the Greens had
proposed a £16 billion programme to rescue the
forests from the effects of industrial pollution.
     The consistency and fundamentalist approach of
the Greens over certain issues holds a powerful
appeal to the idealist supporters of the Green Movement. Moreover, they are being 'proved right' constantly, for instance in their opposition to the
nuclear energy programme. In March 1983, the former
Social Democrat Minister of Research and Technology,
von Buelow, revealed that shortly before his party
was obliged to give up its position in power in
autumn 1982, he had accepted the findings of a
report which called for a re-assessment of the fast
breeder, nuclear reactor project at Kalkar. He
declared that this project, which had already cost
2.5 billion marks and would cost a further 10 billion,
should be brought to a halt. He illustrated how,
since the early seventies, the energy needs of the
country had been over-estimated consistently, and
explained that this was one of the main reasons for
the vast expenditure on projects like the one in
Kalkar.(32) The ecologists had also proved the
experts and politicians wrong over the following
issues: the destruction of forests by 'acid-rain';
the pollution of water supplies; and the dumping of
acid wastes in the North Sea.
     These insights are not, of themselves, the best
guarantee for the future survival of the movements.
They are likely to continue to exist, at least into
the late 1980s, because they have established a
foothold in various parliaments and begun to develop
an interest in the preservation of positions of
power and specific projects and community structures.
Their appeal is likely, however, to remain confined
to less than 10 per cent of the electorate, although
it could increase if there are serious conflicts
within the SPD over future policies. The success of

the Green Party in the 1983 Federal Elections can be
regarded as a decisive electoral result which reveals
a 'sharp alteration in the pre-existing cleavage
within the electorate'.(33) Even before the Green
Party was formed, surveys had shown that around 6.6
per cent of the electorate was prepared to abandon
the major parties and vote for an environmentalist
party. The 1980 Federal Elections occurred too soon
after the formation of the Green Party to allow for
the realisation of this potential. However, in
state elections since then, the Greens gained consistently between 4 and 8 per cent of the vote,
and mainly at the expense of the SPD. In the 1950s
the SPD had made successfully the transition from a
class party to a broader 'people's party' by renouncing its Marxist ideology. In 1983 it was confronted
by a party-political organisation on the Left which
attracted more than two million voters. This will
make it difficult for the party leadership to reconcile the different factions within the party.
Perhaps even more significantly, the Green Movement
which has formed the basis of support for the Green
Party has shown remarkable durability. It has,
despite its loose structures, survived for at least
seven years, since 1976, and has taken up new themes
continually. The relevance of these themes is not
likely to diminish over the next decade. These
factors all suggest a 'durable re-alignment' of the
electorate has taken place, which is based on the
support of the young, well-educated middle classes.

As I have attempted to show, education is an
important determinant and ensures committed support
for the protest movements. Peter Glotz, for example,
has expressed his doubts as to whether the Social
Democrats can attract and motivate the intellectual
sections of the young generation who, although they
may be in a minority, exercise a decisive influence
on the protest movements.(34) What distinguishes
the present realignment in contemporary West German
politics from other examples of alterations in the
pre-existing cleavages within the electorate, is
that significant sections of the supporters of the
protest movement organisations are, apparently,
fundamentally opposed to the existing democratic
order. This has led to a recognition by some policy-
makers and members of public administrative bodies
of the need to incorporate some of the ideas and
integrate some of the issues taken up by the movements into the existing political system. To this
extent, the Greens and other alternative groups do
help to meet the needs of capitalism. Despite their

'fundamental opposition' to the system, they serve
an important functional need of capitalism since
without the warnings issued by these movements, the
state could only adapt to changing needs in society
with great difficulty. This entails, as I have
shown in previous chapters and as I will further
explore in the final chapter, adjustments to changing consumer habits, the discovery of new spheres
for economic growth, innovative approaches to facilitate social integration and socialisation, and new
forms of community and welfare services.

NOTES

1. Taz, 22 Oct. 1980, p. 5.
2. Taz, 1 June 1981, p. 5 and 24 June 1981, p. 5.
3. Taz, 3 Feb. 1982, p. 5.
4. Taz, 4 Dec. 1981, p. 5.
5. Taz, 27 April 1981, p. 5.
6. Taz, 28 April 1981, p. 5.
7. Taz, 4 May 1981, p. 5.
8. Hoplitschek, 'Die Alternativen und die Macht - die
parlamentarischen Erfahrungen der AL Berlin', p. 146ff.
9. Taz, 3 July 1981, p. 6.
10. Taz, 26 Sept. 1981, p. 3.
11. Taz, 18 June 1982, p. 3.
12. Taz, 18 June 1982, p. 3.
13. Der Spiegel, Nr. 41, 1982, p. 42.
14. Ibid., Nr. 42, 1982, pp.131-134.
15. Ibid., Nr. 39, 1982, p. 38.
16. Ibid., Nr. 41, 1982, p. 32.
17. Ibid., Nr. 44, 1982, pp. 31-2.
18. Ibid., Nr. 8, 1983, p. 37ff.
19. Ibid., Nr. 24, 1982, p. 53.
20. Ibid., Nr. 47, 1982, p. 30.
21. Ibid., p. 31.
22. Ibid., Nr. 42, 1982, p. 43f.
23. Ibid., Nr. 8, 1983, p. 37ff.
24. Guardian, 5 March 1983.
25. Die Zeit, 18 Feb. 1983.
26. Der Spiegel, Nr. 50, 1981, p. 106.
27. Das Parlament, 5 March 1983.
28. Taz, 7 April 1983, p. 5.
29. The Economist, 12 March 1983.
30. Der Spiegel, Nr. 7, 1983, p. 76.
31. Ibid.
32. Ibid., Nr. 10, 1983, p. 84.
33. V.O.Key, 'A Theory of Critical Elections' in The
Journal of Politics, Vol. 17, No. 1, February 1955, p. 4.
34. Glotz, 'Dass die SPD Identitaetsprobleme hat'.

Chapter Ten

FUNCTIONAL ASPECTS OF THE GREEN MOVEMENT

Although the emergence of Green and Alternative
parties has posed a threat to the SPD and other
established groups, it has served an important function in integrating the various strands of the
Green Movement. Thus many people who have 'opted
out' of capitalist society have found themselves
voting for a party which has become directly involved in the political machinery of the democratic,
capitalist state. For instance the Alternative List
in Berlin recruits most of its voters from the
'alternative scene' which comprises projects and
autonomous groups that practise an alternative life-
style. The press spokesperson for the party explained that part of this 'scene' wanted nothing at
all to do with the Alternative List because it felt
that 'politics is rubbish'. The party therefore had
to play an integrative role:

> We don't condemn that because we can under-
> stand how people can have such ideas...we
> only criticise it politically and try to
> tell these people that we too basically want
> the same things as them, only one cannot
> step out of politics. If we want to change
> anything we must get involved in politics.(1)

Many supporters of the Green Party take this role
for granted and, as I showed in the previous chapter,
still look towards the SPD to take new initiatives
on the issues raised by the Green Movement and to
co-operate with it. Despite the ideological barriers
between the two sides, the relationship between the
Green Movement and the established groups may be
much more grateful than one might think. This may
also be true of alternative groups which are
'fundamentally' opposed to the prevailing system.

Functional aspects of the Green Movement

Not only are they aware of the need for state subsidies if they are to survive, but they anticipate the needs experienced by many people beyond their own circle for a spiritual justification to their existence and for a more 'humane' system of state welfare.

I Economic pressures on alternative groups

According to most people who were engaged in the initial discussions about the possibilities of state finance for alternative projects, the word 'dialogue' has been misused. Klaus-Juergen Luther, a senior official in the Ministry of Education and Science, felt that the dialogue with young people took place 'behind closed doors' and that practical results had to be achieved in order to convince young people of the sincerity of the state's intentions. However, he was equally sceptical about the motives of the alternative groups:

> Is there really a preparedness by alternative projects to engage in discussions, or is it not pure economic necessity which forces an alternative project to negotiate with the 'devil', whereby I do not wish to describe any of the negotiators as devils. But what we discovered in our discussions was that pure economic necessity allowed several ideological, philosophical and metaphysical barriers to appear secondary.(2)

When I asked an administrator who works in the Netzwerk self-help project about the significance of a dialogue between established political parties and the alternative movement, she replied that dialogue and discussions were only meaningful in order to find out what the other side wanted and with what tricks it tried to 'pull the wool over our eyes'. With dialogue she associated the danger of being 'bought' and of 'integration'. She felt that only if the Green Movement had greater self-confidence, could it allow itself to become involved in a dialogue with the established parties without being caught out.(3) The early stages of dialogue were thus characterised by a deep mistrust, with the alternative groups forced by economic necessity to negotiate with the authorities, and the state faced by a loss of political influence to integrate disaffected groups.

202

The level of self-exploitation in the alternative projects, where long hours of work are accomplished in return for a very low wage, forced many projects to turn to the state for financial assistance. According to one official report, the average monthly income for members of alternative projects was between 500 and 1,000 marks.(4) Most members have to work an average of 40 hours per week. Many projects have been under immense pressure. Two members of a 'Women's Council' which was formed to unite the demands of diverse projects declared, in January 1983, that the projects were no longer prepared to carry out unpaid social and community work because of certain changes in attitudes:

> The impatience is growing because within the women's movement fundamental changes have taken place: the growth in self-confidence has made us recognise more and more the value of our own work...A defensive ideology of poverty which equates money with corruption and makes any political claim untenable, has given way to an offensive strategy to demand money from the state for self-administered projects.(5)

Some groups have justified this demand for state subsidies by referring to them as 'people's money' which has been stolen of 'us' when 'we eat, smoke cigarettes and pay taxes'.(6) One project criticised the Taz for failing to distinguish between 'state' and 'people's' money. The money which flows into the state coffers is regarded as 'our money' which has been created by 'our diligence, our work'. (7) The state is seen as an unjust administrator of taxes. Some alternative projects feel that they are carrying out tasks which should be undertaken by the state or at least subsidised by it. They signal a tax-payers' rebellion from the Left which reflects a general mobilisation of the population in protests against the payment of taxes.(8) The occupants of the 'Factory for Culture, Sport and Handicrafts' in Berlin wanted to 'reclaim' their money:

> When we moved on to the site we said that we will finance our workshops, our own jobs; we will finance a free school...we will do our own social work. These are all spheres that are usually heavily subsidised. If we don't get this money and still pay taxes, we would be paying double.(9)

Functional aspects of the Green Movement

Organisations like the'Working Group for the
Financing of Alternative Projects' (Arbeitskreis
Finanzierung von Alternativprojekten - AFAP) have
been formed to try and unite the basic demands of
alternative projects, to draw attention to the needs
and advantages of state financial aid for these
projects. The AFAP, which comprises members and
sympathisers of alternative groups, has pointed out
that in Berlin the projects have created directly
between 4,000 and 5,000 jobs; they have brought new
life to the small-scale business sector and relate
very well to local communities; they are much more
effective in their consideration of the needs of
young people than state-run institutions; and they
are regarded as an effective form of preventitive
social and community work which is inexpensive and
innovative.(10)   These factors have begun to exercise more and more influence on politicians and
administrators who work in state agencies. However,
the main reason for the preparedness of the projects
to engage in discussions has been the severe economic pressure which has arisen because of the low
wages, lack of expertise, and even competition
between projects like the vast number of printing
presses and bookshops.(11)   There is a real danger
that the projects will become models of pre- rather
than post-industrial society.

II State interest in innovative projects

In the light of the conflicts that have emerged
between traditional institutions and parties and the
Green Movement, any contact between the two sides
could only be established initially by a limited
number of people. Early contacts thus depended on
the preparedness of individuals like Tilman Fichter
(who was carrying out research on the history of the
student movement and had numerous contacts both
within the SPD and the Green Movement) and Peter
Grottian (who was a professor at the Free University
of Berlin, and a founding member of the AFAP) to
mediate between the two sides. It is hardly surprising to find that these people are not necessarily
accepted by both sides.
      One of the main propagators of the idea of
offering money from the state to alternative projects was, not surprisingly, Peter Glotz. This
idea was shared by Bjoern Engholm (when he was the
state secretary to the Minister of Education), who

204

conducted secret negotiations with the projects over the possibility of financing some of them as 'models of educational processes':

> Our starting point was that in the alternative movement significant educational processes are occurring about which we know nothing, but about which we would like to know something since so many young people are apparently attracted by them.(12)

He stressed that the discussions had to be held in secret because of the sensitive nature of the subject. Another reason for this early initiative was, according to K-J. Luther, to try and discover whether both sides could show 'greater tolerance towards each other'. According to some supporters of the projects that took part in the discussions, the aim of the officials was to buy their way into the projects and to gain information about why the existing educational system had failed to integrate young people and to find new ways of 'forcing' them to reintegrate into the social system.(13) All the projects withdrew from the discussions because the officials insisted on keeping them secret. They feared a 'loss of identity' if they made any contact with the bureaucracy and they lacked knowledge about the complexity of the administrative apparatus. According to Luther, the supporters of the projects tended to assume that when they had met the Minister of Education and Science, they had established contact with the entire state, even though he was only one person who was tied up in a total political system, and who faced the danger of 'being suspected by other bureaucrats that he was making contact with revolutionaries'.(14)

Senior officials have made suggestions about how regulations can be improved and made clearer to facilitate the allocation of subsidies.(15) However, the main emphasis under the Social-Liberal Government was to improve 'communication' with the projects since the rules which governed the distribution of taxes were highly complex and could only be tackled through 'continuous dialogue'.(16) At any rate there are clear limits to the possibilities of financial aid from the Ministry of Education and Science for the alternative projects because of the shortage of funds. An official at the Ministry, Gisela Marsen-Storz, pointed out that the regulations which determined the allocation of resources were much simpler at the communal level where there are

far less formal restrictions and controls. It is
precisely at this level that progress in communication between the two sides has been hampered in
various ways. However, the lowest level of administration is, in certain respects, the decisive one
since that is where policies are ultimately put into
practice. There are isolated examples of successful
and fruitful communication, for instance in Nuern-
berg and Bremen, but it is not a process that has
made much headway in the thousands of other communes.
   To some extent, the possibilities of dialogue
were reduced drastically by the activities of terrorist groups in the 1970s. The Ministry of Education
and Science in Bonn is surrounded by barbed wire and
police check-points because of the threats to bomb
the Ministry of Justice which stands nearby. The
demand for an 'opening' of the state by the Green
Movement is difficult in this situation:

> This is one of the contradictions that the
> Baader-Meinhof group set up around the state.
> Terrorism from the Left and from the Right
> have had the effect that between the state
> and society barbed wire has been erected,
> and thus contact has been made more diffi-
> cult if not prevented.(17)

   It has come as a surprise to supporters of
alternative projects that the Christian Democratic
Administration in West Berlin, where supporters
of the party are among the most conservative anywhere, has been anxious to follow up earlier initiatives by the Social Democrats in paying close attention to their demands for financial assistance from
the state. The initiatives by the more liberal-
minded members of the party, led by Mayor von
Weiszaecker, reflect the ideas expressed by the all-
party commission of inquiry into youth protest, that
the state structures should be made more 'trans-
parent' to the population and that certain positive
aspects of the youth protest are relevant to the
whole of society.
   In October 1981 the Christian Democrat Senators
in Berlin launched their own inquiry into groups
that supported alternative life-styles because they
felt that many of these groups made a significant
contribution to social development in the cultural
and social spheres. The CDU declared that it shared
with the projects a belief in the principles of
'self-administration and self-responsibility', as
well as a commitment to 'self-reliance'

(Subsidiaritaet), decentralisation, creativity, individual initiative, communality and a 'unity between collective action and individualism, by means of solidarity, which is alien to socialism'. (18) The concept of 'self-reliance' is particularly important to the CDU since it aims to allow smaller communities and groups (especially the family) to take greater responsibility for their own action. 'Self-reliance' implies less reliance on the central-ised state, which should only intervene in situations where the interests of the wider community are at stake. Otherwise, the situation should be regulated according to the laws and principles of the social market economy.

Thus, whilst all the established political parties perceive the need to change various struct-ures, there is a clear distinction in the proposed remedies. The CDU would like to achieve decentral-isation in conjunction with a curtailment of the spheres for which the state is responsible and of the number of public service employees. The SPD, however, is critical of the conservative attempts to privatise the welfare state. It agrees that altern-ative groups provide an incentive for the state to consider how it can work better and more 'trans-parently' but wants to augment rather than run down its resources. The CDU in Berlin expressed its whole-hearted agreement with the critique by altern-ative groups of the welfare state as it had been shaped by the Social Democrats during the 1970s; it also made a shrewd reference to the critique by the alternative movement of the destruction of communi-ties, an issue which has been neglected by the SPD until recently:

> Today, in an improved welfare state and because of economic prosperity in our country, people have achieved a great deal of what they did not have in former times. But now they lack things which they had previously: the humanity of one's neighbours, a place of emotional security, comprehensible condi-tions of life...In this society everything has become 'bigger' and 'better', whereas the room for human encounter has apparently become small and its quality become worse.(19)

Thus, the critique of technocracy by the Green Move-ment has, with apparent ease, been accommodated by the CDU in Berlin.

The same report goes on to welcome the contri-

bution made by the Green Movement to integrating and
and providing useful activities for the unemployed
and the homeless, and providing training for young
people. The CDU made no attempt to hide the fact
any encouragement of alternative groups was 'part of
a correctly understood policy of integration'.(20)
It also worked out general criteria according to
which projects would be encouraged. The Senator for
Health, Family and Social Welfare, Ulf Fink, even
offered to set aside a vast sum of money - 52 million
marks - to help projects that were carrying out
useful social and community work. Similar ideas
were proposed by the government commission of inquiry
into youth protest.

In its report the government commission stated
that during its visit to West Berlin it visited
various alternative projects and gained the impression that in certain spheres they provide a 'valuable
extension to existing public and private institutions and enterprises' by training young people who
had left school with no qualifications, as well as
carrying out social work with psychologically
disturbed people, with drug addicts and others who
needed help. The commission recommended that
'meaningful' projects should be financed by the state
although they should be encouraged to adhere to minimal norms which generally apply to the conditions of
work and safety. It felt that, although the projects
would have to comply to minimum requirements for
budgetary control,

> no additional tasks which contradict the
> special character of these projects should
> be linked to the encouragement of the pro-
> jects. Here the principles of a 'risky
> furtherance' (Wagnisfoerderung) should serve
> as a model, and budgetary obligations only
> imposed to a limited extent.(21)

III Opportunities for dialogue, mediation and
     integration

Around 1980 the state, faced by increasing disaffection from young people, entered negotiations
with some projects to gain insights into what was
happening in the projects in exchange for financial
aid. Those early discussions did not bear any
immediate results. This was because of the refusal
by alternative groups to become involved in any

'conventional' political compromise. However, according to one editor in the Taz, attitudes began to change:

> the resistance to becoming involved in contemporary politics and the struggle for power, this resistance is increasingly disappearing among alternative groups. This is not only evident with the electoral successes of the Green and Alternative Lists, but there now prevails an awareness among young people of my generation that things are now really serious, that it is really a question of our future survival.(22)

He added that he was referring both to the generation of the sixties' protest movements and to the contemporary alternative groups. Yet the willingness to participate in politics does not mean that the alternative groups are willing to form organisations with general political aims; they point to the failure of the sixties' movement and of its 'march through the institutions', and to the corrupting effect of money and large organisations.

Hence many supporters of alternative groups are reluctant to accept of aid from the state, even if most projects already depend in some manner on subsidies from the state. They point to the danger of developing a vested interest in powerful organisational structures and to the likelihood that will want to become professionals and work only for financial reward. They argue that this would lead to a loss of the committment shown by countless individuals to the original aims of the groups, and to the emergence of new power structures which are anathema to many people within the projects. An editor of the Taz stated that, although he agreed with the critique by left-wing members in the SPD of capitalist conditions, they are 'corrupted in a particular way by their passion for compromise'.(23)

The projects are also fearful that if the state were to make available huge sums of money, they would quarrel amongst themselves over the appropriation of the funds. It would not be easy to implement suggestions that an intermediary organisation like Netzwerk should receive a lump sum and divide it among the projects, and that it alone should be accountable to the authorities. Between 1981 and 1982 there arose, over a period of several months, a bitter dispute between members of Netzwerk and the feminist magazine, Courage. The latter had

requested around one-fifth of the total funds available to Netzwerk in one year to try and rescue the
magazine from financial difficulties. When this
request was turned down there followed months of
acrimonious arguments and efforts to reverse the
decision. Members of alternative groups are very
conscious of how easy it would be for outside forces
to split the movement, precisely by appealing to the
widespread materialist attitudes within it, and thus
offers of money from the state, or of 'people's
money', are treated with great caution.
    A consequence of the initial failure by the
Ministry of Education and Science and the alternative
groups to reach an agreement was the formation of
the AFAP. This organisation aimed to work out a
position among the alternative projects and once
this had been achieved, to negotiate with the state.
(24) This would enable individual projects to apply
for money through a 'representative' organisation
like the AFAP and thus avoid some of the bureaucratic
complexities which accompany any application for
funds. According to Thomas Haertel, who was responsible for the sphere of 'self-help in the health
service' in the Berlin Administration, the demands
by the AFAP were worth considering because they
would provide a basis for the retention of the autonomy of alternative groups.(25) Haertel then
explained what he understood by the idea of 'risky
furtherance' as proposed by the government commission of inquiry into youth protest: the aim was to
provide funds even if there was no guarantee that
they would be repaid, or that they would help
towards successful experimentation by alternative
projects. In addition, a few months after these
comments were made, the Senator for Health, Family
and Social Welfare set up a committee to encourage
self-help groups. Initially this body included
supporters of alternative projects, including Peter
Grottian from the AFAP. However, they all withdrew
from it after a short while.
    Even the AFAP, whose motto proclaims the need
to gain subsidies from the state whilst retaining
the autonomy of the projects, has found it difficult
to persuade the various groups to meet together and
present united demands for money from the state.
There is no single organisation - including the
AFAP - which formally represents the interests of
the alternative projects and this makes it difficult
for a consensus of opinion to emerge. At a meeting
of the AFAP in May 1982, some members explained how
hard they had found it to persuade other groups to

send in a straight-forward application form (designed by the AFAP and not by any large bureaucratic organisation) so that they might be able to draw up a list of the variety of demands for money from the state. Although there was an encouraging rate of response of about 50 per cent from groups in the sphere of health and education, the overall rate was much lower, even though the Berlin Senate was apparently offering millions of marks in subsidies. For example, of the 41 forms which were sent out to women's groups only nine were returned.(26) Members of the AFAP felt that the lack of a common position among the projects would make it easier for the state to negotiate with individual groups and thus to split the movement. Whilst some groups have argued that the distinct character of the autonomous initiatives needs to be maintained, it does appear very likely that a lack of solidarity and a common position among the groups could lead to a situation in which each group, especially those that manage to gain professional qualifications and expertise, will be content to maintain their own progress and relative prosperity. This will probably lead to a loss of the original aims of the alternative movement, namely the realisation of work according to social and ecological principles and even the equality of incomes and of the sexes.

Although many alternative projects survive on, or seek, aid from the state, they are deeply mistrustful of the intentions of the established political parties. Not only are the parties large-scale organisations with hierarchical structures, they are also apparatuses whose existence and survival depends on their ability to bring together under one roof people from all layers of society - in short, they seek to integrate diverse groups into the political and social system. At any rate, the state has been less and less able to set aside funds for alternative projects. The initial offer by the CDU of 52 million marks in Spring 1982 had, by January 1983, been reduced to 7.5 million. According to Peter Grottian:

> The individual projects are sceptical about how far they are going to receive any money at all. And this scepticism is justified, because the projects had hoped that the Senate was really serious about 'self-reliance', less bureaucracy and handing over public money to the projects. This hope is no longer present.(27)

211

Functional aspects of the Green Movement

Grottian has identified two tendencies: the state apparently has less resources to encourage the projects and there is an increase in the number of people who want to take part in them. The decrease in the availability of financial resources constantly leads people to perceive only the need for the survival of their own project so that the overall political and social context cannot effectively be taken into consideration. Grottian was not optimistic about the possibilities for the development of links or of a 'network' between the projects.

None the less, the projects are united in their critique of the welfare state and, as I have shown, this has been taken up by the CDU. This party has often simply ignored the ideology of the Green Movement in so far as it calls for the transformation of the prevailing social system. Members of alternative groups found it difficult to comprehend how established groups and individuals, for instance Peter Glotz, Gerhard Baum and Ulf Fink, were espousing some of their aims even though they did not share the utopian or fundamentalist attitudes of the protestors. The Green Movement had failed to appreciate the capacity of established groups to adapt their demands to the functional needs of the state. The advanced capitalist state has been able to accommodate - one might almost say that it has often welcomed - the critique by social movements since the latter have anticipated and expressed some of the changes in demands by the population.

The government commission of inquiry into youth protest acknowledged the demand by the Green Movement for a 'democratisation of the sphere of reproduction' and for greater consultation of the population:

> The majority of the commission felt that it
> is necessary to broaden the possibilities
> of participation for the citizen who is
> directly affected and to encourage citizens
> to become aware of these possibilities. All
> forms of citizens' participation only fulfil
> their aim if the results of it affect planning
> decisions. The commission recommends a review
> of the regulations on taxes and subsidies, so
> that faulty developments in the course of
> action towards the restoration and modernis-
> ation of housing are avoided.(28)

It also warned the state to adopt policies which would improve social conditions and to carry out its activity on the basis of actions which were considered to be 'humane and just' and not simply irreproachable from a formal-legal perspective. The commission showed that it understood why the Green Movement was critical of 'rationality' and why it saw the state and large organisations as a 'threat to life'; however, it criticised the irrational elements within the protest movements and the 'over-estimation of spontaneity'.(29)

Two issues have not been resolved by the Green Movement: firstly, how to respond to violence that arises from the activities within the movement; and secondly, how to achieve some form of solidarity and suggest alternatives which are of general rather than narrow social relevance and can only appeal to well-educated, young people who are dissatisfied with their situation. Supporters of the alternative movement have continued to insist on the need for autonomy, even though this has made it difficult for them to achieve solidarity. This explains the scepticism of its sympathisers about the likelihood that it will achieve its main aims. Its ideas and practices are thus more likely to be integrated into the 'system' in a similar manner to the ideas of the ecology movement about alternative technology:

> Industry causes damage to the environment and tries to repair it with environmental protection. In a comparable manner, industrial development leads to the dissolution of traditional community life. It produces social decay and tries to repair it with the social services industry.(30)

Self-help projects could thus become not so much pioneers of a 'new partnership between experts and lay people' but of the career development of the professional helper.(31) Although they have prompted new ideas and concepts which have implications for all of society, the projects have been unable to go beyond their preoccupation with their own particular social sphere. Their demands on society are highly contradictory and they have not been able to combine effectively subjective elements and social criticism. The only organised attempt to take up these demands within the context of the new protest movements has occurred with the formation of the Green and Alternative parties.

The Greens have, through their entry into the Federal Parliament, become widely recognised as the representative organisation of the new social movements. To some extent, the Green Party has been

been able to act as a political umbrella organisation, but it is not the main coordinator of activities within the movements. Only a short while before the 1983 Federal Elections, delegates from the Green Party and a whole range of groups that were involved in the peace movement met to discuss a strategy for further activities against the placement of new nuclear missiles later in the year on West German soil. The Greens were particularly anxious to ensure that all activities took place on the basis of non-violence. However, a large proportion of the 'autonomous' groups refused to conform to what they called the 'ideology of non-violence' since it would detract from the 'need for confrontation'.(32) The meeting ended in disarray and again showed the difficulties which accompany the efforts of those who seek to reconcile pragmatic, radical reformism with a fundamentalist and 'uncompromising' critique of existing policies and of society.

The Green Movement has been unable to resolve the question of organisation, although it has managed to create loose structures which have ensured a measure of continuity and success. The most striking manner in which it has made certain its own continutiy has been through the creation of 'alternative communities' where people who are disillusioned with the 'system' find understanding and recognition for their different outlook on life. These communities offered and continue to provide a refuge and retreat after the tiring activities of campaigns. Within these communities, initiatives and projects there has developed an understanding of politics which, at least in the early stages of their development, has enabled many people to participate in decision-making processes. On a small scale these experiments have often been successful. They have not, however, provided an adequate answer to how wider problems which relate to broader sections of the population can be tackled in a coherent and consistent manner. The Green Party and other movement organisations have attempted to establish links between decentral political activities and a wider social context. They have at least succeeded in uniting partially many disparate groups and autonomous initiatives. They have not, however, been able to supersede the need for delegation and for representative politics.

The success of the Green Party in the Federal Elections is likely to make certain the continuation of a process whereby the major institutions and political parties pay heed to and integrate some of

214

the aspirations of the new protest movements. As I have shown, major government inquiries have been carried out on the implications of the protest by young people and on future energy policy. In its final report, the commission of inquiry into youth protest stressed the need to: create perspectives for the future of young people; provide technology and aid to Third World countries in accordance with their particular needs; work towards the integration of isolated spheres of human activity; use new technology to serve human needs like freedom, creativity and self-expression; encourage decentral organisation of work; implement measures to 'humanise the world of work'; encourage cultural and other social activities; preserve housing in areas which enjoy a sound community life; support self-help projects and allow young people a space of their own; use natural resources sparingly; prevent unnecessarily large structures, for instance in the construction of roads and bridges; and develop technologies which will not damage the environment.(33) The commission felt that the youth protest had articulated a growing desire of the population to be consulted in detail about the implementation of political decisions.

However, there was a significant divergence of opinion over how these changes could be achieved. On the one hand, Social Democrat members of the commission felt that the 'positive utopia' they had described, could only be achieved as a consequence of basic structural reforms and conflicts with the 'predominant power structures'. On the other hand, the Christian Democrat members felt that resilience and patience would ensure significant progress in coping with the new challenges. Whilst the latter believed that the 'humane further development of our society on the basis of the social market economy offers the opportunity of coming close to the ideals of freedom, justice and solidarity', the former held a more pessimistic view of the future: more young people would become unemployed and technology would be developed according to the laws of profit and not of the humanisation of the world of work.(34)

The commission expressed the fear that if nothing was done for unemployed people who had very few qualifications, many of them could find an outlet for their frustrations in the new protest movements. This is particularly true of the hundreds of thousands of foreign, especially Turkish, young people who face great difficulties in becoming integrated in West German society.(35)

Functional aspects of the Green Movement

As I have tried to show, the movements display characteristics which can be traced back both to post-war protest movements in advanced industrialised societies and to the critique of modernity as expressed by the German Youth and Expressionist Movements. In particular I have tried to draw attention to the search for 'nature' and 'authenticity' in the alternative culture, and the potential of violence that has arisen out of certain mythological interpretations of social reality. The potential of violence has, until now, not been instrumentalised by any particular group. None the less, a failure by the state to give more than verbal recognition to some of the problems which face young people, and the spread of the protest from well-educated to less educated layers of the population could cause problems for the cohesion of the political and social system. Despite the riots and violent confrontation which have occurred at repeated intervals over the past seven years, contemporary West German society has not experienced the riots which have been supported widely by unemployed, young people of mainly working-class origin in inner city areas in Britain.

The protest movements have articulated both new and old issues. The theme of 'survival' which has usually been adopted successfully by the Right, has now been made topical by left-wing ecologists. The differences between left- and right-wing ecologists lie in their interpretation of the role of the family and the welfare state. Whilst both agree that technocratic society is responsible for the destruction of communities, the Right proposes a reinforcement of traditional family bonds, whilst the Left is more inclined to support experiments in communal living. Similarly, although both sides are critical of the welfare state and centralised, remote bureaucracies, the Right wishes to encourage self-help and to abandon the welfare state, whilst the Left wants to continue with self-help and to expand welfare services. The Left, as it is represented by the Green Movement, signifies a break with some traditional left-wing ideas and practices. The inability of the Left to politicise the theme of nationalism has, to some extent, given way to a renewed interest, especially within the peace movement, in the issue of German sovereignty and nationality. In addition, it has largely abandoned any hopes in traditional working-class struggles, and is either reluctant or unable to offer alternatives for the 'emancipation of the working classes'; it thus calls on them to formulate their own path and to take initiatives 'from below'. Above all, the preoccupation of this section of the Left with communal politics, with grass-roots democracy and with the world of life, marks a significant shift away from the attention that is usually paid to 'abstract theories'. The new emphasis is on involvement in the the community that is 'directly affected' by planning and political decisions which are carried out elsewhere. There is a greater willingness to experiment, to be tolerant; and within the alternative subculture there is less of a tendency to be hateful of one another than among dogmatic left-wing groups.

The themes which preoccupy these groups have attracted the sympathies of the well-educated, middle-class supporters of the SPD. However, it will not be easy for the Social Democrats to move nearer to the utopian aspirations of the Green Movement and, at the same time, to maintain the support of traditional working-class voters; none the less, the departure of Helmut Schmidt, who had successfully co-opted the support of the trade union leadership, has meant that both the unions and the new party leadership have shown a much greater interest in the issues raised, for instance, by the peace movement. The Free Democrats have found it equally, if not more, difficult to reconcile the critique, by some members of the party, of industrial society with more traditional approaches to the solution of economic and social problems. Even among Christian Democrats, especially in Berlin and Baden-Wuerttemberg, the issues raised by the Green Movement have influenced the outlook of senior political figures. It will not be easy for the main parties to re-integrate some of the voters they have lost; many young voters have, at any rate, only ever supported the Greens.

The Social Democrats do have, both in their parliamentary leader, Vogel, and their General Secretary, Glotz, figures who have shown a keen appreciation of the issues raised by the Green Movement. They are well aware of the symbiotic relationship between these issues and the interests of the well-educated, middle-class membership of both the Greens and the SPD. Both have served an apprenticeship in Berlin, one of the main centres of the new protest movements: Glotz, as Senator for Science and Research (1977-80), was engaged in a prolonged effort towards dialogue with members of the Green Movement and Vogel, as leader of the SPD in the Berlin Senate (1981-82), was able to experi-

ence at first hand the activities of the parliamentary representatives of the movement. Similarly, the
Christian Democrats in Berlin have made serious
efforts to propose models to finance alternative
projects. Senator Ulf Fink, who has been mainly
responsible for these initiatives under the CDU
Administration, pointed out that his programmes have
been well-received in his own party throughout the
Federal Republic.(36)

The election of a Centre-Right Government which
includes the Free Democrats means that the polarisation between Left and Right in West German politics
is not likely to be as harsh as it would have been
if the Christian Democrats and the Bavarian Christian
Social Union had gained an absolute majority in the
1983 Federal Elections. Despite their rhetoric,
the Greens,with their entry into the Federal Parliament, are likely to provide further opportunities
for the re-integration of significant sections of
the protest movements into the political culture.
Within the Federal Parliament, they are likely to
come under intense pressure to distance themselves
from violent confrontations, especially in the
campaign to prevent the placement of new nuclear
missiles in West Germany. At the same time they
will not be able to ignore the demands, especially
from activists within the Green Movement, to oppose
the state in an 'uncompromising manner', and to
introduce 'new values' into the existing democratic
order. The suspicion towards the Social Democratic
version of 'technocracy' is being re-directed
towards the Christian Democratic version. This may
well lead many supporters of the Green Movement back
into the SPD.

At any rate it would be mistaken to focus only
on the conflicts and violence between the Green
Movement and established groups and to assume therefore that there is not a grateful relationship
between the two sides. If the state follows a path
similar to the one outlined by an official in the
Berlin Administration, who was echoing the views of
Hans-Jochen Vogel on how to approach the demand by
squatters for an unconditional amnesty for all those
who had been charged with criminal offences, the
chances for the integration of the Green Movement
are very high:

> one must go to young people, listen to
> them, take up their demands and discuss
> them and also be prepared to do things
> which we perhaps do not yet support, and

at the end of such a process there can
be an amnesty. That is a reciprocal
relationship and not just a statement
which declares that there can only be
negotiations once the squatters have
been given an amnesty. Rather the state
should say that it will negotiate and an
amnesty can only be the result of discussions. That is a good path.(37)

It is only through such a reciprocal relationship
and a preparedness by both sides to tolerate and to
listen carefully to each other that the critique by
the Green Movement of contemporary West German
society can bear any fruit and the movement can
develop a more realistic understanding of the const-
raints and limits to the possibilities of a utopian
transformation of society. The move towards a re-
alignment of the electorate in contemporary West
German politics is then likely to lead to practical,
perhaps even far-reaching,reforms rather than to a
serious imbalance in the political system.

NOTES

    1. Interview carried out by the author with Mr. Eschel,
press spokesperson for the Alternative List in Berlin, Jan. 1982.
    2. Luther, Die Bedeutung alternativer Projekte aus
bildungspolitischer Sicht, p. 8.
    3. Interview with 'Sabine' from Netzwerk.
    4. CDU Fraktion, Abgeordnetenhaus von Berlin, Grosse
Anfrage ueber alternatives Leben (Drucksache 9/1607, Bonn,
1982),p. 9.
    5. B.Groeschke and H.Hammel, members of Frauenbeirat AG
Staatsknete in Zitty, Nr. 4, 1983, p. 23.
    6. Taz, 18 March 1981.
    7. Buergerinitiative Energieplanung und Umweltschutz in
Taz, 3 April 1981, p. 6.
    8. For a discussion on the revolt by tax-payers see
F.Rubart, 'Der Steuerprotest' in D.Murphy et al., Protest.
Gruene, Bunte und Steuerrebellen, pp. 69-137.
    9. Taz, 18 March 1981.
    10. Frankfurter Rundschau (Dokumentation), 'Den Berliner
Subventionsstrom anzapfen', 6 July 1981, p. 14.
    11. Interview carried out by the author with Professor
Peter Grottian, Free University of Berlin, January 1982.
    12. Taz, 14 Oct. 1980, p. 7.
    13. Taz, 13 Oct. 1980, p. 6.
    14. Interview carried out by the author
with Klaus-Juergen Luther at the Ministry of Education and
Science in Bonn, May 1982.

15. Luther, Die Bedeutung alternativer Projekte aus bildungspolitischer Sicht, p. 13ff.

16. Interview with Gisela Marsen-Storz, May 1982.

17. Interview with Klaus-Juergen Luther, May 1982.

18. CDU Fraktion, Grosse Anfrage ueber alternatives Leben, p. 2.

19. Ibid., p. 3.

20. Ibid., pp. 10-11.

21. Deutscher Bundestag, Zwischenbericht der Enquete-Kommission, Jugendprotest im demokratischen Staat, p. 14.

22. Interview carried out by the author with Klaus Hartung, editor of the Taz, May 1982.

23. Ibid.

24. Interview with Peter Grottian, January 1982.

25. Interview carried out by the author with Thomas Haertel in the Department of Health, Family and Social Welfare in Berlin, May 1982.

26. Meeting of the AFAP in Berlin on 17 May 1982.

27. Zitty, Nr. 4, 1983, p. 22.

28. Deutscher Bundestag, Zwischenbericht der Enquete-Kommission, Jugendprotest im demokratischen Staat, p. 16.

29. Ibid., p. 10.

30. Huber, Verlorene Unschuld, p. 130.

31. Ibid.

32. Taz, 2 March 1983, p. 4.

33. Deutscher Bundestag, Schlussbericht der Enquete-Kommission, Jugendprotest im demokratischen Staat (Presse- und Informationszentrum, Bonn, 1983), pp.111-126.

34. Ibid., p. 128.

35. Ibid., p. 82ff.

36. Taz, 27 April 1983, p. 7.

37. Interview with Thomas Haertel, Berlin, May 1982.

BIBLIOGRAPHY

Articles, pamphlets, documents

Alternative Liste Berlin.Beschaeftigungspolitisches Sofort-
    programm(Berlin, 1981)
Bartolf,C.Etwas fuer den Frieden tun, unpublished discussion
    paper, Berlin, 1982
——Frieden schaffen ohne Waffen, unpublished seminar paper,
    Free University of Berlin, 1982
Bopp,J.'Trauer-Power. Zur Jugendrevolte 1981', Kursbuch 65
    (Berlin, 1981),pp. 151-68
Bredow von,W.'Zusammensetzung und Ziele der Friedensbewegung in
    der Bundesrepublik Deutschland', aus Politik und Zeitgesch-
    ichte, B24/82 (1982),pp. 3-13
Bundesverband Buergerinitiativen Umweltschutz.Aktionskatalog
    (Karlsruhe, 1979)
Bunte Liste/Bielefelder Stadtblatt.Alternativen in der
    Kommunalpolitik. Kongress am 14-15 Nov. 1980 (Bielefeld, 1980)
CDU Fraktion.Abgeordnetenhaus von Berlin.Grosse Anfrage ueber
    alternatives Leben (Drucksache 9/349, Berlin, 1982)
Deutscher Bundestag.Bericht der Enquete-Kommission, Zukuenftige
    Kernenergie-Politik (Drucksache 8/4341, Bonn, 1980)
——Stenographisches Protokoll der 12 Sitzung der Enquete-
    Kommission, Jugendprotest im demokratischen Staat am 08.02.82
    (Schoeneberg, Berlin, 1982)
——Zwischenbericht der Enquete-Kommission, Jugendprotest im
    demokratischen Staat (Drucksache 9/1607, Bonn, 1982)
——Schlussbericht der Enquete-Kommission, Jugendprotest im
    demokratischen Staat (Presse- und Informationszentrum,
    Bonn, 1983)
Dyson,K.'The West German Party-Book Administration:an evalua-
    tion', Public Administration Bulletin, Nr. 25, Dec. 1977,
    pp. 3-25
Ermittlungsauschuss der Bundesverband Buergerinitiativen
    Umweltschutz.(ed.).Augenzeugenberichte aus Brokdorf - 1976
    (Hamburg, 1976)
Galli,G.'The Student Movement in Italy', The Human Context,

Vol. II, p. 494ff

Goldner,S. et al.'Selbstbestimmt organisiert, gesellschaftlich bezahlt. Anmerkungen zur Staatsknetediskussion in der Alternativbewegung', Paedagogik-extra Sozialarbeit, (Jan. 1982),pp. 42-6

GAL Hamburg.Beschluesse zur Parlamentsarbeit (Hamburg, 1982)

————Programm fuer Hamburg (Hamburg, 1982)

————Stadtentwicklung und Wohnungspolitik (Hamburg, 1982)

————Friedensprogramm (Hamburg, 1982)

Gruenen, Die.Wahlplattform zur Bundestagswahl 1980 (Bonn, 1980)

————Gruene Frauen informieren (Bonn, 1980)

————Das Bundesprogramm (die Gruenen, Munich, 1980)

————Entruestet Euch. Analysen zur atomaren Bedrohung(Bonn,1981)

Habermas,J.'Dialektik der Rationalisierung', Aesthetik und Kommunikation, Heft 45/46,pp. 126-61

Haerlin,B.'Von Haus zu Haus - Berliner Bewegungsstudien', Kursbuch 65 (Berlin 1981),pp. 1-28

Initiativgruppen fuer eine Tageszeitung.Prospekt: Tageszeitung (Frankfurt, 1978)

Jaenicke,M.'Von Demos und Demokraten', Natur, Nr. 1, Jan. 1982, pp. 64-8

Key,V.O.'A Theory of Critical Elections', The Journal of Politics, Vol. 17, Nr. 1, Feb. 1955,pp. 3-18

Landespresse und Informationsamt Nordrhein-Westphalen.Dialog '81. Gespraeche zwischen den Generationen (Duesseldorf, 1981)

Luther,K-J.Die Bedeutung alternativer Projekte aus bildungs- politischer Sicht, revised version of an unpublished paper presented to the 'Fachtagung 1981 der Deutschen Vereinigung fuer politische Wissenschaft',Essen, Oct. 1981

Netzwerk Rundbrief.Ein Gespraech mit Hans Koch, Nr. 15, Dec. 1981

Offe,C.'Am Staat vorbei? Krise der Parteien und neue soziale Bewegungen', Das Argument, Nr. 124, 1980,pp. 809-821

Oxmox.Die Gruenen (K.Schulz, Hamburg, 1980)

Papadakis,E.'The Green Party in Contemporary West German Politics', Political Quarterly, Vol 54, Nr. 3, July-Sept.1983 pp. 302-7

Ridley,H. and Bullivant,K.'A Middle-Class View of German Industrial Expansion, 1853-1900', Oxford German Studies, 7, 1973, pp. 98-108

Schmid,G.'Zur Soziologie der Friedensbewegung und des Jugend- protestes', aus Politik und Zeitgeschichte, B24/82 (1982), pp. 15-30

Seyfried,G.'Spass mit der Wirklichkeit', Titanic, Nr. 1, (1982), pp. 36-43

SPD-Vorstand.Oekologiepolitische Orientierungen der SPD (Bonn, 1982)

Spiegel Umfrage.'Zur Auseinandersetzung um Frieden und Ruestung' Der Spiegel, 1981, Nr. 48, Nr. 49 and Nr. 50

Spindler,W.'Bist du dabei in Brokdorf?', Kursbuch 65 (Berlin, 1981),pp. 117-24

Bibliography

Taz. Gorleben-Dokumentation, 21 June 1980
Taz-Journal.Oekologie (Tageszeitung, Berlin, 1980), Nr. 1
————Sachschaden.Haeuser und andere Kaempfe (Tageszeitung,
    Berlin, 1981), Nr. 3
Tietze,U.'Wissenschaftslaeden in Holland. Keine Bueros sondern
    Teil einer Bewegung', Wechselwirkung, Nov. 1979,pp. 49-54
Wesel,U.'Der friedliche und der unfriedliche Bruch des Friedens'
    Kursbuch 65 (Berlin, 1981),pp. 29-49

Books

Aktion Suehnezeichen Friedensdienste.Bonn 10.10.81 (Lamuv,
    Berlin, 1981)
Ash,R.Social Movements in America (Chicago, 1972)
Bacia,J.et al.Passt bloss auf! Was will die neue Jugend-
    bewegung? (Olle und Wolter, Berlin, 1981)
Bahnemann,S.Ein Tropfen auf den heissen Stein (Freunde der Erde,
    Berlin, 1981)
Bahr,H.et al.Anders Leben, ueberleben (Fischer, Frankfurt, 1977)
Bahro,R.Elemente einer neuen Politik (Olle und Wolter, Berlin,
    1980)
————Socialism and Survival (Heretic, London, 1982)
Banks,J.The Sociology of Social Movements (London, 1972)
Becker,H.S.Outsiders (Free Press, New York, 1963)
Beer,W.Lernen im Widerstand. Politisches Lernen und Sozialisa-
    tion in Buergerinitiativen (Association, Hamburg, 1978)
Benson,L.Proletarians and Parties (London, 1978)
Berger,P.Facing Up To Modernity (Penguin, 1977)
Bergmann,U.et al.Rebellion der Studenten oder die neue
    Opposition (Reinbek, Hamburg, 1968)
Birnbaum,N.et al.Beyond the Crisis (Oxford University Press,
    1977)
Boch,R.et al.'Die alternative Wahlbewegung und die Kommunal-
    politik', in R.Schiller-Dickhut,et al.Alternative Stadt-
    politik, pp. 9-43
Bock,H.M.Geschichte des 'linken Radikalismus' in Deutschland
    (Suhrkamp, Frankfurt, 1976)
Bloch,E.Das Prinzip Hoffnung (Suhrkamp, Frankfurt, 1959)
Brun,R.(ed.).Der Gruene Protest (Fischer, Frankfurt, 1978)
Buchholtz,H.C.Widerstand gegen Atomkraftwerke (Peter Hammer,
    Wuppertal, 1978)
Bullivant,K. and Ridley,H.Industrie und deutsche Literatur
    (DTV, Munich, 1976)
Cobler,S.Law, order and politics in West Germany (Penguin, 1978)
Cohn-Bendit,D.Der grosse Basar (Trikont, Munich, 1975)
Crouch,C. and Pizzorno,A.(eds.).The Resurgence of Class Conflict
    in Western Europe since 1968 (Macmillan, 1978)
Dreitzel,H.P.'On the Political Meaning of Culture', in
    N.Birnbaum,et al.Beyond the Crisis, pp. 83-129
Gay,P.Weimar Culture (Penguin, 1974)

Giddens,A.The Class Structure of the Advanced Societies
(Hutchinson, London, 1973)
Glotz,P.'Staat und alternative Bewegungen', in J.Habermas.(ed.)
Stichworte zur Geistigen Situation der Zeit, Vol. 2, pp. 474-488
——'Dass die SPD Identitaetsprobleme hat, ist ohne Zweifel
richtig', in H.L.Gremliza and H.Hannover.(eds.).Die Linke:
Bilanz und Perspektiven fuer die 80er Jahre(VSA, Hamburg,1980)
——Die Innenausstattung der Macht (Fischer, Frankfurt, 1981)
——Die Beweglichkeit des Tankers (Bertelsmann, Munich, 1982)
Gorz,A.Ecologie et Liberte (editions galilee, Paris, 1977)
Graf,W.The German Left since 1945 (Oleander, Cambridge, 1976)
Grossmann,H.(ed.).Buergerinitiativen - Schritte zur Veraender-
ung? (Frankfurt, 1971)
Gruhl,H.Ein Planet wird gepluendert (Fischer, Frankfurt, 1978)
Guggenberger,B.Buergerinitiativen in der Bundesrepublik
(Kohlhammer, 1980)
Habermas,J.Towards a Rational Society (Heinemann, 1977)
——(ed.).Stichworte zur geistigen Situation der Zeit
(Suhrkamp, Frankfurt, 1979), Vols. 1 and 2
Harich,W.Kommunismus oder Wachstum? (Reinbek, Hamburg, 1975)
Hatzfeldt,H.G.et al.Der Gorleben Report - Auszuege aus dem
Gutachten und dem Hearing der niedersaechsischen Landes-
regierung (Fischer, Frankfurt, 1979)
Hau,W.(ed.).Sponti-Sprueche (Eichborn, Frankfurt)
Hildebrandt,K. and Dalton,R.J.'Die neue Politik. Politischer
Wandel oder Schoenwetterpolitik?', in M.Kaase.(ed.).
Wahlsoziologie heute. Analysen aus Anlass der Bundestags-
wahl 1976 (PVS, 18.J.,H. 2/3, 1976)
Hollstein,W.Die Gegengesellschaft (Neue Gesellschaft, Bonn, 1980)
Hoplitschek,E.'Die Alternativen und die Macht - die parlament-
arischen Erfahrungen der AL Berlin' in R.Schiller-Dickhut,et
al.Alternative Stadtpolitik, pp. 144-55
Huber,J.Wer soll das alles aendern? (Rotbuch, Berlin, 1980
——Die verlorene Unschuld der Oekologie (Frankfurt, Fischer,1982)
Illich,I.Die sogenannte Energiekrise oder die Laehmung der
Gesellschaft (Reinbek, Hamburg, 1974)
Inglehart,R.The Silent Revolution. Changing Values and Political
Styles among Western Publics (Princeton, New Jersey, 1977)
Johnson,N.Government in the Federal Republic of Germany
(Oxford, 1973)
Jonas,H.Das Prinzip Verantwortung (Insel, Frankfurt, 1979)
Jones,A.(ed.).The Jerusalem Bible (Darton, Longman and Todd,
London, 1968)
Jungk,R.Der Atomstaat (Reinbek, Hamburg, 1979)
Kaiser,G.Gas I (1918)
——Gas II (1920)
Kapp,K.W.The Social Costs of Business Enterprise (Spokesman,
Nottingham, 1978)
Kaste,H. and Raschke,J.'Zur Politik der Volkspartei', in Narr,
W-D.(ed.).Auf dem Weg zum Einparteienstaat, pp. 26-74

Bibliography

Kerouac,J.On the Road (Penguin, 1972)

Kretschmann,W.'Die Gruenen im Landtag von Baden-Wuerttemberg', in R.Schiller-Dickhut,et al.Alternative Stadtpolitik,pp.104-10

Langer,T. and Link,R.'Ueber den Umgang mit Defiziten linker Politik in Hamburg', in R.Schiller-Dickhut,et al.Alternative Stadtpolitik, pp. 128-43

Mannheim,K.Ideology and Utopia (Routledge and Kegan Paul, 1979)

Marcuse,H.Der Eindimensionale Mensch (Luchterhand, Neuwied and Berlin, 1975)

——The Aesthetic Dimension (Macmillan, London, 1979)

Mayer-Tasch,P.C.Die Buergerinitiativbewegung (Reinbek, Hamburg, 1976)

Meadows,D.Die Grenzen des Wachstums (Reinbek, Hamburg, 1973)

Mellor,E.H.The Two Germanies - A Modern Geography (Harper and Row, London, 1978)

Michels,R.Zur Soziologie des Parteiwesens in der modernen Demokratie (Stuttgart, 1926)

Mueller,F.'Das Waehlerpotential', in D.Murphy,et al.Protest. Gruene, Bunte und Steuerrebellen, pp. 138-55

Murphy,D.et al.Protest. Gruene, Bunte und Steuerrebellen (Reinbek, Hamburg, 1979)

Narr,W-D.(ed.).Auf dem Weg zum Einparteienstaat (Westdeutscher, Opladen, 1977)

Negt,O.'Alternative Politikformen als politische Alternative?' in Roth,R.(ed.).Parlamentarisches Ritual und politische Alternativen, pp. 147-78

Parkin,F.Middle Class Radicalism (Manchester, 1968)

Paterson,W.E.'Social Democracy - The West German Example' in Kolinsky,M. and Paterson,W.E.(eds.).Social and Political Movements in Western Europe (Croom Helm, London, 1976)

Peters,J.(ed.).Alternativen zum Atomstaat (Rotation, Berlin,1979)

——(ed.).Nationaler 'Sozialismus' von Rechts (Klaus Gruhl, Berlin, 1980)

Rabehl,B.'Im Kampf gegen die Polizei werden sie die Gestalt der Polizei annehmen', in J.Bacia,et al.Passt bloss auf! Was will die neue Jugendbewegung?, pp. 75-88

Raschke,J.Innerparteiliche Opposition. Die Linke in der Berliner SPD (Hoffmann und Campe, 1974)

Rock,P.Deviant Behaviour (Hutchinson, London, 1973)

Ronge,V.Die Gesellschaft an den Grenzen der Natur (AJZ, Bielefeld, 1978)

Roth,J.Armut in der Bundesrepublik (Reinbek, Hamburg, 1979)

Roth,R.(ed.).Parlamentarisches Ritual und politische Alterna-tiven (Campus, Frankfurt, 1980)

——'Notizen zur politischen Geschichte der Buergerinitiativen in der Bundesrepublik Deutschland', in R.Roth.(ed.).Parlamentarisches Ritual und politische Alternative,pp.74-98

Roettgen,H. and Rabe,F.Vulkantaenze - linke und alternative Ausgaenge (Trikont, Munich, 1978)

Rousseau,J-J.Les reveries du promeneur solitaire (Garnier-Flammarion, Paris, 1964)

Rubart,F.'Der Steuerprotest', in D.Murphy,et al.Protest. Gruene,
  Bunte und Steuerrebellen, pp. 69- 137
Schiller-Dickhut,R.et al.Alternative Stadtpolitik (VSA, Hamburg,
  1981)
See,H.'Strukturwandel und Ideologieprobleme der SPD - eine
  empirische Studie', in W-D.Narr.(ed.).Auf dem Weg zum Ein-
  parteienstaat. pp. 75-121
Shell.Studie.Jugend 1981 (Studie im Auftrag des Jugendwerks der
  Deutschen Shell, durchgefuehrt von Psydata, Institut fuer
  Marktanalysen, Sozial- und Mediaforschung GmbH., Hamburg,
  1981, Vol. 1, 2 and 3)
Smith,G.Politics in Western Europe (Heinemann, London, 1972)
Sombart,W.Haendler und Helden (Munich and Leipzig, 1915)
Spielhagen,F.Hammer und Amboss (1869)
Stern,F.The Politics of Cultural Despair (California, Library,
  Berkeley, 1961, reprinted 1974)
Sternstein,W.Ueberall ist Wyhl (Haag und Herchen, Frankfurt,1978)
Toller,E.Masse Mensch (1920)
——Die Maschinenstuermer (1922)
Touraine,A.Le communisme utopique. Le mouvement de mai '68
  (Seuil, Paris)
——The Post-Industrial Society (Butler and Tanner, London, 1971)
——'Crisis or Transformation?', in N.Birnbaum,et al.Beyond the
  Crisis, pp. 17-45
——La prophetie anti-nucleaire (Seuil, Paris, 1980)
Weber,M.The Protestant Ethic and the Spirit of Capitalism
  (Allen and Unwin, 1976)
Wilson,E.Axel's Castle (Fontana, 1974)
Winkler,N.'Gruene Buergerliste fuer Demokratie und Umwelt-
  schutz in Moerfelden-Walldorf', in R.Schiller-Dickhut,at al.
  Alternative Stadtpolitik, pp. 65-75
Zint,G.Gegen den Atomstaat (Zweitausendeins, Frankfurt, 1979)
——Republik Freies Wendland - Ein Dokumentation (Zweitausend-
  eins, Frankfurt, 1980)

Index